The Certified Quality Improvement Associate Handbook

Also available from ASQ Quality Press:

The Certified Manager of Quality/Organizational Excellence Handbook, Fourth Edition
Russell T. Westcott, editor

Principles of Quality Costs: Financial Measures for Strategic Implementation of Quality Management, Fourth Edition
Douglas C. Wood, editor

The ASQ Pocket Guide to Root Cause Analysis
Bjørn Andersen and Tom Natland Fagerhaug

The ASQ Quality Improvement Pocket Guide: Basic History, Concepts, Tools, and Relationships
Grace L. Duffy, editor

Root Cause Analysis: The Core of Problem Solving and Corrective Action
Duke Okes

Modular Kaizen: Continuous and Breakthrough Improvement
Grace L. Duffy

The Executive Guide to Improvement and Change
G. Dennis Beecroft, Grace L. Duffy, and John W. Moran

The Lean Handbook: A Guide to the Bronze Certification Body of Knowledge
Anthony Manos and Chad Vincent, editors

The Quality Toolbox, Second Edition
Nancy R. Tague

Performance Metrics: The Levers for Process Management
Duke Okes

Process Improvement Using Six Sigma: A DMAIC Guide
Rama Shankar

Mapping Work Processes, Second Edition
Bjørn Andersen, Tom Fagerhaug, Bjørnar Henriksen, and Lars E. Onsøyen

The Certified Six Sigma Black Belt Handbook, Second Edition
T.M. Kubiak and Donald W. Benbow

The Certified Six Sigma Green Belt Handbook, Second Edition
Roderick A. Munro, Govindarajan Ramu, and Daniel J. Zrymiak

The Certified Quality Improvement Associate Handbook

Third Edition

Basic Quality Principles and Practices

Russell T. Westcott and Grace L. Duffy, Editors

Supports preparation for the
ASQ *Certified Quality Improvement Associate* (CQIA) certification

Quality Management Division
ASQ The Global Voice of Quality™

ASQ Quality Press
Milwaukee, Wisconsin

First Impression, 2015

Indian edition published by Infotech Standards India Pvt. Ltd.

ISBN 978-81-748-9037-5

Original Edition entitled The Certified Quality Improvement Associate Handbook, 3rd Edition by Russell T. Westcott, Grace L. Duffy, Editors
American Society for Quality, Quality Press, Milwaukee 53203

ASQ Mission: The American Society for Quality advances individual, organizational, and community excellence worldwide through learning, quality improvement, and knowledge exchange.

This edition is authorized for sale in India.

ASQ
AMERICAN SOCIETY FOR QUALITY™

Quality Press
600 N. Plakinton Avenue,
Milwaukee, Wisconsin 53203
Call toll free 800-248-1946
Fax 414-272-1734
www.asq.org
http://qualitypress.asq.org
http:// standarsgroup.asq.org
E-mail: authors@asq.org

INFOTECH STANDARDS INDIA PVT. LTD.
4760-61, 2nd Floor, "SAI SAROVAR"
23, Ansari Road, Daryaganj
New Delhi - 110002, INDIA
Ph. : 011-43586946, 23264946
Fax : 011-43586947
www.standardsmedia.com
E-mail : info@standardsmedia.com

Table of Contents

List of Figures and Tables

Preface

Members and leaders of the Quality Management Division (QMD) of the American Society for Quality (ASQ) acknowledge the continuing evolution of integration and use of organizational and process improvement throughout nearly every type of industry, organization, and organization level. However, within the same time period, numerous occurrences of loss of quality focus are highlighted in the news media, such as:

- Monstrous automobile recalls for faulty parts resulting in deaths and injuries
- Disastrous outcomes caused by segments of the pharmaceutical industry
- Massive fraudulent practices in the field of investments and banking
- Critical failures in the telecommunications arena, disrupting vital connections
- Inadequate controls in the importing of food products, allowing tainted product to be sold
- Building collapses throughout the world, killing hundreds
- Lack of focus on basic quality principles and practices within the governmental sector (federal, state, municipal), with significant impact on organizations and individuals governed; this lack of focus is prevalent in many countries, including the United States

Clearly, much needs to be done to fully integrate quality into every process and aspect of life. In 2000, ASQ introduced the Certified Quality Improvement Associate (CQIA) certification. It is designed to introduce the basics of quality to organizations and individuals not currently working within the field of quality. This book and the Body of Knowledge it supports are intended to form a foundation for further study and application of proven quality principles and practices worldwide. Additionally, preparing for the CQIA exam and becoming certified may be viewed as the first step toward ultimately qualifying for one or several of the ASQ certifications available to ASQ members.

If you are not yet a member of ASQ, we encourage you to consider joining, either you as an individual member or your entire organization as a member. An

ASQ member is entitled to one free selection of a division. A wide range of division choices are available, from those representing a holistic approach to quality management (QMD, the sponsor of the CQIA certification and this book) to divisions representing industries, quality functions, and quality standards. Contact information follows:

- ASQ 800-248-1946, http://www.asq.org (the website offers a plethora of information about ASQ and membership benefits, quality principles and practices, and a membership application)
- ASQ Quality Management Division, http://www.asq-qm.org
- Coeditors' e-mail addresses: russwest@snet.net, grace683@outlook.com

Notes to the Reader

HIGHLIGHTS IN THE EVOLUTION OF QUALITY[1]

The history of quality reaches back into antiquity. This short overview starts with the current quality movement, which began in the 1920s.

The quality profession, as it is called, started with Walter Shewhart of Bell Laboratories. He developed a system known as *statistical process control* (SPC) for measuring variance in production systems. SPC is still used to help monitor consistency and diagnose problems in work processes. Shewhart also created the Plan-Do-Check-Act (PDCA) cycle, which is a systematic approach to improving work processes. When the PDCA cycle is applied consistently, it can result in continuous process improvement.

During World War II, the US War Department hired Dr. W. Edwards Deming, a physicist and US Census Bureau researcher, to teach SPC to the defense industry. Quality control and statistical methods were considered critical factors in a successful war effort. Unfortunately, many companies in the United States stopped using these statistical tools after the war.

Following World War II, the US occupation forces in Japan invited Deming to help Japan with its census. He was also invited to present lectures to business leaders on SPC and quality. The Japanese acceptance and use of Dr. Deming's techniques had a profound positive effect on Japan's economic recovery.

Two other American quality experts, Dr. Joseph M. Juran and Dr. Armand V. Feigenbaum, also worked with the Japanese. Both Deming and Juran (a former investigator at the Hawthorne Works experiments) drew on Shewhart's work and recognized that satisfying the customer 's needs was important and that system problems could be addressed through three fundamental managerial processes: planning, control, and improvement. Feigenbaum stressed the need to involve all departments of a company in the pursuit of quality, a concept he called *total quality control.* The Japanese expanded Juran's customer concept to include internal customers, those people within the organization who depend on the output of other workers.

Kaoru Ishikawa, a Japanese engineer and manager, expanded Feigenbaum's ideas to include all employees, not just department managers, in the total quality control concept. Ishikawa also helped create *quality circles,* small teams of managers, supervisors, and workers trained in SPC, the PDCA cycle, and groupproblem-solving. Applying these techniques created a flow of new ideas for improvement from everyone in the organization and continual incremental improvements that led to better performance. The quality circles were the original model for our current process improvement teams. By the 1970s, most large Japanese companies had adopted what Ishikawa called *companywide quality control* (CWQC), resulting in a changed perception that Japan produced world-class quality products.

The Japanese success prompted American organizations to embrace the teachings of Deming, Juran, Feigenbaum, and other quality gurus and to apply their successful quality management techniques in many types of businesses.

In the mid-1980s, American organizations began to experience improved quality results and enhanced customer satisfaction. In 1987, the criteria for the first Malcolm Baldrige National Quality Award were published. Within the same time period, *ISO 9001, Quality systems—Model for quality assurance in design, development, production, installation, and servicing* was published. These initiatives resulted in profound changes in the way the quality profession applies its principles and practices.

Millions of copies of the *Malcolm Baldrige National Quality Award* criteria have been distributed, and many state and local quality award programs have developed their own programs based on the national award criteria. Although relatively few organizations actually apply for the national award, they use the criteria to evaluate and improve their quality management systems. Healthcare and education versions of the award criteria are now available, further expanding the use and value of the criteria.

In the 1980s, Motorola initiated a Six Sigma methodology. In the mid-1990s, companies such as General Electric and AlliedSignal launched their own Six Sigma initiatives. Since then, many companies have embraced the Six Sigma methodology. The term alludes to focusing on achieving a process that has no more than 3.4 defects per million. As a philosophy, *Six Sigma* is the belief that it is possible to produce totally defect-free products and services. The third edition of *The Certified Quality Improvement Associate Handbook* expands coverage of both Six Sigma and lean.

STRUCTURE OF THIS BOOK

The book follows the CQIA Body of Knowledge (BoK) in both content and sequence. The intent is that this book will serve as a guide to be used in preparation to take the CQIA examination given by ASQ.

Each chapter stands alone, and the chapters may be read in any order. Some material reaching beyond the content of the BoK has been added. Supplemental reading suggestions are provided.

DIVERSITY

The use of the terms "quality" and "continuous improvement" is not considered solely applicable to manufacturing and the traditional engineering and production environment. Most professionals entering the workforce today are required to analyze situations, identify problems, and provide solutions for improved performance. Improving the organization is everyone's job. Teamwork is critical, requiring the participation of members of all cultures, educational levels, and career aspirations.

An attempt has been made to balance the use of personal pronouns as well as provide examples from a variety of organizations. The use of the term "organization" means that the content is considered generic—applicable to any type of entity. Where the term "company" is used, the content is more applicable to a for-profit enterprise.

PRACTICE

An online, interactive sample exam and a paper-and-pencil sample can be found on the ASQ website (http://asq.org/cert/quality-improvement-associate/prepare). There is no cost for either sample exam.

The CQIA BoK is presented in Appendix A and indicates the number of questions that will be asked about each major BoK segment and the maximum cognitive level to which the questions may be asked. Derived from Bloom's taxonomy,[2] the levels are as follows:

1. Remember (Knowledge)
2. Understand (Comprehension)
3. Apply (Application)
4. Analyze (Analysis)
5. Evaluate (Evaluation)
6. Create (Synthesis)

In addition to the content supporting the BoK, the CQIA aspirant is expected to be familiar with the ASQ Code of Ethics, found in Appendix B.

AVAILABILITY OF REFERENCE MATERIALS

All of the texts referenced here should be readily available from normal book sources, many from ASQ Quality Press. A website search will add a plethora of additional information. The US government is an excellent source of quality-related materials.

NOTES

1. J. M. Juran, ed., *A History of Managing for Quality* (Milwaukee, WI: ASQC Quality Press, 1995).
2. B. S. Bloom, ed., *Taxonomy of Educational Objectives: The Classification of Educational Goals, Handbook I, Cognitive Domain* (New York: Longmans, Green, 1956). Additional information about Bloom's taxonomy may be obtained from http://www.coun.uvic.ca/learning/exams/blooms-taxonomy.html.

About the Certified Quality Improvement Associate Exam

Because of ASQ examination rules, no questions or answers to questions may be brought into the room where the examination is given. This handbook, the suggested reference materials, and other references, such as notes from a course, may be brought into the examination room subject to inspection by the examination proctor.

After applying to ASQ to take the exam, the applicant will receive a notice of acceptance. The notice will state the location, date, and time of the exam. If the details are not acceptable, the applicant should contact ASQ for either a change of venue, a postponement, or cancellation.

On the day of the three-hour exam, the applicant can expect the following:

- Other people taking other exams may be in the same room.
- Strict start and stop times will be stipulated.
- "No talking," "leave the exam room," and other rules will be explained.
- The proctor will mention when to expect to receive exam results.
- No electronic devices will be allowed in the exam room. Applicants who rely on a phone or other hand-held device for telling time should bring a simple watch (no functions other than time) in case there is no clock in the room.
- The applicant should bring several sharpened #2 pencils, with working erasers, for recording answers.
- The applicant should ask the exam proctor about anything pertaining to personal needs prior to the start of the exam.
- The exam answer sheet and the exam questions will be turned in to the proctor when the applicant finishes the exam or at the designated stop time. Once these documents are in the hands of the proctor, the applicant may leave.
- The applicant should not engage the proctor in conversation during the exam period.

Good luck!

Acknowledgments

Much gratitude is extended to those who contributed to the third edition:

John E. Bauer—coeditor, first and second editions

Grace L. Duffy—coeditor, third edition

Jd Marhevko—volunteer content reviewer, third edition

Heather McCain—volunteer content reviewer, third edition

Matt Meinholz—ASQ Quality Press acquisition editor

Paul O'Mara—ASQ Quality Press managing editor

Russ Westcott—coeditor, third edition

Part I

Quality Concepts

Look beneath the surface, let not the quality nor its worth escape thee.

Marcus Aurelius

We are what we repeatedly do. Excellence, then, is not an act, but habit.

Aristotle

Quality is about making products that don't come back for customers that do.

Margaret Thatcher

Quality is free. It's not a gift, but it's free. What costs money are the unquality things—all the actions that involve not doing jobs right the first time.

Philip Crosby

Defects are not free. Somebody makes them, and gets paid for making them.

Dr. W. Edwards Deming

Chapter 1

A. Terms, Concepts, and Principles

1. QUALITY

> Define quality and use this term correctly in various circumstances. (Apply)
>
> **CQIA BoK 2014 I.A.1.**

There are many definitions of quality, such as the following:

- Quality is a subjective term for which each person has his or her own definition. In technical usage, quality can have two meanings: (1) the characteristics of a product or service that bear on its ability to satisfy stated or implied needs, and (2) a product or service free of deficiencies.[1]
- Quality is the degree to which a set of inherent characteristics fulfills requirements.[2]
- Quality is conformance to requirements.
- Quality is fitness for use.
- Quality is meeting customer expectations.
- Quality is exceeding customer expectations.
- Quality is superiority to competitors.
- Quality—I'll know it when I see it.

In addition to these various meanings, quality may also be viewed from several dimensions:

- Characteristics such as reliability, maintainability, and availability
- Drivers of quality, such as standards
- Quality of design versus quality of conformance to customer's requirements

- Quality planning, control, and improvement
- Little q and Big Q (product or functional quality versus improvement of all organizational processes)
- Quality as an organizational strategy

Many other quality-related terms are defined in Appendix C, "Quality Glossary."

The two quality management system models most frequently used by quality professionals are the Baldrige Performance Excellence Program Criteria[3] and the ISO family of quality management system standards.[4] These quality models provide insight into the components of a quality management system and define quality as it is practiced today.

Baldrige Performance Excellence Program (2012): Criteria (Business Version)

The business version can be used for both for-profit and not-for-profit organizations.

1 *Leadership*

1.1 Senior Leadership

1.2 Governance and Social Responsibilities

The Leadership category examines how the personal actions of your organization's senior leaders guide and sustain the organization. Also examined are the organization's governance system and how the organization fulfills its legal, ethical, and societal responsibilities and supports its key communities.

2 *Strategic Planning*

2.1 Strategy Development

2.2 Strategy Implementation

The Strategic Planning category examines how your organization develops strategic objectives and action plans. Also examined are how your chosen strategic objectives and action plans are implemented and changed if circumstances require, and how progress is measured.

3 *Customer Focus*

3.1 Voice of the Customer

3.2 Customer Engagement

The Customer Focus category examines how your organization engages its customers for long-term marketplace success. This engagement strategy includes how your organization listens to the voice of its customers, builds customer relationships, and uses customer information to improve and identify opportunities for innovation.

4 Measurement, Analysis, and Knowledge Management

4.1 Measurement, Analysis, and Improvement of Organizational Performance

4.2 Management of Information, Knowledge, and Information Technology

The Measurement, Analysis, and Knowledge Management category examines how your organization selects, gathers, analyzes, manages, and improves its data, information, and knowledge assets and how it manages its information technology. The category also examines how your organization uses review findings to improve its performance.

5 Workforce Focus

5.1 Workforce Environment

5.2 Workforce Engagement

The Workforce Focus category examines your ability to assess workforce capability and capacity and build a workforce environment conducive to high performance. Also examined is how your organization engages, manages, and develops its workforce to utilize its full potential in alignment with its overall mission, strategy, and action plans.

6 Operations Focus

6.1 Work Systems: How do you design, manage, and improve your work systems?

6.2 Work Processes: How do you design, manage, and improve your key work processes?

The Operations Focus category examines how your organization designs, manages, and improves its work systems and processes to deliver customer value and achieve organizational success and sustainability. Also examined is your readiness for emergencies.

7 Results

7.1 Product and Process Outcomes

7.2 Customer-Focused Outcomes

7.3 Workforce-Focused Outcomes

7.4 Leadership and Governance Outcomes

7.5 Financial and Market Outcomes

The Results category examines your organization's performance and improvement in all key areas—product and process outcomes, customer-focused outcomes, workforce-focused outcomes, leadership and governance outcomes, and financial and market outcomes. Performance levels are examined relative to those of competitors and other organizations with similar product offerings.

In recent years the Baldrige Performance Excellence Program has been expanded to include criteria covering healthcare and educational organizations. Information on the programs is available at http://www.quality.nist.gov.

ANSI/ISO/ASQ Q9000 Quality Management System Principles

A *quality management principle* is a comprehensive and fundamental rule or belief for leading and operating an organization; it is aimed at continually improving performance over the long term by focusing on customers while addressing the needs of all other stakeholders. Eight quality management principles form the basis of current international quality management requirements:

1. *Customer Orientation.* Organizations must focus on understanding their customers' needs and requirements. Successful organizations try to anticipate and exceed the customers' expectations.
2. *Leadership.* Organizations need strong leaders to establish common goals and direction. Effective leaders establish open environments in which all employees can participate in meeting their organization's goals.
3. *Involvement.* People are the most important part of any organization. Managers must ensure that employees at all levels of the organization can fully participate and use all their skills to make the organization successful.
4. *Process Management.* The most successful organizations understand that they must manage all their activities as processes.
5. *System Management.* Successful organizations understand that their many individual processes are interrelated and that, in addition to being managed individually, they must be managed within an overall system.
6. *Continual Improvement.* Continual improvement is the key to long-term success and high performance. Successful managers recognize that processes must be reviewed and improved continually to ensure that their organization stays competitive.
7. *Fact-Based Decisions.* Organizations that base their decisions on factual data are more likely to make the correct decision than those that do not.
8. *Close Supplier Relationships.* Organizations that partner and work closely with their suppliers ensure that both the organization and the suppliers are better able to achieve success.

A side-by-side review of the Baldrige and the ISO 9001:2008 quality models reveals many similarities. They both stress strong organizational leadership; a focus on customers; the development and involvement of the organization's people; gathering, analyzing, and using information to make decisions; and process management. Together these characteristics define quality as it is practiced in many successful organizations.

2. QUALITY PLAN

> Define a quality plan, describe its purpose for the organization as a whole, and identify the various functional areas and people that have responsibility for contributing to its development. (Understand)
>
> **CQIA BoK 2014 I.A.2.**

Quality planning is the process of developing a master plan that is linked to organizational strategy, goals, and objectives that pertain to the quality of products or services to be delivered to customers. The quality plan includes key requirements, performance indicators, and commitment of resources to ensure that customer needs are met. The quality plan often consists of several related documents.

Although it is separate from the three phases of organizational planning (strategic, tactical, and operational), quality planning is dependent on the decisions and processes established by management during those phases. Key quality requirements and performance indicators must be established in the design, development, and implementation of all products and services for final customer delivery. Quality initiatives must be understood in their relation to all three levels of the organization: strategic planning, tactical planning, and operational planning.

Strategic planning deals with developing the long-range strategies of the organization, including:

- The organization's overall strategic goals and objectives
- External customers' needs and expectations
- The needs and expectations of internal stakeholders (employees, shareholders, and so on)
- Risks that must be taken into account
- Regulatory requirements
- Competitors' capabilities
- Business systems needed to operate the organization effectively and efficiently

Tactical planning (sometimes called action or project planning) deals with translating strategic objectives into actionable activities that must occur, on a short-term basis, to support the achievement of the strategic plans. There are measurable steps and events that result from the downward deployment of the strategic plans.

Operational planning deals with developing day-to-day operating procedures that ensure the quality of individual products and services. Operational plans address areas such as:

- Resources needed to develop and create the organization's products and services

- Materials and supplies required for creating and delivering the products and services
- Knowledge and skills required of employees
- Processes and procedures required to create the organization's products and services as well as to run the business effectively in transactional areas such as finance, human resources, engineering, legal, and so on.
- Unique tools or equipment required
- Documentation (specifications, standards, drawings, visual aids, and so on) required
- Examination, inspection, or testing requirements
- Administrative support and follow-up for customer communication
- Records required to document the creation of the organization's products and services
- Process improvement methods to continually improve the organization's deliverables

Customer-Specific Quality Planning

At the day-to-day level, meeting a specific customer's requirements sometimes requires a *quality plan* for an individual contract or purchase order. To develop such a working plan means looking at the particular requirements of the order and determining the resources (time, materials, equipment, process steps, skills, etc.) that will be required to complete the individual transaction to the customer's satisfaction and provide an adequate return on the resource investment. This type of quality plan is usually completed as part of the process that organizations use to provide quotes on new or repeat work for their customers.

Overall, a consistent planning, monitoring, and reviewing approach is required for organizations using established quality systems based on criteria such as the Baldrige Performance Excellence Program or the ISO 9001:2008 standard. The approach taken by an organization becomes the guiding policy in producing a valued product or service that remains competitive in the marketplace. The planning must include:

- A comprehensive focus on customer needs and expectations
- Support of quality goals and strategies by upper management
- A balance of resources between short-term and long-term requirements, including capital expenditures, training, and continual improvement
- Ongoing interpretation of long-term goals into tactical and operating plans
- Development and execution of processes for evaluation and process improvement
- Integration of quality activities into the daily work of the frontline associates

3. EMPLOYEE INVOLVEMENT AND EMPOWERMENT

> Define and distinguish between employee involvement and employee empowerment, and describe the benefits of both concepts. (Understand)
>
> **CQIA BoK 2014 I.A.3.**

The two predominant quality models (Baldrige and ISO 9000) stress the importance of the participation of all employees in an organization's quality efforts. Organizations work to motivate and enable their employees to develop and utilize their full potential in support of the organization's overall goals and objectives. Organizations also work to build and maintain work environments that support their employees and create a climate conducive to performance excellence and personal and organizational growth. People at all levels are the essence of any organization, and empowering them to fully use their abilities and to be fully involved in the organization's processes benefits the organization.

Empowerment means that employees have the authority to make decisions and take action in their work areas without prior approval, within established boundaries. Allowing employees to work as active members of a process improvement team is one way to empower them to fully use their collective wisdom and decision-making skills. But they must also be given the training, tools, materials, equipment, processes, and procedures to accomplish their individual tasks. Providing these critical resources shows employees that the organization truly values their minds, not just their bodies.

Each employee must recognize that the outputs of his or her individual activities provide the inputs to the next person's process. Employee involvement allows employees to participate in decision making at some level, provides the necessary skills to accomplish the required task, and carefully defines responsibilities and authority. Employee involvement also provides recognition and rewards for accomplishments and enables communication with all levels of the organization's structure.

Managers must do more than just tell employees that they have the authority to participate fully in processes. They must also relinquish some of their authority and show by their actions that they expect full employee involvement and that they support actions taken by employees and decisions made by them to further the organization's goals and objectives. Giving employees the authority to act also gives them responsibility and accountability for what they do. To fully participate, employees must understand the organization's mission, values, and systems.

It is also important to understand the difference between *job enlargement* and *job enrichment*. Enlarging a job means expanding the variety of tasks performed by an employee. Enriching a job means increasing the worker's responsibilities and authority in work to be done. Two examples are as follows:

> In addition to staffing a customer transaction window, a bank teller's job is expanded to tidying up the tables used by customers to fill out forms and also ensuring that all brochure displays are restocked. (job enlargement)

A waitperson's job is increased in scope to include helping the cook determine the next day's menu. (job enrichment)

Organizations sometimes have formal suggestion systems that allow employees to provide input on problems and suggestions on how to improve existing processes. Many of these systems are tied to incentives or rewards for suggestions that are implemented.

4. SYSTEMS AND PROCESSES

> Define and distinguish between a system and a process and describe the interrelationships between them. Describe the components of a system—supplier, input, process, output, customer (SIPOC)—and how these components impact the system as a whole. (Analyze)
>
> **CQIA BoK 2014 I.A.4.**

A *system* is a set of interrelated or interacting processes. A *process* is a set of interrelated or interacting activities that transforms inputs into outputs. For example:

The quality audit process uses various inputs (trained auditors, procedures, employee interviews, checklists, and so on) to develop an output (the audit report) that is used to improve the organization's overall quality management system. The quality management system is composed of many individual processes that interact with each other and contribute to improving the organization's overall performance.

Using a system of interrelated processes to manage an organization is called a *process approach to management*, or simply *process management*. The process management approach is based on the organization's ability to identify all its processes, recognize the inputs and outputs of each process, document the processes so they can be easily implemented, identify the owners of each process, implement the processes, measure the outcomes of the implementation, and continually improve the efficiency and effectiveness of the processes. The organization's objectives are achieved more efficiently when related resources and activities are managed as processes and when the individual processes work together to form an integrated management system.

Processes can be divided into various categories:

- Product/service development processes deal with how the organization:
  - —Designs new and improved products and services
  - —Changes old products and services to meet new customer requirements

— Incorporates improvements in technology

— Anticipates customers' future needs

- Product/service production processes deal with how the organization:

  — Produces products and services in the most efficient and economical way

  — Ensures that the products and services meet all technical requirements

  — Delivers the products and services in the time frame required by the customer

  — Uses customer and employee feedback

- Business processes deal with how the organization:

  — Accounts for its resources

  — Develops and uses measures of performance

  — Continually improves its operations

  — Trains, evaluates, recognizes, and rewards its employees

Process documentation might include these components:

1. A short, simple description of the process and its purpose
2. A description of the process's starting and ending activities
3. A list of inputs required at the process starting point and who provides the inputs, or the process supplier
4. A list of outputs at the process ending point and who receives the outputs, or the process customer
5. A flowchart of the process—that is, a process map identifying the interfaces of the process with other functions of the organization
6. Identification of the process owner, establishing clear responsibility, authority, and accountability for managing the process
7. The measurements used to identify that the process has been completed successfully
8. A statement of the overall capability of the process

Using the process approach to management leads to more predictable results, better use of resources, prevention of errors, shorter cycle times, and lower costs, as well as a better understanding of the capability of processes and more predictable outputs.

The Baldrige and ISO models encourage the use of a process and system approach to management. They also stress the importance of integrating different business processes, such as design, production, quality, packaging, and shipping, into one interlinked system. All processes have inputs and outputs. The inputs of a process being worked on usually come as outputs from another process, and the outputs of the process being worked on usually serve as the inputs to another process. For example:

> Parts manufactured and inspected to meet customer requirements are sent to the packaging department for preparation for shipment. The packaged parts are sent to the shipping department for transfer to a transportation company. The outputs of the manufacturing and inspection processes are inputs to the packaging process. The outputs of the packaging process are inputs to the shipping process. These interrelationships must be understood by managers in order to develop an efficient overall system.

This business methodology, sometimes called a *system of processes* or a *process approach*, is critical to the efficient (timely) and effective (correct) operation of modern organizations. (Lean systems regularly deal with system efficiencies, and Six Sigma systems often deal with the effectiveness of those systems. Lean and Six Sigma processes each have many activities that meld into the other.) Also critical to this methodology is the concept that all processes generate data (which are transformed into information) that must be "fed back" to other interrelated processes. Information about a deficient product found at inspection must be "fed back" to the manufacturing process, and possibly to the design process, so that corrective action can be taken to cure the process defect that created the deficient product.

SIPOC Analysis

Process improvement efforts are often focused on removing a situation that has developed in which a process is not operating at its normal level. However, much of continual improvement involves analyzing a process that may be performing as expected, but where a higher level of performance is desired. A fundamental step in improving a process is to understand how it functions from a process management perspective. This can be understood through an analysis of the process to identify the supplier-input-process-output-customer (SIPOC) linkages (see Figure 1.1).

It begins with defining the process of interest. The outputs that the process creates that go to customers, are listed on the right side. Suppliers and what they provide to enable the process (the inputs) are similarly shown on the left side. Once this fundamental process diagram is developed, two additional items can be discussed: (1) measures that can be used to evaluate performance of the inputs and outputs, and (2) the information and methods necessary to control the process.

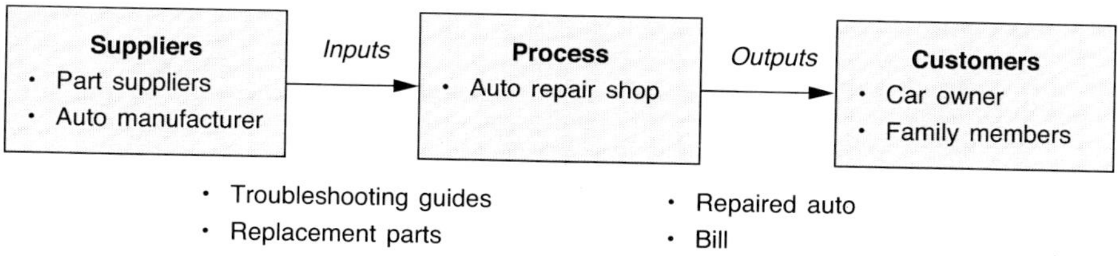

Figure 1.1 SIPOC diagram.

5. VARIATION

> Define and distinguish between common and special cause variation in relation to quality measures. (Understand)
>
> **CQIA BoK 2014 I.A.5.**

Variations are differences, usually minor, from the designed and expected outputs of a process. Some variation is found in all processes. (Even the earth wobbles as it completes its daily orbit.) The key to controlling processes is to control variation as much as possible.

All variation has some cause. Knowing the causes is important in order to determine the actions that must be taken to reduce the variation. It is most important to distinguish between *special cause* variation and *common cause* variation.

Special cause variation results from unexpected or unusual occurrences that are not inherent in the process. As an example:

> A school bus driver is on her way to pick up her first student in the morning when the engine stalls because of a fuel-line leak.

This occurrence is not inherent in the student pickup process. Special causes of variation account for approximately 15% of the observed variation in processes. They are usually very easy to detect and correct. No major modifications to the process are required. These special causes are sometimes called *assignable causes,* because the variation they result in can be investigated and assigned to a particular source.

Common cause variation results from how the process is designed to operate and is a natural part of the process. As an example:

> A school bus driver starts her route of assigned streets on time, makes her required stops, and arrives at the school nine minutes later than usual but within the overall time allowance of her schedule. She experienced a slowdown due to the timing of traffic lights. (A cause inherent in the process.)

Common causes of variation account for approximately 85% of the observed variation in processes. When the process is in control, as it was in the school bus example, there is no need to take action. Common causes are sometimes called *system causes* or *chance causes,* because the variations they result in are inherent in the system.

Making minor adjustments to a process because of perceived common cause variation is called *tampering.* Tampering can drive a process into further variation due to unnecessary changes being made to a stable process because of a misunderstood special cause that is actually a common cause.

Process owners should recognize that the special cause variations in production or quality within manufacturing or service processes can usually be detected and removed by the individuals operating the process and that the common cause variations usually require management action to change some inherent feature of the process. This is sometimes called the "85/15 rule," recognizing that management is responsible for providing the necessary inputs to correct the majority of variation problems, that is, common causes.

One of the first goals of successful organizations is to develop reliable processes. A *reliable process* is one that produces the desired output each time with very little variation. Once reliable processes are established and the system becomes stable, the next goal is to continually improve the process (further reduce variation) to produce output that is even better able to meet customer requirements.

Many processes, particularly long-term, high-quantity production processes, lend themselves to the use of *statistical process control* (SPC). SPC is a method of monitoring a process during its operation in order to control the quality of the products or services while they are being produced rather than relying on inspection of the products or services after completion. SPC involves gathering data about the product or service as it is being created, graphically charting the data on one of several types of control charts, and tracking this information on the progress of the process to detect unwanted variation.

Once a process is under control and shows very little variation, process capability studies can be run to calculate the maximum capability of the process. Once a process is running near its maximum capability, making any additional changes to the process is usually not economical.

NOTES

1. Donald L. Siebels, *The Quality Improvement Glossary* (Milwaukee, WI: ASQ Quality Press, 2004).
2. ASQ, *ANSI/ISO/ASQ Q9000:2000, Quality management systems—Fundamentals and vocabulary* (Milwaukee, WI: ASQ Quality Press, 2000).
3. National Institute of Standards and Technology, *Baldrige Performance Excellence Program* (Gaithersburg, MD: National Institute of Standards and Technology, Technology Administration, United States Department of Commerce). The criteria are available in three categories: business, healthcare, and education. One copy of the criteria, any category, is available free of charge. Contact the National Institute of Standards and Technology: telephone 301-975-2036, e-mail nqp@nist.gov, or website http://www.baldrige.nist.gov. Bulk copies are available from ASQ: telephone 800-248-1946, e-mail asq@asq.org, or website http://www.asq.org. Call ASQ for pricing. (The criteria change periodically. The 2012 version is cited in this book.)
4. ASQ, *ANSI/ISO/ASQ Q9000:2005, Quality management systems—Fundamentals and vocabulary* (Milwaukee, WI: ASQ Quality Press, 2006); ASQ, *ANSI/ISO/ASQ Q9001:2008, Quality management systems—Requirements* (Milwaukee, WI: ASQ Quality Press, 2008); ASQ, *ANSI/ISO/ASQ Q9004:2009, Quality management systems—Managing for the sustained success of an organization* (Milwaukee, WI: ASQ Quality Press, 2009). Available from ASQ: telephone 800-248-1946, e-mail asq@asq.org, or website http://www.asq.org. Available in print form, for downloading (PDF), and in English and Spanish. Call ASQ for pricing.

ADDITIONAL RESOURCES

Duffy, Grace L., ed. *The ASQ Quality Improvement Pocket Guide.* Milwaukee, WI: ASQ Quality Press, 2013.

Juran, J. M., and A. B. Godfrey, eds. *Juran's Quality Handbook.* 5th ed. New York: McGraw-Hill, 1999.

Naval Leader Training Unit. *Introduction to Total Quality Leadership.* Washington, DC: US Department of the Navy, 1997.

Navy Total Quality Leadership Office. *Handbook for Basic Process Improvement.* Washington, DC: US Department of the Navy, 1996.

Westcott, Russell T., ed. *The Certified Manager of Quality/Organizational Excellence Handbook.* 4th ed. Milwaukee, WI: ASQ Quality Press, 2014.

Chapter 2
B. Benefits of Quality

Quality is not the exclusive province of engineering, manufacturing, or, for that matter, services, marketing, or administration. Quality is truly everyone's job.

John R. Opel (IBM)

By far the largest costs that outstanding service saves are those of replacing lost customers.

William Davidow and Bro Uttal

Quality is the absence of compromise.

Unknown

Be a yardstick of quality. Some people aren't used to an environment where excellence is expected.

Steve Jobs

> Describe how using quality techniques to improve processes, products and services can benefit all parts of an organization. Describe what quality means to various stakeholders (e.g., employees, organization, customers, suppliers, community) and how each can benefit from quality. (Understand)
>
> **CQIA BoK 2014 I.B.**

High quality affects all of an organization's stakeholders. Employees, the organization itself, customers, suppliers, and the community benefit from total quality performance.

EMPLOYEES

Quality benefits the employees involved in producing high-quality products and services by enhancing their feeling of accomplishment in knowing they have done their jobs to the best of their ability. It also strengthens the security of their position by ensuring continued work to meet the demands of satisfied customers. High-quality products and services sometimes demand higher prices, which can result in higher wages. Well-documented quality systems and processes make the employee's job easier and less frustrating, reduce errors, and allow employees to grow because they are given ready access to the information they need to acquire the skills and knowledge to succeed. By participating in the development of the organization's processes, employees can see their experience, skills, and ideas being put to use for the benefit of everyone in the organization. Accurate, complete documentation reduces errors. And with instant access, documentation allows unplanned problems to be dealt with quickly and safely. Well-informed employees have less risk of on-the-job injuries. Employees benefit from the positive organizational culture that exists in a high-quality organization. The reputation, prestige, and image of a high-quality organization make it easier to recruit new employees, and play an important part in employee job satisfaction. Satisfied employees are less likely to want to move on to other organizations.

THE ORGANIZATION

Quality benefits the organization because it represents the productive and cost-effective use of the organization's resources. Processes that generate high-quality products and services result in lower costs from repair, rework, and warranty actions. High quality can lead to repeat orders from current customers, and it often enables an organization to win an enhanced reputation and additional orders in the marketplace.

A lack of quality can not only result in losing the current order but also damage the supplier's reputation and result in the loss of future orders. It's widely believed that one dissatisfied customer will tell at least 9–15 other people how poor the organization's product or service is, and the loss of future orders could be substantial. The lack of a quality system can create the need for extensive rework, repair, and warranty actions. These actions add extra costs and delays and reduce the productivity of the system. When components are scrapped or services have to be repeated, it is not only the time and material cost that are lost but also the cost of all the work done on the product or service (the added value) up to the point at which it is scrapped. Poor quality costs money. Good quality may cost money, too, but in most cases the costs of poor quality exceed those of good quality.

According to a survey sponsored by the Automotive Industry Action Group (AIAG) and the ASQ Automotive Division, "Companies certified to the automotive industry version of ISO 9000 estimated their average certification cost at $118,100 per site, while they estimated their benefit was $304,300 per site."[1]

Good quality can be a very powerful marketing tool. Recognition by third-party sources can enhance an organization's ability to market its products and services in ways that competitors can't. Here's an example from a recent automotive advertisement:

> Over the past few years, Buick has steadily and quietly been improving its vehicles to where last year it received the highest ranking among domestic manufacturers for quality from JD Power and Associates.

> Buick's Regal, which comes in either the LS or more elaborate GS trim, has benefited from this move to quality, which begins with the versatile 3.8 liter V-6 fuel-injection workhorse engine that powers several models.

A high-quality organization can focus on continuous improvement—assessing what's happening in the organization and preventing bad product and service quality—rather than just reacting to problems and cases of customer dissatisfaction. This proactive style of management will result in a much more profitable organization than a style that reacts only to problems. It greatly increases the probability of the organization's survival.

CUSTOMERS

Customer satisfaction is defined as meeting or exceeding the customer's requirements for product and service features, price, timeliness, and performance. Quality benefits the customer by increasing customer satisfaction. Fewer defects could also add to customers' satisfaction. Higher service quality will also make the customer's experience much more pleasant.

Customers dealing with an organization that has a strong quality program will have fewer complaints because they are being supplied a product or service from better-trained staff following clearer processes and thus making fewer errors. As the organization progressively reduces the time it is forced to devote to correcting mistakes, it can turn to reengineering its processes to make them more customer friendly and more cost-effective. Customers will better trust the organization because they know that it takes quality seriously and gives a better level of service.

Every organization has customers. Quality organizations differentiate themselves from their competitors by providing their customers with high levels of personalized customer care service. Evidence has shown it's easier and much less costly to retain current satisfied customers than to replace lost customers.

Though increased sales and growing profits are generally seen as an accurate measurement of success, customer retention may be the most inclusive measurement. High-quality organizations build lasting long-term customer relationships.

An increasing number of organizations, both public and private, continually measure customer satisfaction. A national, cross-industry measure of customer satisfaction is the American Customer Satisfaction Index (ACSI), an economic indicator of customer satisfaction with the quality of goods and services available to consumers in the United States. Results of the surveys are posted on the ACSI website (http://www.theacsi.org).

See Chapter 11 for more information relating to customers.

SUPPLIERS

Quality organizations work closely with their suppliers and share information to ensure that the suppliers fully understand the organization's requirements and that the organization knows the capabilities of its suppliers. Suppliers' sales, marketing, and service personnel know what the organization needs and can communicate with the appropriate personnel at their customers' facilities to resolve potential problems before they become serious concerns.

Suppliers benefit from working with quality organizations because of the close relationships that the organizations and the suppliers establish to accomplish their mutual goals. Good supplier–organization collaboration tends to have a common set of characteristics, including:

- Reduced cost of inspections
- Less frequent customer audits
- Open sharing of organization and supplier quality information
- Frequent visits to both the organization's and the supplier's facilities to ensure mutual understanding of each party's relative responsibilities
- Supplier shipments of materials directly to the organization's production line for immediate use, such as actions to lower customers' internal inventory
- Decreased expenses from cost sharing
- Reduced risk to the organization because of its ability to use the supplier's knowledge and skills to improve its product or service

See Chapter 12 for more information relating to suppliers.

THE COMMUNITY

The individual communities in which high-quality organizations operate share in the benefits just mentioned. Successful employees, organizations, and suppliers are taxpayers. They contribute to the community by stabilizing the economy. Think of the many communities and regions that have been devastated by the failure of organizations and industries. The quality, productivity, and competitiveness of high-quality organizations directly affect the viability of the communities they occupy.

Communities are very aware of the benefits of having high-quality organizations. Many state and local government jurisdictions provide incentives, including training and consulting, for organizations to fully develop their potential and to assist employees in gaining the necessary training and skills to work in the highly competitive environment of today's economy.

QUALITY BENEFITS TO SOCIETY AS A WHOLE

Everyone can help make communities better places in which to live and work. The process of improvement requires proactive participation by all members of the community: technical societies, neighborhood associations, government agencies, religious organizations, educational institutions, corporations, and businesses.

In many locations, community quality councils provide a forum for improving the quality of life in communities and regions through the use of total quality management (TQM) principles. Embracing TQM principles is a major step forward for all types of organizations. The next step involves society itself. Applying improvement principles to a community is a leading-edge concept in the quality movement.

Quality brings other factors into play, such as vision, leadership, and lifelong learning. It is important because it gives people the opportunity to cooperate and gives their enterprises the means to strive for excellence. The essential ingredient for community improvement is a network of civic and government entities focused on quality and improvement principles. The benefit of propagating quality and improvement principles and practices through a community quality council is that success helps preserve jobs—truly a win–win situation.

Successful experiences in life are almost always the result of careful planning and thorough preparation. People are using quality principles in their communities, providing a pragmatic, holistic approach to making fundamental improvements in the way community problems are addressed. Their experiences are lessons that can be shared for the benefit of all.

Many state and local governments also sponsor quality awards, usually based on the Baldrige Performance Excellence Program criteria, to encourage organizations to advance the level of the quality management processes in their respective communities. Following is an example of stakeholder involvement in a healthcare process:

> A Northern Virginia hospital system recently initiated a process improvement effort to address the issue of patient sepsis. Sepsis is a potentially fatal whole-body inflammation (a systemic inflammatory response syndrome [SIRS]) caused by severe infection. Sepsis is a significant cause of mortality in healthcare patients. Treatment of sepsis also results in an extended length of stay, a measure tracked by the regulating bodies and used as part of hospital reimbursement.
>
> The hospital director of pharmacy chartered a process improvement team to reduce the incidence of sepsis within the hospital. In establishing the charter, the team identified the following stakeholders:
>
> 1. Patients and patient families (considered the primary customers of healthcare)
> 2. Nurses, pharmacists, physicians, and hospital support staff (employees)
> 3. Hospital billing department, insurance providers, and the Centers for Medicare and Medicaid [CMS] (organization)
> 4. Rehabilitation centers, referring physicians, and other hospitals (suppliers)
> 5. Northern Virginia counties supported by the hospital system, professional societies, other healthcare organizations also addressing the sepsis issue, and The Joint Commission (community)
>
> The team members recognized that the project affected more than the patient and internal hospital professionals. They included external stakeholders such as hospital rehabilitation partners that referred critical sepsis patients to the hospital for treatment. Although the team started the project tracking sepsis only in patients arriving through the emergency department, its success led it to broaden the scope of the project to train

the rehabilitation center staff on the recognition and initial treatment of sepsis. As a result of interim reduction in mortality, the project team was included in a nationwide pilot program run by The Joint Commission. Members of the process improvement team have published papers documenting their successes and lessons learned in professional journals, society newsletters, and conference proceedings.

Contact the ASQ Quality Information Center (QIC) for reference to books and publications incorporating quality improvement with the stakeholders discussed above.

NOTE

1. M. Economou, "Quality's Not Costly," *Manufacturing Engineering* 120, no. 3 (1998): 20.

Chapter 3

C. Quality Philosophies

Describe and distinguish between the following theories and philosophies. (Remember)

1. The Shewhart cycle: plan, do, check, act (PDCA)
2. Deming's 14 points
3. The Juran trilogy
4. The Ishikawa diagram
5. Crosby's zero defects

CQIA BoK 2014 I.C.

A *quality philosophy* is defined as "a system of fundamental or motivating principles that form a basis for action or belief." A quality philosophy should reflect how an organization acts in its day-to-day business operations. It should reflect the organization's ideas, values, principles, attitudes, and beliefs. The organization's quality philosophy sets the cultural background in which the organization operates. The philosophy should focus on improving the organization and helping it grow to meet its full potential.

A quality philosophy will be the background for developing the organization's mission, strategic goals, objectives, and plans and will assist the organization's employees in understanding what is expected of them. Given these documents, employees can work in an environment with guidelines for understanding and responding to the day-to-day variables in their work experiences.

A philosophy with a strong focus on quality requires managers to develop well-defined management systems with an emphasis on process management. In developing a quality philosophy, managers need to focus on:

- What their customers consider the most important quality characteristics of the organization's products and services
- What their customers', other stakeholders', and society's needs and expectations are
- What ethical principles should govern how the organization operates

- How the quality philosophy affects the overall operation of the organization's other management systems (financial, health and safety, environmental, etc.)
- What statutory, regulatory, and technical specification requirements affect the organization's operations
- Which of the currently available quality tools should be used in developing and supporting the organization's quality management system

The principles for modern quality management have evolved over the past 50 plus years based on the work of a number of experts who are sometimes referred to as quality gurus. These experts have developed a number of theories and principles that assist organizations in developing their own quality philosophies.

1. DR. WALTER A. SHEWHART

Walter A. Shewhart was born in New Canton, Illinois, on March 18, 1891. He received his bachelor's and master's degrees from the University of Illinois and his PhD in physics from the University of California at Berkeley in 1917. He taught at the Universities of Illinois and California, and he briefly headed the Physics Department at the Wisconsin Normal School in La Crosse.

Shewhart spent most of his early professional career as an engineer at Western Electric (1918–1924) and later worked at Bell Telephone Laboratories, where he served as a member of the technical staff from 1925 until his retirement in 1956. He lectured on quality control and applied statistics at the University of London, at the Stevens Institute of Technology, at the graduate school of the US Department of Agriculture, and in India.

Called on frequently as a consultant, Dr. Shewhart served the War Department, the United Nations, and the government of India, and he was active with the National Research Council and the International Statistical Institute. He served for more than 20 years as the first editor of the *Mathematical Statistics* series published by John Wiley and Sons. He is considered by many to be the father of statistical quality control. Dr. Shewhart died on March 11, 1967, in Troy Hills, New Jersey.

Walter Shewhart first introduced a scientific method for process improvement in 1939. Originally described as a three-step process of specification, production, and inspection for mass production that "constitutes a dynamic scientific process of acquiring knowledge," these steps correspond to the scientific method of hypothesizing, carrying out an experiment, and testing the hypothesis. Shewhart depicted this process graphically as a circle to convey the importance of continual improvement. Deming modified Shewhart's idea and presented it during his seminars in Japan in 1950 as the Plan-Do-Study-Act (PDSA) or Deming Cycle (Chapter 7).

2. DR. W. EDWARDS DEMING

William Edwards Deming was born on October 14, 1900, in Sioux City, Iowa. His family then moved several times, ending up in Powell, Wyoming. Deming attended the University of Wyoming, earning a bachelor's degree in engineering in 1921. He went on to receive a master's degree in mathematics and physics from the University of Colorado in 1925, and he earned a doctorate in physics from Yale University in 1928. During the summers of 1925 and 1926, he worked for the Western Electric Company's Hawthorne plant in Chicago. It was at Hawthorne that he met Walter A. Shewhart and became interested in his work to standardize the production of telephone equipment. After receiving his PhD, Deming went to work for the US government. He applied Shewhart's concepts to his work at the National Bureau of the Census. Routine clerical operations were brought under statistical process control in preparation for the 1940 population census. This led to sixfold productivity improvements in some processes. As a result, Deming started to run statistical courses to explain his and Shewhart's methods to engineers, designers, and others in the United States and Canada.

In 1938, he published a technical book[1] and taught courses on the use of his statistical methods. The beneficial effects of Deming's programs, such as reductions in scrap and rework, were seen during World War II. However, his techniques were generally abandoned after the war as emphasis shifted to producing quantities of consumer goods to alleviate the shortages that had been experienced during wartime.

After World War II, Deming was invited to Japan as an advisor to the Japanese census. He became involved with the Union of Japanese Scientists and Engineers (JUSE) after its formation in 1946. As a result, Deming's name became known and JUSE invited him to lecture to the Japanese on statistical methods. In the early 1950s he lectured to engineers and senior managers, including in his lectures ideas now regarded as part of modern quality principles. In 1956, Deming was awarded the Shewhart medal by the American Society for Quality Control. Four years later, Deming's teachings were widely known in Japan, and the emperor awarded him the Second Order of the Sacred Treasure.

In the late 1970s, Deming started to work with major American organizations. However, his work was relatively unknown in the United States until June 1980, when NBC aired a documentary entitled "If Japan Can, Why Can't We?" Following this exposure, he became well known and highly regarded in the quality community. Deming's first popular book, *Out of the Crisis*, was published in 1986. The following year, he was awarded the National Medal of Technology in America. Dr. Deming died in 1993 at the age of 93.

Deming's Philosophies

Deming's teachings reflected his statistical background. He encouraged managers to focus on variability and to understand the difference between special causes and common causes.

Deming's writings, teachings, and work also extended beyond statistical methods. He encouraged organizations to adopt a systematic approach to problem solving, which later became known as the Deming cycle, or the PDSA cycle. He also pushed senior managers to become actively involved in their companies' quality improvement programs. Work done by Deming and his followers in the United States and elsewhere has attempted to make major changes in the style of Western management.

Dr. Deming taught that management should have a full understanding of his philosophies in order to achieve sustainable progress in an organization. He constantly improved and refined his ideas, and he also used the ideas of others. He is considered by many to be the father of the modern quality revolution.

In his landmark 1986 book, *Out of the Crisis,* Dr. Deming delineated a "chain reaction" philosophy: improve quality → decrease costs → improve productivity → increase market share with better quality, lower price → stay in business → provide more jobs. In the book, he discusses management's failures in planning for the future and foreseeing problems. These shortcomings waste resources, which in turn increases costs and ultimately affects the prices to customers. When customers do not accept paying for such waste, they go elsewhere, resulting in loss of market for the supplier. See Figure 3.1 for an adapted version.

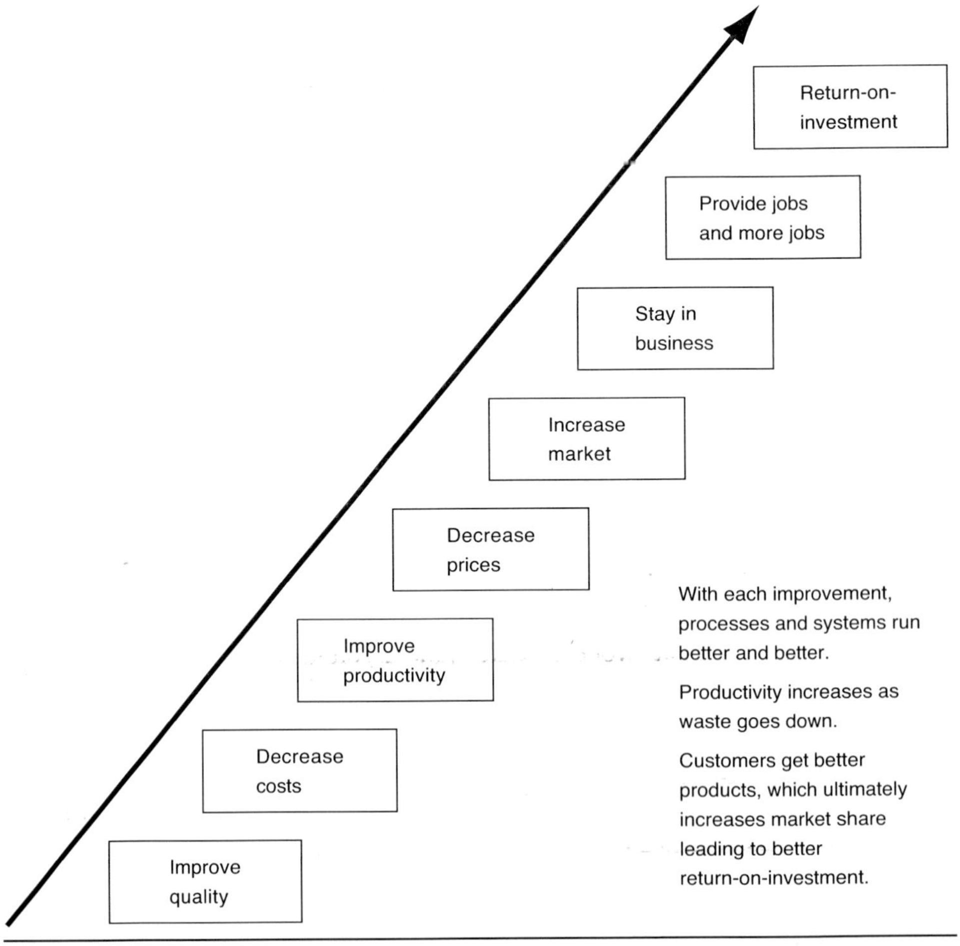

Figure 3.1 Deming's "Chain Reaction."

Source: Adapted from W. Edwards Deming, *Out of the Crisis* (Cambridge, MA: MIT, Center for Advanced Engineering Study, 1986).

In the introduction to *Out of the Crisis,* Deming discusses the need for an entirely new structure, from the foundation upward, to achieve the needed transformation and replace the typical American reconstruction or revision approach. He proposed a new structure in his renowned 14 points of management:

1. Create constancy of purpose toward improvement of product and service, with the aim to become competitive and to stay in business, and to provide jobs.
2. Adopt the new philosophy. We are in a new economic age. Western management must awaken to the challenge, must learn their responsibilities, and take on leadership for change.
3. Cease dependence on inspection to achieve quality. Eliminate the need for inspection on a mass basis by building quality into the product in the first place.
4. End the practice of awarding business on the basis of price tag. Instead, minimize total cost. Move toward a single supplier for any one item, on a long-term relationship of loyalty and trust.
5. Improve constantly and forever the system of production and service, to improve quality and productivity, and thus constantly decrease costs.
6. Institute training on the job.
7. Institute leadership. The aim of supervision should be to help people and machines to do a better job. Supervision of management is in need of overhaul, as well as supervision of production workers.
8. Drive out fear, so that everyone may work effectively for the company.
9. Break down barriers between departments.
10. Eliminate slogans, exhortations, and targets for the work force asking for zero defects and new levels of productivity. Such exhortations only create adversarial relationships, as the bulk of the causes of low quality and low productivity belong to the system and thus lie beyond the power of the work force.
11. (A.) Eliminate work standards (quotas) on the factory floor. Substitute leadership. (B.) Eliminate management by objectives. Eliminate management by numbers, numerical goals. Substitute leadership.
12. (A.) Remove barriers that rob the hourly worker of his right to pride of workmanship. The responsibilities of supervisors must be changed from sheer numbers to quality. (B.) Remove barriers that rob people in management and in engineering of their right to pride of workmanship. This means abolishment of annual or merit rating and of management by objectives.
13. Institute a vigorous program of education and self-improvement.
14. Put everybody in the company to work to accomplish the transformation. The transformation is everybody's job.

In *Out of the Crisis*, Deming also discusses the seven "deadly diseases," which include lack of constancy of purpose, focus on short-term profits, management that is too mobile, and excessive medical and legal costs.

Deming's System of Profound Knowledge

In 1993, Deming outlined his *system of profound knowledge* in his final book, *The New Economics for Industry, Government, and Education*. This is the knowledge needed for transformation from the present style of management to one of optimization. Deming's system of profound knowledge includes management's need to understand systems, to have knowledge of statistical theory and variation, to plan based on past experience, and to have an understanding of psychology.

3. DR. JOSEPH M. JURAN

Joseph Moses Juran was born to a poor family in Braila, Romania, in December 1904. Five years later his father Jakob left Romania for America. By 1912, he had earned enough money to bring the rest of the family to join him in Minnesota. Joseph did well in school and showed a high level of proficiency in math and science; in fact, he did so well that he was able to skip the equivalent of four grade levels. In 1920, he enrolled at the University of Minnesota, the first member of his family to pursue higher education. In 1925, he received a BS in electrical engineering and began working at Western Electric in the inspection department of the famous Hawthorne Works in Chicago. In 1926, he was selected from a group of 20 trainees to become one of two engineers for the Inspection Statistical Department, one of the first such divisions created in American industry. In 1937, Juran became the chief of industrial engineering at Western Electric's home office in New York. During World War II, Juran received a temporary leave of absence from Western Electric to assist the US government with the war effort. He served in Washington, DC, as an assistant administrator for the Office of Lend-Lease Administration. He and his team improved the efficiency of the process, eliminating excessive paperwork and thus hastening the arrival of supplies to the United States' overseas friends. Juran did not return to Western Electric. Rather, he chose to devote the remainder of his life to the study of quality management. As early as 1928, Juran had written a pamphlet entitled *Statistical Methods Applied to Manufacturing Problems*. By the end of the war, he was a well-known and highly regarded statistician and industrial engineering theorist. After he left Western Electric, Juran became the chairman of the Department of Administrative Engineering at New York University, where he taught for many years. In 1951, the first edition of the *Juran's Quality Control Handbook* was published and led him to international eminence. Still a classic standard reference work for quality managers, it is now in its sixth edition.

JUSE invited Juran to come to Japan to teach them the principles of quality management as they rebuilt their economy after World War II. He arrived in 1954 and conducted seminars for top and middle-level executives. His lectures had a strong managerial flavor and focused on planning, organizational issues, management's responsibility for quality, and the need to set goals and targets for improvement. He emphasized that quality control should be conducted as an integral part of management control. In 1979, Juran founded the Juran Institute to better facilitate broader exposure of his ideas. The Juran Institute is today one of the leading quality management consultancies in the world. In 1981, Juran received the Second Order of the Sacred Treasure award from Emperor Hirohito for "the development of quality control in Japan and the facilitation of U.S. and Japanese friendship."

His books have collectively been translated into 13 languages. He received more than 30 medals, honorary fellowships, and awards from 12 different countries. Dr. Juran, who continued working to promote quality management, died at age 103, in 2008.

Juran's Philosophies

Juran taught a project-by-project, problem-solving, team method of quality improvement in which upper management must be involved. He believed that quality does not happen by accident; it must be planned. And he asserted that quality improvements come from a project-by-project approach.

Juran's book *Planning for Quality* is perhaps the definitive guide to Juran's thoughts and his structured approach to company-wide quality planning. Juran taught that quality planning is the first step in a three-level approach to quality management within the organization. Along with planning comes quality control, which involves assessing quality performance, comparing performance with established goals, and closing the gap between actual performance and stated goals. Juran saw the third level—quality improvement—as an ongoing and continual process that includes the establishment of the organizational infrastructure necessary to make cyclical quality improvements. He recommended using teams and project-by-project activities to maintain a continual effort toward both incremental and breakthrough improvement. Juran viewed quality planning as part of a *quality trilogy* that also includes quality control and quality improvement.

His key points in implementing organization-wide quality planning include identifying customers and their needs; establishing optimal quality goals; creating measurements of quality; planning processes capable of meeting quality goals under operating conditions; and producing continuing results in improved market share, premium prices, and reduction of error rates in an office or factory.

Juran's more recent work involved creating an awareness of the quality crisis, establishing a new approach to quality planning, training, assisting companies to replace existing processes to avoid quality deficiencies, and establishing mastery within companies over the quality planning process, thus avoiding the creation of new chronic problems. In the fifth edition of *Juran's Quality Handbook*, Juran contrasts the concepts of Big Q (transactional or business processes) and little q (operation or production processes).[2]

Dr. Juran believed that the majority of quality problems are the fault of poor management rather than poor workmanship on the shop floor. In general, he believed that management-controllable defects account for over 80% of all quality problems.

He was the first to incorporate the human aspect of quality management, which is now embraced within the concept of total quality management. Juran's process of developing his ideas was gradual. Top management involvement, the need for widespread training in quality, the definition of quality as fitness for use, the project-by-project approach to quality improvement, the distinction between the "vital few" and the "useful many," and the trilogy (quality planning, quality control, and quality improvement)—these are the ideas for which Juran is best known.

4. DR. KAORU ISHIKAWA

Kaoru Ishikawa was born in 1915 and graduated in 1939 from the Engineering Department of Tokyo University, having majored in applied chemistry. In 1947, he was made an assistant professor at the university. He obtained his doctorate of engineering and was promoted to professor in 1960. He was awarded the Deming Prize and the Nihon Keizai Press Prize, the Industrial Standardization Prize for his writings on quality control, and the Grant Medal from the American Society for Quality Control in 1971 for his education program on quality control. He died in April 1989.

Ishikawa is best known as a pioneer of the "quality circle" movement in Japan in the early 1960s. In a speech at a convention to mark the 1000th quality circle in Japan in 1981, he described how his work took him in this direction: "I first considered how best to get grassroots workers to understand and practice quality control. The idea was to educate all people working at factories throughout the country but this was asking too much. Therefore I thought of educating factory foremen or on-the-spot leaders in the first place."

In 1968, Ishikawa produced a nontechnical quality analysis textbook for quality circle members. The book, *Guide to Quality Control*, was subsequently translated into English in 1971, with a second edition published by the Asian Productivity Organization in 1982. He subsequently published *What Is Total Quality Control? The Japanese Way*, which was also translated into English (Prentice Hall, 1985).

Ishikawa's Philosophies

In his teachings, Ishikawa emphasized good data collection and presentation. He is best known for his promotion of the use of quality tools such as the Pareto diagram (to prioritize quality improvements) and the cause-and-effect diagram (also known as the Ishikawa or fishbone diagram).

Ishikawa saw the cause-and-effect diagram, like other tools, as a device to assist groups or quality circles in quality improvement. As such, he emphasized open group communication as critical to the construction of the diagrams. Ishikawa diagrams are useful as systematic tools for finding, sorting out, and documenting the causes of variation of quality in production and for organizing mutual relationships between them.

Dr. Ishikawa is associated with the company-wide quality control movement that started in Japan in the years 1955–1960, following the visits of Deming and Juran. Under this system, quality control in Japan was characterized by company-wide participation, from top management to lower-ranking employees. Quality control concepts and methods were used for problem solving in the production process, for incoming material control and new product design control, for analysis to help top management decide policy and verify that policy was being carried out, and for solving problems in sales, personnel, labor management, and clerical departments. Quality audits, internal as well as external, formed part of this activity.

5. PHILIP B. CROSBY

Philip B. Crosby was born in Wheeling, West Virginia, on June 18, 1926. He served two tours in the US Navy, separated by attendance at Western Reserve University.

He worked as a technician in the quality department for the Crosley Corporation from 1952 to 1955. He then moved to the Martin-Marietta facility in Mishawaka, Indiana, where he was a reliability engineer on a government missile program. Later Crosby moved to the Martin-Marietta facility in Orlando, Florida, as a quality manager. During his time at the Orlando facility, he created the "zero defects" concept. In 1965, he began working for ITT. During his 14 years as corporate vice president for ITT, he worked with many ITT subsidiary manufacturing and service divisions around the world, implementing his philosophy.

In 1979, he founded Philip Crosby Associates (PCA). PCA taught management courses on how to establish a quality improvement culture. Large corporations such as GM, Chrysler, Motorola, and Xerox and many other organizations worldwide came to PCA to understand quality management. The courses were taught in many languages in locations around the world.

Crosby's first book, *Quality Is Free*, sold over 2 million copies and was translated into 15 languages. Many organizations around the world began their quality improvement activities because of the popularity of *Quality Is Free* and because of Crosby's reputation for clear and to-the-point advice. Much of *Quality Is Free* is devoted to the concept of zero defects, which is a way of explaining to employees the idea that everything should be done right the first time, that there should be no failures or defects in work outputs.

Crosby left PCA in 1991 and founded Career IV. In 1997, he bought back PCA, a consultancy that now operates throughout the world.

He published his second best-seller, *Quality without Tears*, in 1984, and he is also the author of *The Art of Getting Your Own Sweet Way*. More recently, he published a group of three management books: *Running Things, The Eternally Successful Organization*, and *Leading: The Art of Becoming an Executive*.

Philip B. Crosby died in August 2001.

Crosby's Philosophies

According to Crosby, quality is conformance to requirements, and it can only be measured by the price of nonconformance. This approach means that the only standard of performance is zero defects.

Cost of quality refers to all costs involved in the prevention of defects, assessment of process performance, and measurement of financial consequences. Management can use cost of quality to document variations against expectations and to measure efficiency and productivity. Crosby believed that tracking cost of quality takes the business of quality out of the abstract and brings it sharply into focus as cold hard cash.

Crosby claimed that all nonconformances are caused—they don't appear without reason. Anything that is caused can be prevented. Therefore, organizations should adopt a quality "vaccine" to prevent nonconformance and save money. The three ingredients of the vaccine are determination, education, and implementation.

The Points, or Steps to Quality Improvement

The points that Crosby considered essential involve the following ideas:[3]

- Management commitment
- Education and training
- Measurements
- Cost of quality
- Quality awareness
- Corrective action
- Zero defects
- Goal setting
- Recognition

Crosby's points offer a way to implement the quality improvement process in an organization. They are management tools that evolved from a conviction that an organization's quality improvement policy should be defined, understood, and communicated in a practical manner to every member of the organization.

Crosby's perception of a continuing successful organization embraces the ideas that employees in the organization routinely perform their tasks right the first time, that the organization continues to grow and prosper, that new offerings to customers are created as needed, that change is viewed as an opportunity, and that the people in the organization enjoy working there.

The Four Absolutes of Quality Management

Crosby articulated four absolutes of quality management as the basic concepts of a quality improvement process. The essence of these absolutes is contained in the following statements:

1. Conformance to requirements is the only definition of quality
2. What causes quality is prevention, not appraisal
3. Zero defects is the only acceptable performance standard
4. The price of nonconformance is how quality should be measured

Crosby is best known for his concepts of *do it right the first time* and *zero defects.* He considered traditional quality control, acceptable quality limits, and waivers of substandard products to represent failure rather than assurance of success. He believed that because many organizations have policies and systems that allow deviation from what is actually required, the organizations lose vast amounts of revenue by doing things wrong and then doing them over again. He estimated the loss to be 20% of revenues for manufacturing companies and up to 35% of revenues for service organizations.

6. OTHER GURUS

Dr. Armand V. Feigenbaum

Armand V. Feigenbaum was born in New York City in 1920. He attended Union College and Massachusetts Institute of Technology (MIT), graduating in 1951 with a PhD in engineering. He wrote *Total Quality Control* while he was a doctoral student at MIT. The book has been published in more than a score of languages, including French, Japanese, Chinese, Spanish, and Russian, and has been widely used throughout the world as a foundation for quality control practice. A 40th anniversary edition was published in 1991.

Feigenbaum worked for the General Electric Company from 1942 until 1968. He was worldwide director of manufacturing operations and quality control from 1958 to 1968, when he left to found General Systems Company with his brother Donald.

Feigenbaum was elected to the National Academy of Engineering of the United States in 1992. The citation presented at his election read, "For developing concepts of 'total quality control,' and for contributions to 'cost of quality' and quality systems engineering and practice."

He was the founding chairman of the International Academy for Quality and is a past president of the American Society for Quality Control, which presented him with the Edwards Medal and the Lancaster Award for his international contribution to quality and productivity. In 1988, the US secretary of commerce appointed Feigenbaum to the first Board of Overseers of the Malcolm Baldrige National Quality Award Program.

Feigenbaum is considered by many to be the originator of total quality control. He argued for a systematic or total approach to quality, requiring the involvement of all functions, not just manufacturing, in the quality process. The idea was to build in quality at an early stage rather than inspecting and controlling quality after the fact.

Feigenbaum's Philosophies

In his teachings, Feigenbaum strove to move away from the then primary concern with technical methods of quality control to quality control as a business method. He emphasized the administrative viewpoint and considered human relations to be a basic issue in quality control activities. Individual methods, such as statistics and preventive maintenance, are seen only as segments of a comprehensive quality control program. He saw quality control as an effective system for coordinating the quality maintenance and quality improvement efforts of the various groups in an organization so as to enable production at the most economical levels that allow for full customer satisfaction.

He stated that quality does not mean "best" but "best for the customer use and selling price." The word "control" in the term "quality control" represents a management tool that includes setting quality standards, appraising conformance to the standards, acting when standards are violated, and planning for improvements in the standards.

Dr. Feigenbaum emphasized in his work that total quality programs are the single most powerful tool for organizations and companies today. For quality programs to work, organizational management must assume the responsibility of making the leadership commitment and contributions that are essential to the growth of their respective organizations.

Dr. Genichi Taguchi

Genichi Taguchi was born in 1924. After service in the Astronomical Department of the Navigation Institute of the Imperial Japanese Navy from 1942 to 1945, he worked in the Ministry of Public Health and Welfare and the Institute of Statistical Mathematics, Ministry of Education. He learned much about experimental design techniques from the prizewinning Japanese statistician Matosaburo Masuyama, whom he met while working at the Ministry of Public Health and Welfare. This led to his early involvement as a consultant to Morinaga Pharmaceuticals and its parent company, Morinaga Seika.

In 1950, Taguchi joined the newly founded Electrical Communications Laboratory of the Nippon Telephone and Telegraph Company. He stayed for more than 12 years, during which he began to develop his methods. While working at the laboratory, he consulted widely in Japanese industry. As a result, Japanese companies, including Toyota and its subsidiaries, began applying Taguchi methods extensively from the early 1950s. His first book, which introduced orthogonal arrays, was published in 1951.

From 1954 to 1955, Taguchi was a visiting professor at the Indian Statistical Institute. During this time, he met the well-known statisticians R. A. Fisher and Walter A. Shewhart. In 1957/1958, he published his two-volume book, *Design of Experiments.* His first visit to the United States was in 1962 as a visiting research associate at Princeton University, during which time he toured the AT&T Bell Laboratories. Also in 1962, he was awarded his PhD by Kyushu University.

In 1964, Taguchi became a professor at Aoyama Gakuin University in Tokyo, a position he held until 1982. In 1966, he and several coauthors wrote *Management by Total Results.* At this stage, Taguchi's methods were still essentially unknown in the West, although applications were taking place in Taiwan and India. In this period and throughout the 1970s, most applications of his methods were on production processes; the shift to product design occurred in the last decade.

In the early 1970s, Taguchi developed the concept of the *quality loss function.* He published two other books in the 1970s as well as the third (current) edition of *Design of Experiments.* He won the Deming Application Prize in 1960 and the Deming Award for Literature on Quality in 1951 and 1953.

In 1982, Taguchi became an advisor at the Japanese Standards Association. In 1984, he again won the Deming Award for Literature on Quality. He died on June 2, 2012, in Japan.

Taguchi's Philosophies

Taguchi methods are concerned with the routine optimization of product and process prior to manufacture rather than reliance on the achievement of quality through inspection. Concepts of quality and reliability are pushed back to the design stage, where they really belong. The method provides an efficient technique to design product tests prior to entering the manufacturing phase. However, it can also be used as a troubleshooting methodology to sort out pressing manufacturing problems.

In contrast to Western definitions, Taguchi worked in terms of quality loss rather than quality. Quality loss is defined as "loss imparted by the product to society from the time the product is shipped." It includes not only the loss to the company through costs of reworking or scrapping, maintenance costs, downtime due to equipment failure, and warranty claims, but also the costs to the customer through poor product performance and reliability, leading to further losses to the manufacturer as its market share falls. Taking a target value for the quality characteristic under consideration as the best possible value of this characteristic, Taguchi associated a simple quadratic loss function with deviations from this target. The loss function showed that a reduction in variability about the target leads to a decrease in loss and a subsequent increase in quality.

Taguchi methodology is fundamentally a prototyping method that enables the engineer or designer to identify the optimal settings to produce a robust product that can survive manufacturing time after time, piece after piece, in order to provide the functionality required by the customer. Two major features of the Taguchi methodology are that it was developed and is used by engineers rather than statisticians, thus removing most of the communication gap and the problems of language traditionally associated with many statistical methodologies, and that the methodology is also tailored directly to the engineering context.

SUMMARY

Dr. Deming emphasized statistical process control and uniformity and dependability at low cost. "Work smarter, not harder," he said. Dr. Juran stressed the human elements of communication, organization, planning, control, and coordination and said that problems should be scheduled for solution. Mr. Crosby introduced the concept of zero defects and argued that quality is conformance to requirements and that prevention is the best quality management technique.

All three of these quality management experts agreed that quality means meeting customer requirements and that increased productivity is the result of quality improvement. They all advocated management commitment and employee involvement to improve systems and avoid problems, identification of the most critical problems, use of statistics and other problem-solving tools, and the focus of all activities on the customer.

It is important to understand that the philosophies of Deming, Juran, Crosby, and the many other quality and management gurus are starting points to the development of an organization's quality philosophy. Each organization has unique products, services, cultures, and capabilities. The philosophies of the gurus can help an organization get started, but management, working with all the organization's stakeholders, must develop a philosophy that fits the unique needs of the organization. No one philosophy is totally correct or incorrect. All must be studied and used in the context of how they apply to each individual organization.

Additional information about each of the mentioned gurus may be found by doing an internet search using their full names.

7. QUALITY MODELS

For the quality profession, 1987 was a very significant year, as two events occurred that dramatically changed the way many quality professionals operate. The first was the publication of the original *Malcolm Baldrige National Quality Award Criteria* (now called the *Baldrige Performance Excellence Program*). The second event was the publication of the first edition of the ISO 9000 series of quality management system requirements and guideline documents. Both events resulted in the establishment of hundreds of thousands of documented quality management systems based on the models outlined in the two publications. The following is a brief review of the two models.

The Baldrige Quality Award Program

The Malcolm Baldrige National Quality Award was created by Public Law 100–107 and signed into law on August 20, 1987. The award is named for Malcolm Baldrige, who served as secretary of commerce from 1981 until his tragic death in a rodeo accident in 1987. His managerial excellence contributed to long-term improvement in the efficiency and effectiveness of government.

The quality award program was established to assist in:

- Helping to stimulate American companies to improve quality and productivity for the pride of recognition while obtaining a competitive edge through increased profits
- Recognizing the achievements of those companies that improve the quality of their goods and services and provide an example to others
- Establishing guidelines and criteria that can be used by business, industrial, governmental, and other organizations in evaluating their own quality improvement efforts
- Providing specific guidance for other American organizations that wish to learn how to manage for high quality by making available detailed information on how winning organizations were able to change their cultures and achieve eminence

The awards are given to organizations based in the United States to recognize their achievements in quality and business performance and to raise awareness about the importance of quality and performance excellence as a competitive edge. The award is not given for specific products or services. In 1998, the president and the US Congress approved legislation that made education and healthcare organizations eligible to participate in the award program. Up to three awards may be given annually in each of five categories: manufacturing, service, small business, healthcare, and education.

Though the Baldrige Award and its recipients form the very visible centerpiece of the US quality movement, a broader national quality program has evolved around the award and its criteria. *Building on Baldrige: American Quality for the 21st Century*, a report by the private Council on Competitiveness, said, "More than any other program, the Baldrige Quality Award is responsible for making quality a national priority and disseminating best practices across the United States."[4] The US Commerce Department's National Institute of Standards and Technology (NIST) manages the Baldrige Performance Excellence Program in close cooperation with the private sector. The American Society for Quality assists in administering the award program under contract to NIST.

The Baldrige Performance Excellence Criteria are a framework that any organization can use to improve overall performance. Seven categories make up the award criteria. Comparisons of the Baldrige Award Criteria for each of the three major segments are listed in Table 3.1.

Table 3.1 Comparisons of Baldrige Award Criteria (2011–2012).

Baldrige National Quality Program—2012 Criteria Categories		
Manufacturing, Services, and Small Business	**Healthcare (same as col. 1, except for category 7)**	**Education (same as col. 1, except for category 7)**
1. Leadership 1.1 Senior Leadership 1.2 Governance and Social Responsibilities		
2. Strategic Planning 2.1 Strategy Development 2.2 Strategy Implementation		
3. Customer Focus 3.1 Voice of the Customer 3.2 Customer Engagement		
4. Measurement, Analysis, and Knowledge Management 4.1 Measurement, Analysis, and Improvement of Organizational Performance 4.2 Management of Information, Knowledge, and Information Technology		
5. Workforce Focus 5.1 Workforce Environment 5.2 Workforce Engagement		
6. Operations Focus 6.1 Work Systems 6.2 Work Processes		
7. Results 7.1 Product and Process Outcomes 7.2 Customer-Focused Outcomes 7.3 Workforce-Focused Outcomes 7.4 Leadership and Governance Outcomes 7.5 Financial and Market Outcomes	7. Results 7.1 Health Care and Process Outcomes 7.2 Customer-Focused Outcomes 7.3 Workforce-Focused Outcomes 7.4 Leadership and Governance Outcomes 7.5 Financial and Market Outcomes	7. Results 7.1 Student Learning and Process Outcomes 7.2 Customer-Focused Outcomes 7.3 Workforce-Focused Outcomes 7.4 Leadership and Governance Outcomes 7.5 Budgetary, Financial and Market Outcomes

The award program promotes quality awareness, recognizes quality achievements of US organizations, and provides a vehicle for sharing successful strategies. The Baldrige Award Criteria focus on results and continual improvement. They provide a framework for designing, implementing, and assessing a process for managing all business operations.

The criteria are used by thousands of organizations of all kinds for self-assessment and training and as a tool to develop performance and business processes. Millions of copies have been distributed since the first edition in 1988, and extensive reproduction and electronic access multiply the distribution many times.

For many organizations, using the criteria results in better employee relations, higher productivity, greater customer satisfaction, increased market share, and improved profitability. Studies by NIST, universities, business organizations, and the US General Accounting Office have found that investing in quality principles and performance excellence pays off in increased productivity, satisfied employees and customers, and improved profitability—for both customers and investors. For example, NIST has tracked a hypothetical stock investment in Baldrige Award winners and applicants receiving site visits. The studies have shown that these companies significantly outperform Standard & Poor's 500.

Information about the Baldrige program is available at http://www.nist.gov/baldrige.

ISO 9000 Series

ISO 9000 is a series of international standards first published in 1987 by the International Organization for Standardization, in Geneva, Switzerland. Organizations can use the standards to help determine what is needed to maintain an efficient quality management system (QMS). For example, the standards describe the need to have an effective quality system, to ensure that measuring and testing equipment are calibrated regularly, and to maintain an adequate record-keeping system, as well as many other elements of a complete quality management system. Note: "ISO" is not the abbreviation of the organization; it is derived from the Greek word *isos*, meaning equal.

The ISO 9000 family of standards represents an international consensus on good management practices that ensure an organization has a system that can deliver a product or service that meets the customer's quality requirements. The ISO 9000 series is a set of standardized requirements and guidelines for a QMS applicable to any type of organization, regardless of what the organization does, how big it is, and whether it's in the private or public sector.

Under ISO 9000, organizations establish written QMSs based on the quality elements listed in the ISO 9001 requirement document. Once the QMS has been documented and is in regular use, the organization can have an independent third-party registrar do an audit to assess the system to determine whether it, in fact, meets the requirements of the ISO 9008 standard. If the written QMS meets the standard and is operating as written, the registrar will certify the QMS as meeting ISO 9008 requirements and will register the organization on an international list of organizations that have met the QMS standard.

The ISO 9000 series contains two additional documents. The three documents are:

- *ISO 9000:2005, Quality management systems—Fundamentals and vocabulary.* This document gives the basic quality management principles upon which the new series is based and defines the fundamental terms and definitions used in the ISO 9000 family.
- *ISO 9001:2008, Quality management systems—Requirements.* This document is the requirement standard that outlines the QMS elements that must be addressed to meet customer and applicable regulatory requirements. It is the standard in the ISO 9000 family for which third-party certification can be granted.
- *ISO 9004:2009, Quality management systems—Managing for the sustained success of an organization.* A quality management approach that describes and provides guidance on the principles of quality management to enhance performance improvements.

Because the 2008 edition of the ISO 9001 standard presents only one generic QMS model—ISO 9001—the organization itself determines which elements of the standard apply to its business operations and develops a QMS to meet those applicable requirements. Registrars will then indicate on the certificates issued to each organization what the scope of the registration is and any quality management elements of ISO 9001 that have been excluded.

The ISO 9001 standard lays out requirements in broad, general terms. Each company must interpret them within the context of its own business and develop its own QMS to comply. A brief outline of key requirements follows:

- The QMS addresses:
  - —Overall management system requirements
  - —Documentation requirements (quality manual requirements)
  - —Control of document requirements
  - —Control of records requirements
- Management responsibility addresses top management's commitment to the QMS: communicating, quality policy, quality objectives, quality planning, and continual improvement
- Resource management addresses:
  - —Providing adequate resources to maintain the QMS
  - —Ensuring competence, awareness, and training of human resources
  - —Providing suitable infrastructure and work environment
- Processes for producing products and services ("product realization") address:
  - —Planning for product realization; requirements for customer-related processes

  - Requirements for designing and developing product; purchasing processes
  - Controlling production and service; controlling devices used for monitoring
  - Measuring
- Processes for measurement, analysis, and improvement address:
  - Monitoring and measuring relative to satisfaction of customers
  - Internal auditing of the QMS
  - Monitoring, measuring, analyzing, and controlling data
  - Continually improving (corrective and preventive action)[5]

Additional information about the ISO 9000 family of quality management standards can be found at the International Organization for Standardization website, http://www.iso.org/iso/home.

NOTES

1. W. E. Deming, *Statistical Adjustment of Data* (New York: John Wiley and Sons, 1938, 1943; Dover, 1964).
2. J. M. Juran and A. B. Godfrey, eds., *Juran's Quality Handbook*, 5th ed. (New York: McGraw-Hill, 1999).
3. Derived from P. B. Crosby, *Quality Is Free: The Art of Making Quality Certain* (New York: McGraw-Hill, 1979) and *Quality without Tears: The Art of Hassle-Free Management* (New York: New American Library, 1984).
4. Fiscal Year 2012 Budget Hearing, Baldrige Performance Excellence Program, before the House Committee on Appropriations Subcommittee on Commerce, Justice, Science and Related Agencies, March 11, 2011 (statement of E. David Spong, Foundation for the Malcolm Baldrige National Quality Award, American Society for Quality).
5. Adapted from R. T. Westcott, ed., *The Certified Manager of Quality/Organizational Excellence Handbook*, 4th ed. (Milwaukee, WI: ASQ Quality Press, 2014).

ADDITIONAL RESOURCES

Crosby, P. B. *Quality Is Free: The Art of Making Quality Certain.* New York: McGraw-Hill, 1979.

———. *Quality without Tears: The Art of Hassle-Free Management.* New York: New American Library, 1984.

Deming, W. E. *The New Economics for Industry, Government, and Education.* Cambridge, MA: MIT, 1993.

———. *Out of the Crisis.* Cambridge, MA: MIT Center for Advanced Engineering Study, 1986.

Evans, James R., and William M. Lindsay, *Managing for Quality and Performance Excellence.* 9th ed. Cincinnati, OH: South-Western/Cengage Learning, 2014.

Federal Quality Institute. *Federal Total Quality Management Handbook.* Washington, DC: US Office of Personnel Management, 1990.

Feigenbaum, A. V. *Total Quality Control.* 3rd ed., rev. New York: McGraw-Hill, 1991.

Ishikawa, K. *Guide to Quality Control.* 2nd ed., rev. Tokyo: Asian Productivity Organization, 1986.

———. *What Is Total Quality Control? The Japanese Way.* New York: Prentice-Hall, 1985.

Juran, J. M. *Juran on Planning for Quality.* New York: The Free Press, 1988.

———. *Management of Quality.* 4th ed. Wilton, CT: Juran Institute, 1986.

Juran, J. M., and A. B. Godfrey, eds. *Juran's Quality Handbook.* 5th ed. New York: McGraw-Hill, 1999.

Latzko, W. J., and D. M. Saunders. *Four Days with Dr. Deming: A Strategy for Modern Methods of Management.* Reading, MA: Addison-Wesley, Longman, 1995.

Naval Leader Training Unit. *Introduction to Total Quality Leadership.* Washington, DC: US Department of the Navy, 1997.

Nilsson Orsini, Joyce. *The Essential Deming: Leadership Principles from the Father of Quality.* Milwaukee, WI: ASQ Quality Press, 2013.

Pyzdek, Thomas, and Paul Keller. *The Handbook for Quality Management: A Complete Guide to Operational Excellence,* 2nd ed. New York: McGraw-Hill, 2013.

Westcott, R. T., ed. *The Certified Manager of Quality/Organizational Excellence Handbook.* 4th ed. Milwaukee, WI: ASQ Quality Press, 2014.

Part II

Team Basics

Teams outperform individuals acting alone or in larger organizational groupings, especially when performance requires multiple skills, judgments, and experiences.

John Katzenbach and Douglas Smith

Competition leads to loss. People pulling in opposite directions on a rope only exhaust themselves: they go nowhere.

W. Edwards Deming

A U.S. Government team adopted "CHAMPIONS" as its definition of "team":

C ustomer oriented
H ard working
A mbitious
M ake sure the job's done right
P roud of their work
I nnovative
O pen to new ideas
N ever shirk assignments
S old on quality

V. Daniel Hunt (*Quality Management for Government*)

Chapter 4
A. Team Organization

1. TEAM PURPOSE

> Describe why teams are an effective way to identify and solve problems, and describe when, where, why, and how teams can be used more effectively than other groups of workers. (Apply)
>
> **CQIA BoK 2014 II.A.1.**

The Definition of Team

- A team is a group of individuals organized to work together to accomplish an objective
- A team is a group of two or more people who are equally accountable for the accomplishment of a task and specific performance goals
- A team is a small number of people with complementary skills who are committed to a common purpose
- A team combines individuals' knowledge, experience, skills, aptitude, and attitude to achieve a synergistic effect

A team is *not:*

- An organizational work unit that is not functioning cohesively; however, a team may comprise members of a work unit
- An informal gathering of people, a crowd
- Members of a club, an association, or a society who are not interacting toward a common goal
- Top management of an organization, even though they may be referred to as the "management team," unless they truly function as a team
- A staff meeting, a conference, a seminar, or an educational course, unless functioning as a team

Teams may be initiated for a variety of purposes, some of which are to:

- Improve a process—for example, a cycle-time-reduction team
- Complete a project—for example, a relocation task force to relocate a manufacturing plant
- Conduct a study of a best practice—for example, a benchmarking team
- Solve a problem—for example, a hospital "tiger team" to hunt for the cause of fatalities
- Produce a special event—for example, a team to plan, organize, and conduct an employee recognition evening
- Investigate a discrepancy—for example, a team to determine the root cause of inventory shrinkage
- Participate in a competitive sport—for example, an organization's softball team

A team is appropriate when:

- Achieving an objective involves (or should involve) more than one organizational function. For example, a team to improve the procurement process might involve members from purchasing, materials management, finance, production, and key suppliers.
- Some degree of isolation from the mainstream work is desirable in order to focus on a specific objective or problem. For example, a team to launch a year-long project to implement a quality management system.
- Specially trained and experienced people are "on call" when a specific need arises. Three examples are a proposal response team that is quickly assembled to address a request for proposal from a potential customer/client, a material review board that assembles when there is nonconforming product to review and determine disposition, and an in-plant volunteer fire brigade.

How long a team remains active in a functioning mode depends on several factors, such as:

- The nature of the purpose of the team
- An anticipated or predetermined time span
- Available resources
- The progress being made by the team
- The value of the planned outcomes
- The effectiveness of the team itself

One fault that may occur with a team is when it remains in effect after its purpose and objectives are met. The following are examples:

1. A company has a policy that states that process improvement teams should meet for 14 weeks for any given improvement effort.

2. A project team continues to find reasons to meet long after the original project has been completed. (Members like the comradeship. Some members may fear returning to their regular work after a long hiatus.)

2. TYPES OF TEAMS

> Define and distinguish between various types of teams: process or continuous improvement teams, workgroups or workcells, self-managed teams, temporary or ad hoc project teams, and cross-functional teams. (Apply)
>
> **CQIA BoK 2014 II.A.2.**

Work Group, Work Cell, or Natural Team

A natural team (such as a work group, department, or function) is made up of persons who have responsibility for a specific process or function and who work together in a participative environment. Unlike the process improvement team, which is discussed next, the natural team is neither cross-functional nor temporary. The team leader is generally the person responsible for the function or process performed within the work area. The natural team is useful in involving all employees in a work group in striving for continual improvement. Starting with one or two functions, successful natural teams can become role models for expansion of natural teams throughout an organization. A natural team example follows:

> The information technology (IT) department serves all the functions within the 4000-person Mars Package Delivery's countrywide operations. The IT department's work units (technical system maintenance, application systems design and programming, data entry, computer operations, data output, and customer service—internal, technology help desk, and administration) function as an internal team. Selected representatives from each work unit meet weekly to review the IT department's performance and to initiate corrective and preventive actions.

Process Improvement Teams

Process improvement teams—or PITs, as they are often called—focus on creating or improving specific business processes. A PIT may attempt to completely reengineer a process or may work on incremental improvements (see "Incremental and Breakthrough Improvement" in Chapter 8). If attempting a breakthrough, the team is usually cross-functional in composition, with representatives from a number of different functions and with a range of skills related to the process to be improved. A PIT working on incremental improvements is often composed of persons having a functional interest in improving a portion of the overall process, such as representatives from a specific functional work unit. Two examples follow:

> BPC, which manufactures a flexible packaging product, periodically convenes a cycle-time-reduction team (CTRT) under the leadership of a pressroom supervisor, with four or five operators from the supervisor's pressroom. A trained facilitator helps bring about the team's formation and keeps the meeting process on track during the weekly meetings. Each CTRT defines its objectives and the procedures and tools to be used to improve its process. The CTRT typically meets for 10–12 weeks, but it may disband earlier if its objectives have been met. Pressrooms rotate so that only one CTRT is functioning at any one time. A technical trainer provides training as necessary, either for members new to improvement tools or for the whole team when a new tool or technique is needed. The CTRT may call on anyone in the company to provide needed information. At BPC, it is considered a privilege to be invited to join a CTRT.

> At A&H, a provider of group accident and health insurance in the southwestern United States, originators of significant process improvement suggestions (with an estimated savings of $100,000 per year or more) are invited to participate in a PIT to address their suggestions. A trained facilitator is assigned to help with team formation and team process issues. A&H finds that this approach not only recognizes and rewards those with suggestions, but also stimulates involvement in the suggestion system. The synergy of the PITs often results in savings exceeding the original estimates.

A variation used in many fast-paced organizations is the *kaizen blitz* or *kaizen event.* This accelerated work-team approach focuses intensely on achieving improvements in a three-to five-day time frame. Reducing cycle time and waste and increasing productivity are examples in which improvements of as much as 70% have been reported.

Becoming more prevalent are teams consisting of qualified Green Belt and Black Belt employees that are formed to improve processes using the techniques and tools of Lean-Six Sigma. Such teams serve three purposes: They nurture the philosophy of continuous improvement, they substantiate the continual investment in Lean-Six Sigma methodology, and they sustain the training and development of qualified Lean-Six Sigma personnel. This type of team is frequently cross-functional in composition and involved in *breakthrough improvements.* (See Chapter 8.)

In some organizations, cross-functional teams carry out all or nearly all of the functions. In such cases, the organization resembles a matrix- or project-type organization. In attempting to eliminate internal competition among functional groups, organizations have adopted cross-functional teams for many areas, including product design. For example:

> Macho Motors, a leading manufacturer of off-road service vehicles, integrates its marketing, engineering, production, support services, shipping, and customer service functions into product families. Employing quality function deployment tools and concurrent engineering-production techniques, each family (cross-functional team) works together to meet

> customers' needs. Representatives from each family meet quarterly to share process improvement information.

The smaller the organization, the more likely employees are to work together, often doing others' designated jobs as the need arises. Each employee wears many hats. In recent times, larger organizations have come to recognize the value of smaller, cross-functional entities. In a fast-paced economy, these more flexible organizations can often move more swiftly than larger competitors to reconfigure themselves and their products and services to meet changing needs. An example is the following:

> Williams Air Service's employees own the regional air passenger service firm. Nearly everyone, from the airline's president to the people staffing the check-in counter, is trained to rotate among jobs in performing passenger check-in, baggage handling, fueling, flight attendant functions, and clerical functions. Only the pilots, mechanics, and the bookkeeper have specialized functions not delegated to other personnel. The entire airline is a cross-functional team.

Project Teams

A project team is formed to achieve a specific mission. The project team's objective may be to create something new, such as a facility, product, or service; or to accomplish a complex task, such as to implement a quality management system certified to ISO 9001 requirements; or to upgrade all production equipment to be computer-controlled. Typically, a project team employs full-time members, on loan, for the duration of the project. The project team operates in parallel with the primary organizational functions. The project team may or may not be cross-functional in member composition, depending on its objectives and competency needs. Often the project leader is the person to whom the ultimate responsibility for managing the resulting project outcome is assigned. An example follows:

> Abel Hospital, a community healthcare organization of 250 employees, has established a task force (project team) to select a site and design and build a new hospital to replace the existing 112-year-old facility. New governmental regulations make a new facility imperative. The "Must Build It" (MBI) project team includes representatives from each hospital department, an external consulting firm, an architectural design firm, and a legal firm. A full-time facilitator-consultant provides team training and facilitates meetings. The team leader is the former assistant director of Abel Hospital and will likely assume the role of director when the present director retires (coincidental with the planned occupation of the new facility). The MBI team has a three-year window in which to complete the facility and move the existing services and patients. Care is taken to conduct team building and provide training in the tools and techniques the team members will need, especially project planning and management. Team members have been replaced in their former positions until the project is completed. The MBI team is located in a rental site that is removed from the present premises of Abel Hospital. The MBI leader provides weekly project status reports to senior management and quarterly project summary presentations to the board of directors.

Self-Directed Teams

Self-directed (self-managed) teams are groups of employees authorized to make a wide range of decisions about how they will handle issues regarding safety, quality, scheduling of work, allocation of work, setting of goals, maintenance of work standards, equipment maintenance, and resolution of conflicts. Often called high-performance work teams, these teams offer employees a broader spectrum of responsibility and ownership of a process. Often the team members select the team leaders; sometimes leadership is rotated among members. Two examples are the following:

> Med Plastics has structured its new manufacturing operations for medical devices on the principles of cell manufacturing and self-managed teams. Each cell manufactures one complete category of products. Within a cell, each operator is fully trained to perform all operations. Self-led and making their own decisions, the members of the teams in each cell determine how and when to rotate tasks and are responsible for the quality of the products shipped.

> District 4 of Alabaster County's K–12 educational system allows the editorial offices of each of the three high schools' student newspapers to manage its own operations, within the rules and regulations of the district. Each school's newspaper office is responsible for recruiting its own student staff, selecting its editor, arranging for team and technical training, allocating assignments, and producing a high-quality student newspaper. Each newspaper office has adopted some unique approaches to managing its operations. The achievements of the student newspaper offices are publicized in local community media. Awards for significant contributions are given annually, sponsored by the *Alabaster Chronicle*.

Because of the level of empowerment afforded, careful planning and training are key to a successful self-directed team. The most success usually occurs when a new business or process is initiated. Transforming a traditional work culture to one of self-management is a lengthy process and can cause serious workforce turmoil.

Virtual Teams

A virtual team is a group of two or more persons who are usually affiliated with a common organization and have a common purpose. The nature of the virtual team is that its members conduct their work either partly or entirely via electronic communication. Virtual teams are a hybrid in that they may or may not be cross-functional in terms of competencies. These teams may or may not be partly or entirely self-managed. Typically, the virtual team is geographically dispersed, often with individual members working from their homes. For example:

> A virtual team of two members of ASQ's Quality Management Division (QMD) (one member in Florida and one in Connecticut) edited this book, augmented by two QMD content reviewers (one from Michigan and the other from Kansas).

3. VALUE OF TEAMS

> Identify how a team's efforts can support an organization's key strategies and effect positive change throughout the organization. (Understand)
>
> **CQIA BoK 2014 II.A.3.**

A key principle is that no team should be formed unless its purpose (mission) and objectives can be traced upward in supporting the organization's strategies and plans.

This alignment with organizational strategies, goals, and objectives should be shown through measurements directly related to the customer requirements of the company. Tools such as the balanced scorecard, voice of the customer (house of quality), customer or employee surveys, and focus groups are all effective vehicles for documenting the ultimate value of the team's work within the organization. Further, teams should be capable of demonstrating value. Every team, regardless of type, should plan to address one or more of the following purposes or missions:

- Fulfilling a mandate (law, regulation, owners' requirements)
- Producing a favorable benefits-to-cost ratio
- Providing a return on investment (ROI) for the organization that is equal to or greater than an alternative project
- Improving customer satisfaction and retention
- Meeting or exceeding competitive pressures in the marketplace
- Introducing new processes, products, or services
- Improving a process (cycle-time reduction, cost saving/avoidance, reduce waste)
- Improving or expanding the organization's core competencies
- Building an effective and efficient workforce through training, education, and individual development
- Involving key suppliers and customers in improvement initiatives
- Continually innovating processes, products, and services
- Supporting the communities in which the organization operates
- Enhancing the organization's reputation for delivering quality products/services

Chapter 5
B. Team Roles and Responsibilities

The team concept conveys the message that PQI [= Productivity and Quality Improvement] is everybody's business.

John Hradesky

Major gains in quality and productivity most often result from teams.

Peter R. Scholtes

> Describe the roles and responsibilities of various team stakeholders. (Understand)
>
> **CQIA BoK 2014 II.B.**

Of the seven roles described in Table 5.1, those of timekeeper and scribe are the only optional ones, depending on the mission of the team. Though the remaining five roles are essential, they may be combined in a variety of ways. However, the most crucial roles for the success of the team, once it is formed, are those of the team leader and the facilitator. The team leader is responsible for the content, the work done by the team. The facilitator is responsible for ensuring that the process affecting the work of the team is the best for the stage and situation the team is in.

The need for a trained facilitator depends on whether:

- The team has been meeting for some time and is capable of resolving conflicting issues
- A new member has been added, thus upsetting established relationships
- A key contributor to the group has been lost
- Other disturbing factors have occurred, such as lack of adequate resources, the threat of project cancellation, or a major change in requirements

Obviously, the team member role is also important, but it is somewhat less critical than those of team leader and facilitator. Supplementing the team with "on call" experts can often compensate for a shortfall in either the number of members or

Table 5.1 Roles, responsibilities, and performance attributes.

Role Name	Responsibility	Definition	Attributes of Good Role Performance
Sponsor	Backer; risk taker	The person who supports a team's plans, activities, and outcomes.	• Believes in the concept/idea • Has sound business acumen • Is willing to take risk and responsibility for outcomes • Has authority to approve needed resources • Will be listened to by upper management
Champion	Advocate	The person promoting the concept or idea for change/improvement.	• Is dedicated to seeing it implemented • Holds absolute belief it is the right thing to do • Has perseverance and stamina
Facilitator	Helper; trainer; advisor; coach	A person who: • Observes the team's processes and team members' interactions and suggests process changes to facilitate positive movement toward the team's goals and objectives • Intervenes if discussion develops into multiple conversations • Intervenes to skillfully prevent an individual from dominating the discussion or to engage an overlooked individual in the discussion • Assists the team leader in bringing discussions to a close • May provide training in team building, conflict management, and so forth	• Is trained in facilitating skills • Is respected by team members • Is tactful • Knows when to and when not to intervene • Deals with the team's process, not content • Respects the team leader and does not override his or her responsibility • Respects confidential information shared by individuals or the team as a whole • Will not accept facilitator role if expected to report to management any information that is proprietary to the team • Will abide by the organization's Code of Ethics and principles

Team leader	Change agent; chair; head	A person who: • Staffs the team or provides input for staffing requirements • Strives to bring about change/improvement through the team's outcomes • Is entrusted by followers to lead them • Has the authority for and directs the efforts of the team • Participates as a team member • Coaches team members in developing or enhancing necessary competencies • Communicates with management about the team's progress and needs • Handles the logistics of team meetings • Takes responsibility for team records	• Is committed to the team's mission and objectives • Has experience in planning, organizing, staffing, controlling, and directing teams • Is capable of creating and maintaining communication channels that enable members to do their work • Is capable of gaining the respect of team members; serves as a role model • Is firm, fair, and factual in dealing with a team of diverse individuals • Facilitates discussion without dominating • Actively listens • Empowers team members to the extent possible within the organization's culture • Supports all team members equally • Respects each team member's individuality
Timekeeper	Gatekeeper; monitor	A person designated by the team to watch the use of allocated time and remind the team members when their time objective may be in jeopardy.	• Is capable of assisting the team leader in keeping the team meeting within the predetermined time limitations • Is sufficiently assertive to intervene in discussions when the time allocation is in jeopardy • Is capable of participating as a member while still serving as a timekeeper

(*continued*)

Table 5.1 Roles, responsibilities, and performance attributes. *(continued)*

Role Name	Responsibility	Definition	Attributes of Good Role Performance
Scribe	Recorder; note taker	A person designated by the team to record critical data from team meetings. Formal "minutes" of the meetings may be published and distributed to interested parties.	• Is capable of capturing on paper, or electronically, the main points and decisions made in a team meeting and providing a complete, accurate, and legible document (or formal minutes) for the team's records • Is sufficiently assertive to intervene in discussions to clarify a point or decision in order to record it accurately • Is capable of participating as a member while still serving as a scribe
Team members	Participants; subject matter experts	The persons selected to work together to bring about a change/improvement, achieving this in a created environment of mutual respect, sharing of expertise, cooperation, and support.	• Are willing to commit to the purpose of the team • Are able to express ideas, opinions, and suggestions in a nonthreatening manner • Are capable of listening attentively to other team members • Are receptive to new ideas and suggestions • Are even-tempered and able to handle stress and cope with problems openly • Are competent in one or more fields of expertise needed by the team • Have favorable performance records • Are willing to function as team members and forfeit "star" status

members' competencies. Selected members must willingly share their expertise, listen attentively, and support all team decisions.

Selecting a team member to serve as timekeeper may be helpful, at least until the team becomes adept at monitoring its use of time. When a timekeeper is needed, the role is often rotated, giving consideration to whether the selected member has a full role to play in the deliberations at a particular meeting.

In some team missions for which formal documentation is required, a scribe or notetaker may be needed. This role can be distracting for a member whose full attention is needed on the topics under discussion. For this reason, an assistant, not a regular member of the team, is sometimes assigned to "take the minutes" and publish them. Care should be taken not to select a team member for this role solely on the basis of that team member's sex or position in the organization.

Very frequently, a team must function in parallel with day-to-day assigned work and with the members not relieved of responsibility for the regularly assigned work. This places a burden and stress on the team members. Both the day-to-day work and the work of the team must be conducted effectively. The inability to be in two places at one time calls for innovative time management, conflict resolution, negotiation, and delegation skills on the part of the team members.

Several roles within a team may be combined, depending on the size of the team and its purpose. Following are some examples:

- The team has begun to function smoothly, and the team leader has become more skilled under the guidance of a facilitator. It is decided that the facilitator is no longer needed.
- A three-person team self-selects the person who sold the idea to management (the champion) as team leader.
- A self-managed, cross-functional PIT of eight persons elects to rotate the team leader role at two-week intervals.
- A departmental work group (natural team) rotates timekeeper and scribe roles at each meeting so as not to discriminate based on gender, job held, age, schooling, and so forth.
- The backer of the project team serves as the team leader because the project is confined to his or her area of responsibility.
- Specialists, such as a material-handling systems designer or a cost accountant, are periodically requested to temporarily join a team as needed.

Chapter 6

C. Team Formation and Group Dynamics

1. INITIATING TEAMS

> Apply the elements of launching and sustaining a successful team, including establishing a clear purpose and goals, developing ground rules and schedules, gaining support from management and commitment from the team members. (Apply)
>
> **CQIA BoK 2014 II.C.1.**

The underlying principles pertaining to launching most any team are as follows:

- There must be a clearly understood purpose for having the team. This purpose must be communicated to all individuals and organizations potentially impacted by the work of the team.
- The team must be provided with or generate a mission statement and a clear goal—the expected outcome of the team's efforts. The mission and the goal must support the organization's strategic plans.
- The team must document objectives, with time lines and measurement criteria, for the achievement of the goal.
- The team must have the support of management, including the needed resources, to achieve its objectives.
- The team must be given or define for itself the ground rules and schedules under which it will operate.
- The team must be empowered, to the extent allowed by the sponsor, to perform its scheduled activities.
- The team must build into its plans a means for interim measurement of progress and the means for improving its performance.
- The team must commit to achieving its mission, goals, and objectives.
- The sponsor must provide a mechanism for recognizing both the efforts and the outcomes of the team's activities.

Though an ideal team size could be five members, team size will vary depending on the following:

- Purpose for the team—its mission
- Size and complexity of the task that the team is to perform
- Size of the organization in which the team will be formed
- Type of team
- Duration of the team's work and the frequency of its meetings
- Degree of urgency for the outcomes of the team's efforts
- Resource constraints, such as funding, availability of appropriate personnel, facilities, and equipment
- Team management constraints, such as minimum and maximum number of team members needed to achieve the team's mission
- Organizational culture—organizational policies and practices
- Predominant managing style of the organization to which the team reports
- Regulatory requirements
- Customer mandates

When a whole function or department works as a natural team, the team size is the number of persons in the department. If three persons band together to operate a charter air-taxi service and they work as a team, the team is the three persons. When a cross-functional project team is formed to design and build a new shopping center, the team could be very large and be subdivided into a number of smaller teams. In a municipal public library, when a quality/process improvement team is formed to reduce retrieval and reshelving cycle times, it is likely to be cross-functional but limited to one representative from each function within the process cycle and constrained by the availability of staff.

All team members must adhere to expected standards of quality, fiduciary responsibility, ethics, and confidentiality. (See Appendix B for the ASQ Code of Ethics.) It is imperative that the most competent individuals available are selected for each role.

Guidelines for Team Formation

A formal charter may be appropriate. The charter could include the following:

- The purpose for the team and overall outcome anticipated
- The sponsor
- Approval to launch the team (including release of funding)
- Criteria for team member selection
- Methodology and technology to be used
- Degree of autonomy granted and team member empowerment boundaries

- Any constraints pertinent to the team's work and conduct
- Start and end times (as applicable)
- Techniques and tools of project planning and management to be used
- Tracking, measuring, and reporting procedure to be implemented
- Risk assessment criteria to be established, and contingency plans with periodic assessments conducted
- The means that will be put in place to recognize, reinforce, and reward the team for work done well

2. SELECTING TEAM MEMBERS

> Describe how to select team members based on their knowledge and skill sets and team logistics, such as a sufficient number of members in relation to the size or scope of the project, appropriate representation from affected departments or areas, and diversity. (Apply)
>
> **CQIA BoK 2014 II.C.2.**

The basis for a strong, successful team is careful selection of its members. See Table 5.1 for the attributes of good role performance.

Team members are often selected because of their knowledge and past achievements. Membership choices for smaller and shorter-duration teams are frequently based on informal referrals. Some instruments and formal methods may be employed in staffing larger and longer-duration teams, especially when candidates are unknown to the sponsor or team leader.

In our fast-paced environment, most organizations seek team leaders who are both visionary and flexible—team leaders who can inspire an eclectic, high-performance group of followers. Needed are team leaders who can coach as well as cajole, captain as well as crew, control as well as collaborate, criticize as well as commend, confess as well as confront, consummate as well as concede, create as well as conform—these attributes and others are those of a flexible leader. Although they may help, neither charisma nor superiority (in terms of position, education, longevity, or political clout) should be the primary criterion for choosing a potentially effective team leader.

> A floundering project team formed to design and implement a substantive information technology project failed to reach any of its first-year goals, other than spending the $100,000 (1970 time period) allocated for the project. The small team of three, augmented by personnel from a software design firm, was led by a person who had in-depth knowledge of present systems, the organization, and the principal people in the organization. He

had been with the company his entire working career and was within two years of retirement when first assigned. A systems analyst and an accomplished computer programmer were the other in-house team members.

When the CEO became concerned that nothing visible was occurring, he ordered that a new project manager be assigned with the directive to find out what was going on and then recommend either continuance with restructuring or abandonment. The new project manager assessed the situation and confirmed that the three project incumbents had sufficient expertise, with help from the software house, to complete the project with a one-year extension and with additional funding.

The recommendation was approved, and the now four-person team proceeded under new direction. Formal project management practices were instituted, and a tight time line with interim milestones and clear objectives for the work were established. Measurements and monitoring were instituted along with weekly progress reviews. Much of the earlier work had to be discarded. Assurances had to be obtained for the analyst and the programmer to ensure their reentry to their former work units when the project was completed. The contract with the software house had to be renegotiated, with penalty clauses for failure to meet the organization's requirements. Working conditions for the team were improved. Means for recognizing their contribution were created.

Relieved of his project manager responsibility, the former leader poured newfound energy and his extensive knowledge into the detailed design of the system, eager to retire with a success. Ensured of their jobs after the project was completed, the analyst and the programmer committed to making the project successful.

The key to the successful completion of the project, 10 months later, was due in large part to the new team leader's leadership and management attributes and approach.

Ideally, a profile of what attributes are sought for each member of a team establishes the criteria for guiding selection. Résumés of candidates and records of past performance are reviewed, and potential members are interviewed. Member selection may be augmented by the following instruments:

- The Myers-Briggs Type Indicator (MBTI), an instrument for assessing personality "type" based on Carl Jung's theory of personality preferences. The test results, analyzed by a trained practitioner, can aid in structuring either the diversity or the similarity desired in a potential team. There are four bipolar scales:

  — (E) Extroverted or (I) Introverted

  — (S) Sensing or (N) Intuitive

  — (T) Thinking or (F) Feeling

  — (J) Judging or (P) Perceiving

  These scales form 16 possible styles, for example, ENFP, INTJ, and ISFJ.

- The DiSC profiling instrument, based on William Marston's theories, measures characteristic ways of behaving in a particular environment.

The DiSC dimensions are dominance, influence, steadiness, and conscientiousness.

- A KESAA factors analysis is a method for capturing and analyzing the factors that are important for performing a specific job or task. The factors are knowledge, experience, skills, aptitude, and attitude.[1]

In addition to the composition of the team, another key consideration for its success is whether the team will function as an autonomous parallel organization or as an adjunct to the daily operation of the organization. The stand-alone team is often located away from the parent organization and is also sometimes exempt from some of its restrictive rules. Members of such a team are typically on temporary assignment to the team and do not continue their former daily responsibilities. When the team must function with members retaining their day-to-day responsibilities, conflicts can arise over which activity takes precedence. If such conflicts are not carefully resolved, team effectiveness can be severely compromised.

"Pills-are-us," a cross-functional PIT in a small community hospital, was established to find ways to reduce the time it took to obtain medications from the hospital's pharmacy. The nine-person team, consisting of nurses from each of the larger departments, was to meet for one hour once a week "until they found a way to substantially reduce the cycle time."

From the outset, the team was plagued with absences and late arrivals. Each absent or tardy nurse had a legitimate reason for his or her behavior. Regardless, team effectiveness suffered and the team dragged on without an end in sight.

Repeatedly, the team leader attempted to get department heads to help resolve the conflict, but their concerns were elsewhere. Finally, the team's sponsor, a vice president, convened a meeting of department heads to reaffirm their commitment and reach agreement as to how their nurses' participation would be handled. Priorities were established, resource-sharing agreements were reached, and supervisors were advised of the decisions. Project team participation now had its assigned priority and the appropriate management commitment to back it up. The team members—the nurses—were relieved of the decision as to which "master" to serve first and under what conditions.

3. TEAM STAGES

> Describe the classic stages of team evolution: forming, storming, norming, and performing. (Understand)
>
> **CQIA BoK 2014 II.C.3.**

According to B. W. Tuckman, teams move through four stages of growth as they develop maturity over time.[2] Each stage may vary in intensity and duration.

Stage 1: Forming

The cultural background, values, and personal agenda of each team member come together in an environment of uncertainty. New members wonder, "What will be expected of me? How do I, or can I, fit in with these people? What are we really supposed to do? What are the rules of the 'game,' and where do I find out about them?" Fear is often present but frequently denied. Fear may be about personal acceptance, possible inadequacy for the task ahead, and the consequences if the team fails its mission. These fears and other concerns manifest themselves in dysfunctional behaviors such as:

- Maneuvering for a position of status on the team
- Undercutting the ideas of others
- Degrading another member
- Trying to force one's point of view on others
- Bragging about one's academic credentials
- Vehemently objecting to any suggestion but one's own
- Abstaining from participation in discussions
- Distracting the work by injecting unwanted comments or trying to take the team off track
- Retreating to a position of complete silence

Because of the diversity of some teams, there may be a wide variety of disciplines, experience, academic levels, and cultural differences among the members. This can result in confusion, misunderstanding of terminology, and language difficulties. A technique for moving the team through this stage is to clearly state and understand the purpose of the team, identify the roles of the members, and establish criteria for acceptable behavior ("norms").

Stage 2: Storming

In the storming stage, team members still tend to think and act mostly as individuals. They struggle to find ways they can work together, and sometimes they belligerently resist. Each member's perspective appears to be formed from his or her own personal experience rather than based on information from the whole team. Uncertainty still exists, defenses are still up, and collaborating is not yet the accepted mode of operation. Members may be argumentative. They frequently test the leader's authority and competence. Members often try to redefine the goal and direction of the team and act as individual competitors.

Stage 3: Norming

True teamwork begins at the norming stage. Members shift from dwelling on their personal agendas to addressing the objectives of the team. Competitiveness, personality clashes, and loyalty issues are sublimated, and the team moves toward willingness to cooperate and openly discusses differences of opinion. The leader, with aid from a facilitator, focuses on process, promoting participation and team decision making, encouraging peer support, and providing feedback. A potential danger at this stage is that team members may withhold their good ideas for fear of reintroducing conflict.

Stage 4: Performing

Now the members, functioning as a mature and integrated team, understand the strengths and weaknesses of themselves and other members. The leader focuses on monitoring and feedback, letting the team take responsibility for solving problems and making decisions. The team has become satisfied with its processes and is comfortable with its working relationships and its resolution of team problems. The team is achieving its goals and objectives. However, reaching this stage does not guarantee smooth operating indefinitely.

Typically, a team moves through these four stages in sequence. However, a team may regress to an earlier stage when something disturbs its growth. The addition of a new member may take a team back to stage 1 as the new member tries to become acclimated and the existing team members "test" the newcomer. Loss of a respected member may shift the apparent balance of power so that the team reverts to stage 2. A change in scope or the threat of cancellation of a team's project may divert the team to an earlier stage to redefine direction. Exposure of an individual team member's manipulation of the team can cause anger, retrenchment to silence, or a push to reject the offending member, along with a revert to stage 1.

Some teams find difficulty in sustaining stage 4 and oscillate between stages 3 and 4. This may be a matter of inept team leadership, unsupportive sponsorship, less-than-competent team members, external factors that threaten the life of the team's project, or a host of other factors.

> Big Risk, an insurer of off-road construction and pleasure vehicles, has a strategic plan to reduce administrative expenses by 30% over the next three years. In support of this goal, the vice president of administration sponsors a project: a claim-processing team (CPT) to reduce the claim-processing cycle time (mission) from three weeks to four days within one year. A team leader is selected. She gathers data and estimates savings of $250,000 per year and an estimated project cost of $25,000.
>
> The CPT members are selected from functions affected by any potential change. A facilitator is retained to conduct team-building training and to guide the team through its formative stages until it reaches a smooth-functioning level of maturity. The CPT prepares a project plan, including monthly measurement of progress, time usage, and costs. The president approves the plan. The CPT fine-tunes its objectives, sets ground rules, and allocates the tasks to be performed. The project is launched.
>
> The CPT reviews its progress weekly, making any necessary adjustments. The CPT presents a monthly summary review to the vice president of administration, giving the status of time usage, costs, and overall progress toward the goal. Any problems requiring the vice president's intervention or approval are discussed (such as the need for more cooperation from the manager of field claims adjusters or the need to contract for the services of a computer systems consultant).

The CPT completes the process reengineering and successfully implements the changes. A formal report and presentation are presented to the senior management. The outcomes of the CPT are publicized, and team member contributions are recognized and rewarded. Appropriate documentation is completed and the CPT is disbanded.

Adjourning

Other authors have added adjourning to Tuckman's original model. This stage is the process of closure that occurs when a team has accomplished its mission. The actions include reviewing lessons learned, assessing the achievement of the outputs and outcomes intended, completing documentation, recognizing the team's efforts and celebrating, and formally disbanding the team. This stage is often skipped or inadequately addressed in the team's haste to disband and move on.

4. TEAM CONFLICT

> Describe the value of team conflict and recognize how to resolve it. Define and describe groupthink and how to overcome it, understand how poor logistics, agendas and lack of training become barriers to team success. (Analyze)
>
> **CQIA BoK 2014 II.C.4.**

Conflict among team members can occur at any of the stages but is more likely to surface during the forming and storming stages. Conflict can, and does, occur in cooperative as well as competitive relationships. It is part of human life. Conflict is inevitable—make it work for the team.

Authors Schmidt and Tannenbaum list five stages of the evolution of conflict:[3]

1. Anticipation
2. Conscious but unexpressed difference
3. Discussion
4. Open dispute
5. Open conflict

The team leader, with guidance from a facilitator, if needed, can help transform a conflict into a problem-solving event by:

- Welcoming differences among team members
- Listening attentively with understanding rather than evaluation
- Helping to clarify the nature of the conflict
- Acknowledging and accepting the feelings of the individuals involved

- Indicating who will make the final decision
- Offering process and ground-rule suggestions for resolving the differences
- Paying attention to sustaining relationships between the disputants
- Creating appropriate means for communication between the persons involved in the conflict

A commonly used instrument for assessing individual behavior in conflict situations is the Thomas-Kilmann Conflict Mode Instrument.[4] This instrument assesses behavior on two dimensions: assertiveness and cooperativeness. These dimensions are then used to define three specific methods for dealing with conflicts: avoiding (accommodating, competing), collaborating, and compromising.

"Conflict is common and useful. It is a sign of change and movement. Conflict is neither good nor bad. The effort should not be to eliminate conflict but to refocus it as a productive rather than destructive force. Conflict can be a vital, energizing force at work in any team."[5] Therefore, if conflict is approached as an opportunity to learn and move forward, it really isn't a barrier; it's more an enabler.

Active listening is a key attribute for team leaders in managing conflict. Active listening is used to:

- Reduce defensiveness
- Help others feel understood
- Defuse emotional situations
- Build rapport and trust
- Help focus energy on problem solving

Active listening involves two steps:

1. Accept what the individual is saying (which does not imply agreement) and his or her right to say it
2. Offer an understanding of both the content of what was said and the feelings observed and heard, giving no unsolicited advice

Groupthink

In the team selection process, as well as in the team's day-to-day functions, care must be taken to avoid groupthink. Groupthink occurs when most or all of the team members coalesce in support of an idea or a decision that hasn't been fully explored, or one on which some members secretly disagree. The members are more concerned with maintaining friendly relations and avoiding conflict than in becoming engrossed in a controversial discussion.

Actions to forestall groupthink may include:

- Brainstorming alternatives before selecting an approach
- Encouraging members to express their concerns
- Ensuring that ample time is given to surface, examine, and comprehend all ideas and suggestions

- Developing rules for examining each alternative
- Appointing an "objector" to challenge proposed actions

Other Barriers

Logistics is defined as a process involving planning, implementing, and controlling an efficient, cost-effective flow and storage of raw materials, in-process inventory, finished goods, and related information from point of origin to point of consumption for the purpose of conforming to customer requirements.[6] Breakdowns in the planning and implementing phases can substantially and negatively impact the work of a team. For example, consider some of the issues for team members regarding meetings:

- If team members are not in the same building, what connectivity and communication problems can arise?
- The logistics of getting people together for kaizen events can be frustrating (who carries on the work when the member is at the event?).
- Selecting conference rooms, technology, room setup, and so on, creates logistic nightmares (who coordinates these arrangements?).
- Agendas, notes, action items, and so on, are part of the logistics of team meetings (who attends to these functions?).

For example:

> HandiWare, a manufacturer of household tools designed especially for women, has assembled its first team to design, procure, and install an exhibit at an upcoming home show. The team completes the exhibit design on schedule, procures the needed materials to assemble the exhibit, and arranges for the shipping to and erection of the exhibit at the site—all on schedule.
>
> The HandiWare salespeople arrive at the site to set up, but the exhibit does not. Phone calls, e-mails, and frantic texting finally confirm the exhibit is on a truck four states away and heading even farther away. The sales team cobbles together a makeshift exhibit that fails to portray the quality products they wish the consumers to buy.
>
> A post-exhibition "lessons learned" debriefing concluded the following:
>
> - No risk assessment had been done
> - No contingency plans were made based on potential scenarios
> - No exhibition-savvy person was involved in the planning
> - No attempt had been made to query other, more experienced exhibitors
> - No representative of the HandiWare exhibition team had been invited to sit in on the design team meeting
> - The exhibit design was beautifully and cost-effectively designed, and was never used

Hidden agendas are another common barrier. If a team member is hiding a purpose for participating that conflicts with the mission and objectives of the team, it can result in a dysfunctional team. Such hidden agendas may be politically motivated or motivated for self-gain.

Disruptive behavior is another barrier. A member who continually disrupts the work of the team with behavior that is offensive to other members can cause rebuffs, resentment, and/or retaliation. Such behavior can seek to:

- Get personal attention
- Gain control of the team
- Disrespect the team leadership or a specific member
- Take the team "off track"
- Destroy the team environment

It is vital that the team leader, perhaps with assistance from the facilitator, deal with these agendas as soon as they are detected. Best scenario: a brief, straight-to-the-point talk with the individual, away from the team, focusing on a positive behavior change. Worst scenario: the person becomes belligerent, resists attempts to correct the disruptive behavior, and requires disciplinary action, even removal from the team.

Lack of training is yet another common barrier. Lack of the "soft" or interpersonal skills as well as lack of skills in the use of appropriate tools can impede a team's progress. Unless team members have had previous experience on teams, it is wise to provide training on teamwork and team dynamics. A team should strive to move through the stages of team development in as effective a way as possible. It usually pays to spend the effort, time, and expense to carefully train the team members for the roles they will need to fulfill.

With most adults, just-in-time training works well. This means that skill training takes place immediately before the trainee will use the skill.

5. TEAM DECISION-MAKING

> Describe and use different decision-making models such as voting (majority rule, multi-voting) and consensus, and use follow up techniques to clarify the issue to be decided, to confirm agreement on the decision, and to come to closure on the decision made. (Apply)
>
> **CQIA BoK 2014 II.C.5.**

Definitions

Decision making is a process for analyzing pertinent data to make the optimum choice. *Decisiveness* is the skill of selecting a decision and carrying it through.

Fans of the Star Trek: The Next Generation *television program may recall the decision-making process of the captain. He solicited input (information and recommendations) from his subordinate officers, thought about it, made a decision, and ordered "Make it so."*

HALF PRICE BOOKS®

Half Price Books
1835 Forms Drive
Carrollton, TX 75006
OFS OrderID 19804548

Thank you for your order, Sinead Arrieta!

Thank you for shopping with Half Price Books! Please contact Support@hpb.com. if you have any questions, comments or concerns about your order (114-2320344-8175408)

Visit our stores to sell your books, music, movies games for cash.

SKU	ISBN/UPC	Title & Author/Artist	Shelf ID	Qty	OrderSKU
S329512324	9788174890375	The Certified Quality Improvement Associat... Russell T. Westcott and Grace L. Duffy	07--05--4	1	

SHIPPED STANDARD TO:
Sinead Arrieta
3428 E WINDSONG DR
PHOENIX AZ 85048-7887
bkw7lb72gxqfc2w@marketplace.amazon.com

ORDER# **114-2320344-8175408**
AmazonMarketplaceUS

The Decision-Making Process

1. Clearly state the decision purpose
2. Establish the criteria (basis for decision and results required)
3. Assess criteria for those that would be acceptable and measurable (identify the desirable criteria in order of priority)
4. Create a list of alternatives to consider, and collect data about each
5. Assess the alternatives (relate each alternative solution back to the criteria, eliminate those that are unacceptable, and weigh and prioritize remaining alternatives)
6. Conduct a risk analysis of the remaining alternatives (identify what could go wrong)
7. Assess the risks (probability and seriousness of impact)
8. Make the decision (a decision with manageable and acceptable risk)

Decision-Making Styles

- Top-down (The boss makes the decisions.)
- Consultative (Top-level employees solicit input from lower levels.)
- Proactive consultative (Lower-level employees propose ideas and potential decisions to the top level for final decision.)
- Consensus (Intelligence and alternatives are widely discussed in the team. When everyone agrees they can support a single decision, without opposition, it is considered final.)
- Delegation
  - —Delegation with possible veto (Top level retains right to reject decision made at a lower level.)
  - —Delegation with guidelines (Lower levels may make decisions within established constraints.)
  - —Total delegation (Lower levels are free to make decisions however they wish.)
- Voting (Each team member has a vote. Each member stating his or her rationale for his or her vote may expand this method. Voting is acceptable for fairly unimportant decisions. It is fast but lacks the rigor necessary for critical and more complex decisions.)

Team Decision-Making Tools

Consensus

Consensus is a form of group decision making in which everyone agrees with—or can at least live with—the decision. If even one person says, "I'm sorry, but I can't support this decision," then the team needs to keep working toward consensus.

Consensus can be more time-consuming than deciding by simple majority, but organizations around the world have learned that the decisions that come from building consensus are generally in the long run much more effective. The most important rule in coming to consensus is honesty. A consensus decision is one that everyone on the team agrees to support. This means that no one can say later, "I never really liked that decision, so I'm not going to support it." A consensus vote is "thumbs-up" for everyone:

- Thumbs-up means, "I like this option and I fully support it."
- Thumbs-sideways means, "I'm not thrilled with this option, but I can live with it and will support it fully."
- Thumbs-down means, "I cannot live with this option and cannot support it."

If there are many thumbs-sideways votes, it may be wise to spend the time to find a more appealing option. If someone does not vote, take it as an automatic thumbs-down, because it is important that the entire team agrees to support the decision fully. Generally, teams should talk about consensus as a decision making process, and people should agree that they will use it and abide by it.

Multivoting

Multivoting is a quick and easy way for a group to identify the highest-priority items in a list. This technique helps a team to:

- Prioritize a large list without creating a win-lose situation in the group that generated the list
- Separate the "vital few" items from the "useful many" on a large list

The basic steps involved in multivoting are as follows:

1. Give each team member a number of votes equal to approximately half the number of items on the list (e.g., 10 votes for a 20-item list).
2. Have the members vote individually for the items they believe have high priority. Voters can "spend" their votes as they wish, even giving all to one item.
3. Compile the votes given to each item and record the quantity of votes beside each item.
4. Select the four to six items receiving the highest number of votes.
5. Discuss and prioritize the selected items relative to each other. If there is difficulty in reaching agreement, remove the items that received the fewest votes from the list and then conduct another vote.

Multivoting is best suited for use with large groups and long lists. Its simplicity makes it very quick and easy to use.

Nominal Group Technique

The *nominal group technique* (NGT) is a structured process that identifies and ranks major problems or issues that need addressing. It can be used to identify the major strengths of a department/unit/institution or to make decisions by consensus when selecting problem solutions in a business. This technique provides each participant with an equal voice.

The basic steps involved in using NGT are as follows:

1. Request that all participants (usually 5–10 persons) write or say which problem or issue they feel is most important.
2. Record all problems and issues in a master list and omit any duplicates.
3. Generate and distribute to each participant a form that numbers the problems or issues in no particular order.
4. Request that each participant select the top five problems or issues and rank them by importance, with "5" for highest and "1" for lowest.
5. Tally the rankings of all participants by aggregating the points for each problem or issue.
6. The problem or issue with the highest aggregated number is the most important one for the team as a whole.
7. Discuss the results and generate a final ranked list for process improvement action planning.

Figure 6.1 is an example of NGT.

Attributes of a Good Decision

- It represents the optimum in operational feasibility.
- It involves a minimum of undesirable side effects and trade-offs.
- It is technically free from flaws.
- It delineates specific action commitments.
- It is within the capacity of the affected people to comprehend and execute.
- It is acceptable to those involved.
- It is supportable with the resources that can be made available.
- It includes provision for alignment, audit, and measurement.

	Individuals and rankings					
Restaurant	Tom	Joe	Mary	Sue	Terry	**Total**
Marlow's	1	2	3	1	2	9
Grunge Café	3	1	1	2	3	10
Stew & Brew	2	4	2	4	4	16
Fancaé	4	3	4	3	1	15

Figure 6.1 An example of NGT.

Source: Reproduced by permission from R. T. Westcott, ed., *The Certified Manager of Quality/Organizational Excellence Handbook*, 4th ed. (Milwaukee, WI: ASQ Quality Press, 2014), 342.

Considerations

- Fact-finding is often confused with decision making. Technical questions can be answered with a "yes or no" or a "go or no go" decision. There are no alternatives; the answer is right or wrong.
- Decision making is selecting the most effective action from among less favorable actions.
- Decisions can be no better than the intelligence supporting them.
- Determine the dollar value of decision-making intelligence and then determine what a better decision is worth.
- Decision making is a process rather than a single act.
- Good team leaders don't make decisions; they manage decision makers and decision making.
- No team leader in today's world knows enough to make major decisions without reliable help from others.
- Good decision makers hold off decisions until they are needed, but they do think about decisions they will make, and they don't delay the gathering of intelligence.
- A decision made today may be totally inappropriate in tomorrow's changed environment.

Team Meetings

The structure of team meetings depends on the team's purpose, its size, its duration, its projected outcomes, and the degree of urgency of results required. Teams may range from having no formal meetings to having frequent scheduled meetings with extensive agendas and formal minutes. Certain rules and regulations as well as client requirements may specify the extent of meetings to be held. For example:

> A company whose quality management system is certified under the ISO/TS 16949 automotive QMS standard is expected to conduct periodic design reviews (meetings) as a product is being developed. Evidence that such reviews have been conducted and documented is examined. Failure to comply could place the certification in jeopardy.

In a typical formal team meeting, the team leader arranges for an agenda to be prepared and sent to all team members. The agenda states the time, place, and intent of the meeting. Additional material may be attached as pre-meeting reading for participants to prepare themselves for discussion. In some cases, the agenda states the role of each team member, why his or her input is needed, and decisions that must be made relative to the topics for the meeting. The logistics of obtaining the meeting venue and equipping the meeting room are the responsibility of the team leader, but the task is often delegated to an assistant.

All team members have a responsibility to assist the team in reaching consensus when differences of opinion arise, yet also to challenge assumptions that could endanger the outcome of the team. Further, each member must respect and cooperate with others on the team.

Inasmuch as a team should function as a process, a team meeting process self-assessment (Figure 6.2) can be a useful tool to critique the overall effectiveness of a team meeting. The value lies in having each team member and the facilitator complete the assessment and then having the group as a whole discuss the results, reach consensus, and set one or more improvement objectives for the next meeting.

Team Leader as Coach

Leaders often complain about employees, saying they have poor work habits, have little respect for authority, require constant supervision, arrive late and leave early, lack drive and initiative, want more money for less work—the list goes on.

Circle a number to represent your perception of the team's process in this meeting.
10 = *high*, 1 = *low*

We had no agenda or we did not follow the agenda we had.	***TEAM ON TRACK*** 1 2 3 4 5 6 7 8 9 10	An agenda was distributed in advance of the meeting and we followed it exactly.
Members who were supposed to attend didn't show. Others straggled in late.	***ATTENDANCE AND PROMPTNESS*** 1 2 3 4 5 6 7 8 9 10	All expected members attended and arrived on time. The meeting started at the scheduled time.
Some members tended to dominate and others did not participate.	***PARTICIPATION*** 1 2 3 4 5 6 7 8 9 10	Member participation was evenly balanced; everyone contributed to decisions and openly discussed ideas.
More than one person talked at a time; disruptive remarks were made; side conversations occurred. Overall disrespect of person speaking was evident.	***LISTENING*** 1 2 3 4 5 6 7 8 9 10	One person talked at a time; others helped clarify and build on ideas; all were attentive to person speaking. Respect for one another was evident.
No attempt was made to redirect the team to the agenda or to encourage balanced participation.	***SHARED LEADERSHIP*** 1 2 3 4 5 6 7 8 9 10	Both the team leader and team members intervened to keep the team focused on the agenda and to stimulate participation when needed.
When conflicts arose, chaos resulted. Differences of opinion were allowed to escalate to inappropriate behavior and lack of adequate resolution.	***CONFLICT MANAGEMENT*** 1 2 3 4 5 6 7 8 9 10	The energies involved with differing opinions were directed toward understanding conflicting views and seeking consensus.
Team decisions were inferior to what individuals would have produced. There was no attempt to summarize main ideas/decisions or future actions/responsibilities.	***RESULTS*** 1 2 3 4 5 6 7 8 9 10	Team expertise and decisions were superior to individual judgments. Main ideas/decisions were summarized, and action assignments were made at end of meeting.
Team was totally ineffective in achieving its purpose for this meeting.	***OVERALL RATING*** 1 2 3 4 5 6 7 8 9 10	Team was totally effective in achieving its purpose for this meeting. All agenda items were addressed or properly tabled for the next meeting.

Figure 6.2 Team meeting process self-assessment.

"If only they were more motivated" is the common lament. The fact is that most people start a new job already motivated. Something makes them want to take the job in the first place. It's what happens to employees after they are hired that demotivates them. To better lead people, a team leader needs to become an effective coach.

A basic principle is that one person cannot "motivate" another. Motivation comes from within a person and is a consequence of one's environment. This environment may consist of past experiences, the present situation, competency to do the job, knowledge of what's expected by management, working conditions, whether and how recognition is received, the degree to which decisions and suggestions are allowed and accepted, the degree to which one feels empowered to act on behalf of the business, perception of management's actions (e.g., punishing), opportunity to develop and make more money, conditions outside of work, and personal health. Each person has a unique set of needs that vary depending on circumstances and that, if fulfilled, will motivate him or her. An effective leader can provide an environment in which an employee feels motivated. To do this, consider the "6 Rs":

1. *Reinforce.* Identify, recognize, and positively reinforce work done well.
2. *Request information.* Discuss team members' views. Is anything preventing expected performance?
3. *Resources.* Identify needed resources, the lack of which could impede quality performance.
4. *Responsibility.* Customers make paydays possible; all employees have a responsibility to the customers, both internal and external.
5. *Role.* Be a role model. Don't just tell; demonstrate how to do it. Observe learners' performances. Together, critique the approach and work out an improved method.
6. *Repeat.* Apply the previous principles regularly and repetitively.

Coaching is an ongoing process. But it doesn't have to be a burden. A team leader can become an effective, quality-driven coach by following these action steps:

- Catch team members doing something right and positively reinforce the good behavior in that specific situation.
- Use mistakes as learning opportunities.
- Recognize and reward team members who take risks in changing their behavior, even if they sometimes fail while learning a new behavior.
- When discussing situations, position yourself for relaxed conversation. Respond with words such as "I see/I understand," "What do you suggest we do?" "How can I help you make this happen?"
- Acknowledge the team member's reason for action, but don't agree to it if it's inappropriate, and do explain your rationale for not agreeing.
- When giving correctional performance feedback, state the expectation or requirement, state the employee's behavior, describe any behavior

change needed and explain why it is needed, mention consequences for not changing, and discuss how and when change must occur.

- When giving complimentary performance feedback, state what the employee did properly and the requirement or expectation met, explain why it is important (the results of the action), and compliment the employee for work done well. Discuss any further improvements that may be desirable. If for a significant achievement, arrange for wider-range recognition and perhaps a reward.
- Encourage members to make suggestions for improving. Always give credit to the member making the suggestion.
- Treat team members with even more care than other organization resources.

Potential Perils and Pitfalls of Teams

- The purpose of the team is not linked to the organization's strategic direction and goals
- Management commitment and personal involvement are nonexistent or inadequate
- The team environment is hostile or indifferent
- Assigned members lack the needed competence (knowledge, skills, experience, aptitude, and attitude)
- Training for team members is not made available or is inadequate for the tasks to be done
- Team leadership is inadequate to lead the team in meeting its objectives
- Team-building action is nonexistent or inadequate
- Team facilitation action is nonexistent or inadequate
- Team ground rules are nonexistent or inadequate
- Team process is ignored or improperly managed
- Members do not behave as a team
- Team members are unsure of what's expected of them
- Recognition and reward for work done well are nonexistent or inappropriate
- Adequate resources are not provided (e.g., support personnel, facilities, tools, materials, information access, and funding)
- Conflicts between day-to-day work and work on the team have not been resolved
- The team cannot seem to move beyond the "storming" stage
- Team members constantly need to be replaced

- Team members show little respect for each other's competency
- The decision to form a team is not the best approach for the situation
- The team leader is reluctant to give up absolute control and unquestioned authority
- Day-to-day operations personnel perceive the team as a potential threat
- The union objects to the forming of a team
- The team, if self-directed, lacks the training and knowledge to handle situations that may be off-limits, such as hiring/firing and compensation
- Planning the process and managing the process by which the team will operate has been done poorly, if at all
- The team leader does not understand two primary concepts: how to lead a team and how to manage the team process
- The team is allowed to continue beyond the time when it should have been disbanded
- Team members have been selected involuntarily
- The basis for team member selection is not consistent with the goals and objectives and the expected outcomes of the team
- Team members' roles and organizational levels in day-to-day operations are carried into team activities, upsetting the "all are equal" environment desired
- The team assumes an unauthorized life of its own
- The team fails to keep the rest of the organization apprised of what it's doing and why
- Team members are cut off from their former day-to-day functions, losing opportunities for professional development, promotions, and pay raises
- The size of the team is inappropriate for the intended outcome—too limited or too large
- The team's actions are in violation of its contract with the union or in violation of labor laws and practices

What Makes a Team Work?

- All team members agree on the expected outputs and outcomes of the team.
- Each member is clearly committed to the goals and objectives of the team and understands why he or she is on the team.
- Each member fully accepts the responsibilities assigned and makes an overall commitment to help with whatever needs to be done to ensure the team's success.

- Members agree to freely ask questions and openly share their opinions and feelings, with no hidden agendas and with respect for other team members.
- Information is not hoarded or restricted. Each member has access to what is needed, and when it is needed, to get the work accomplished.
- Building and maintaining trust is of paramount importance to the team's successful achievement of its purpose.
- Every member feels he or she can make a difference with his or her contribution.
- Management is committed to supporting the team's decisions, as is each team member.
- Conflict within the team, when properly managed, produces a win–win outcome.
- The team maintains a dual focus: its process as a team and its anticipated outcomes.
- Serving on the team can increase a member's expertise and reputation but should never be a detriment to his or her personal development (such as promotional opportunities, compensation increases, and training to maintain job skills).

NOTES

1. Russell T. Westcott, *Simplified Project Management for the Quality Professional* (Milwaukee, WI: ASQ Quality Press, 2005), pp. 79–81.
2. Defined by B. W. Tuckman, "Developmental Sequence in Small Groups," *Psychological Bulletin* 63, no. 6 (November–December, 1965): 384–399.
3. W. Schmidt and R. Tannenbaum, "Management of Differences," *Harvard Business Review*, November–December 1960: 107–115.
4. Kenneth W. Thomas and Ralph H. Kilmann, *Thomas-Kilmann Conflict Mode Instrument* (Tuxedo, NY: XICOM, 1974).
5. G. Dennis Beecroft, Grace L. Duffy, and John W. Moran, eds., *The Executive Guide to Improvement and Change* (Milwaukee, WI: ASQ Quality Press, 2003), p. 91.
6. Adapted from the Council of Logistics Management.

ADDITIONAL RESOURCES

Bauer, Robert W., and Sandra S. Bauer. *The Team Effectiveness Survey Workbook.* Milwaukee, WI: ASQ Quality Press, 2005.

Beecroft, G. Dennis, Grace L. Duffy, and John W. Moran, eds. *The Executive Guide to Improvement and Change.* Milwaukee, WI: ASQ Quality Press, 2003.

Bens, Ingrid M., ed. *Facilitation at a Glance.* 3rd ed. Salem, NH: GOAL/QPC, 2012.

Dreo, Herb, Pat Kunkel, and Thomas Mitchell. *The Virtual Teams Guidebook for Managers.* Milwaukee, WI: ASQ Quality Press, 2003.

Evans, J. R., and W. M. Lindsay. *The Management and Control of Quality.* 9th ed. Cincinnati, OH: South-Western College Publishing, 2013.

GOAL/QPC and Joiner Associates. *The Team Memory Jogger.* Salem, NH: GOAL/QPC, 1995.

Hallbom, Tim, and Nick LeForce. *Coaching in the Workplace.* Salem, NH: GOAL/QPC, 2008.

Hitchcock, D. *The Work Redesign Team Handbook: A Step-by-Step Guide to Creating Self-Directed Teams.* White Plains, NY: Quality Resources, 1994.

Scholtes, Peter R., Brian L. Joiner, and Barbara J. Streibel. *The Team Handbook.* 3rd ed. Madison, WI: Joiner Associates, 2003.

Westcott, Russell T., ed. *The Certified Manager of Quality/Organizational Excellence Handbook.* 4th ed. Milwaukee, WI: ASQ Quality Press, 2014.

———. *Simplified Project Management for the Quality Professional.* Milwaukee, WI: ASQ Quality Press, 2005.

Part III

Continuous Improvement Techniques

The largest room in the world is room for improvement.

Anonymous

Continuous improvement is simply the way the company does business.

Mary Walton

Even if accurate data are available, they will be meaningless if they are not used correctly. The skill with which a company collects and uses data can make the difference between success and failure.

Masaaki Imai

Improvement means the organized creation of beneficial change; the attainment of unprecedented levels of performance. A synonym is breakthrough.

Joseph M. Juran

Chapter 7
A. Continuous Improvement

> Define and use continuous improvement tools and techniques. (Understand)
>
> **CQIA BoK 2014 III.A.**

Continuous quality improvement (CQI) is a management approach to improving and maintaining quality that emphasizes internally driven and relatively constant (as contrasted with intermittent) assessments of potential causes of quality defects, followed by action aimed at either avoiding a decrease in quality or correcting it in an early stage. CQI could use most, if not all, of the tools discussed in this chapter at some point in a quality improvement initiative.

1. BRAINSTORMING

Brainstorming is a group process used to generate ideas in a nonjudgmental environment. Group members are presented with the issue and are asked, first, to be wide-ranging in their own thinking about the issue and, second, not to criticize the thinking of others. The purpose of the tool is to generate a large number of ideas about the issue. Team members interact to generate many ideas in a short time period.

As the goal of brainstorming is to generate ideas, make sure everyone in the group understands the importance of postponing judgment until after the brainstorming session is completed.

The basic steps involved in brainstorming are as follows:

1. Write the problem or topic on a whiteboard or flip chart where all participants can see it
2. Write all ideas on the board and do as little editing as possible
3. Number each idea for future reference
4. Choose from several brainstorming techniques: structured brainstorming, unstructured (or free-form) brainstorming, or silent brainstorming

Structured brainstorming follows the one-at-a-time or round-robin method:

- One idea is solicited from each person in sequence
- Participants who don't have an idea at the moment may say "pass"
- A complete round of passes ends the brainstorming session

The advantage of structured brainstorming is that each person has an equal chance to participate, regardless of rank or personality. The disadvantage of structured brainstorming is that it lacks spontaneity and can sometimes feel rigid and restrictive. Encourage participation and building on the ideas of others.

In *unstructured* (or free-form) brainstorming, participants simply contribute ideas as they come to mind. The advantage of free-form brainstorming is that participants can build on each other's ideas. The atmosphere can be very informal and sometimes hectic.

The disadvantage of free-form brainstorming is that less assertive or lower-ranking participants may not contribute. An ideal approach is to combine these two methods. Begin the session with a few rounds of structured brainstorming and finish up with a period of unstructured brainstorming.

In *silent* (or "write it down") brainstorming:

- The participants write their ideas individually on sticky notes or small slips of paper
- The papers are collected and posted for all to see

The advantage of silent brainstorming is that it prevents individuals from making disruptive "analysis" comments during the brainstorming session and provides confidentiality. It can help prevent a group from being unduly influenced by a single participant or common flow of ideas. The disadvantage of silent brainstorming is that the group loses the synergy that comes from an open session. Silent brainstorming is best used in combination with other brainstorming techniques.

After brainstorming:

- Reduce your list to the most important items
- Combine items that are similar
- Discuss each item in turn—on its own merits
- Eliminate items that may not apply to the original issue or topic
- Give each person one final chance to add items

There are several points to remember about brainstorming:

- Never judge ideas as they are generated. The goal of brainstorming is to generate a lot of ideas in a short time. Analysis of these ideas is a separate process, to be done later.
- Don't quit at the first lull. All brainstorming sessions reach lulls, which are uncomfortable for the participants. Research indicates that most of the best ideas occur during the last part of a session. Try to encourage the group to push through at least two or three lulls.

- Try to write down all the ideas exactly as they are presented. When you condense an idea to one or two words for ease of recording, you are doing analysis. Analysis should be done later.
- Encourage outrageous ideas. Although these ideas may not be practical, they may start a flow of creative ideas that can be used. This can help break through a lull.
- Try to have a diverse group. Involve process owners, customers, and suppliers to obtain a diverse set of ideas from several perspectives.

2. PLAN-DO-CHECK-ACT (PDCA) OR PLAN-DO-STUDY-ACT (PDSA) CYCLE

The key steps involved in the implementation and evaluation of quality improvement efforts are symbolized by the PDCA/PDSA cycle (see Chapter 8, Figure 8.7). The goal is to engage in a continuous endeavor to learn about all aspects of a process and then use this knowledge to change the process to reduce variation and complexity and improve the level of process performance. Process improvement begins by understanding how customers define quality, how processes work, and how understanding the variation in those processes can lead to wise management action. The major process improvement techniques and tools are discussed throughout this chapter and Chapter 9.

3. AFFINITY DIAGRAM

An *affinity diagram* is a tool to facilitate consideration and organization of a group of ideas about an issue by a team through a consensus decision. The team members take turns writing each of their ideas on separate slips of paper. The team then gathers all the ideas into natural (affinity) groups; in other words, it groups the ideas in a manner that allows those with a natural relationship or relevance to be placed together in the same group or category.

An affinity diagram is used to organize verbal information into a visual pattern. An affinity diagram starts with specific ideas and helps work toward broad categories. Affinity diagrams can help:

- Organize and give structure to a list of factors that contribute to a problem
- Identify key areas where improvement is most needed

The steps to generate an affinity diagram are as follows:

1. Identify the problem. Write the problem or issue on a whiteboard or flip chart.
2. Generate ideas. Use an idea-generation technique, such as brainstorming, to identify all facets of the problem. Use index cards or sticky notes to record the ideas.

3. Cluster ideas, on cards, paper, or a wall, into related groups. Ask, "Which other ideas are similar?" and "Is this idea somehow connected to any others?" to help group the ideas together.
4. Create an affinity card (header card) for each group with a short statement describing the entire group of ideas.
5. Attempt to group the initial affinity cards into even broader groups (clusters). Continue until the definition of an affinity cluster becomes too broad to have any meaning.
6. Complete the affinity diagram. Lay out all the ideas and affinity cards on a single medium. Draw borders around each of the affinity clusters. The resulting structure will provide valuable insights about the problem.

Figure 7.1 shows a completed affinity diagram after the team has completed step 6.

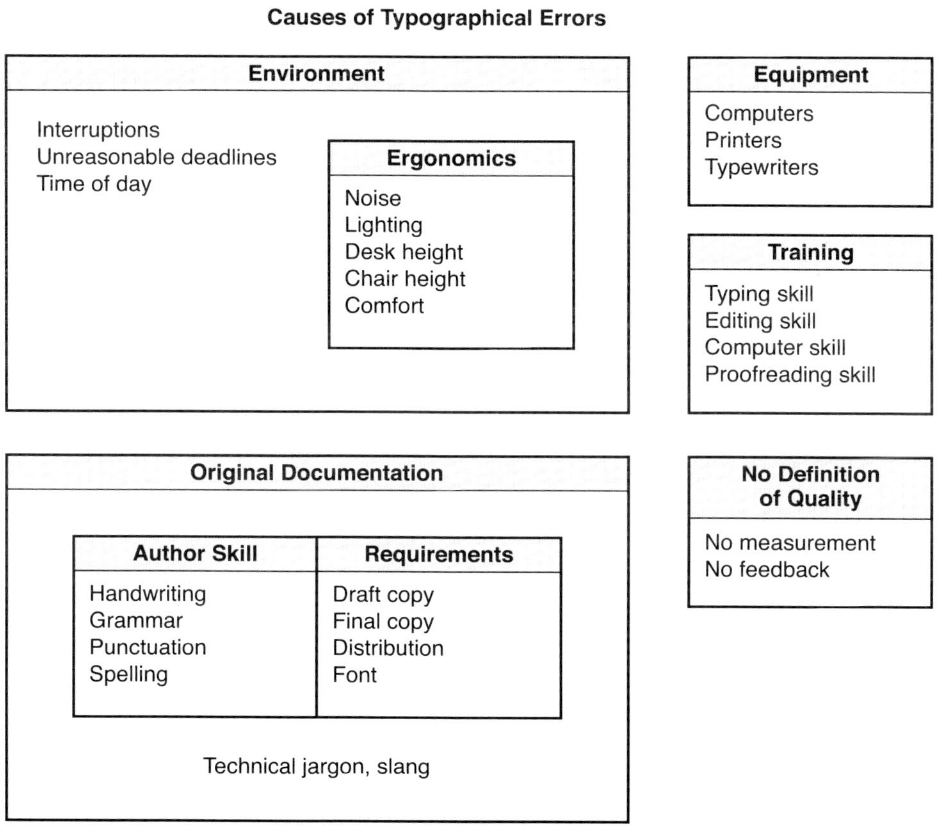

Figure 7.1 Affinity diagram.

4. COST OF QUALITY

Cost of quality is a methodology that allows an organization to determine the extent to which organizational resources are used for activities that prevent poor quality, that appraise the quality of the organization's products or services, and that result from internal and external failures. Having such information allows an organization to determine the potential savings to be gained by implementing process improvements.

Quality-related activities that incur costs may be divided into prevention costs, appraisal costs, and internal and external failure costs.

- *Prevention costs* are costs incurred to prevent or avoid quality problems. These costs are associated with the design, implementation, and maintenance of the quality management system. They are planned and incurred before actual operation, and they could include:
  - —Product or service requirements—establishment of specifications for incoming materials, processes, finished products, and services
  - —Quality planning—creation of plans for quality, reliability, operations, production, and inspection
  - —Quality assurance—creation and maintenance of the quality system
  - —Training—development, preparation, and maintenance of programs
- *Appraisal costs* are costs associated with measuring and monitoring activities related to quality, such as the suppliers' and customers' evaluation of purchased materials, processes, products, and services to ensure that they conform to specifications. They could include:
  - —Verification—checking of incoming material, process setup, and products against agreed specifications
  - —Quality audits—confirmation that the quality system is functioning correctly
  - —Supplier rating—assessment and approval of suppliers of products and services
- *Internal failure costs* are costs incurred to remedy defects discovered before the product or service is delivered to the customer. These costs occur when the results of work fail to reach design quality standards and are detected before they are transferred to the customer. They could include:
  - —Waste—performance of unnecessary work or holding of stock as a result of errors, poor organization, or communication
  - —Scrap—defective product or material that cannot be repaired, used, or sold
  - —Rework or rectification—correction of defective material or errors
  - —Failure analysis—activity required to establish the causes of internal product or service failure

- *External failure costs* are costs incurred to remedy defects discovered by customers. These costs occur when the products or services fail to reach design quality standards but are not detected until after transfer to the customer. They could include:
  - —Repairs and servicing—both of returned products and of those in the field
  - —Warranty claims—failed products that are replaced or services that are re-performed under a guarantee
  - —Complaints—all work and costs associated with handling and servicing customers' complaints
  - —Returns—handling and investigation of rejected or recalled products, including transport costs

The costs of doing a quality job, conducting quality improvements, and achieving goals must be carefully managed so that the long-term effect of quality on the organization is a desirable one. These costs must be a true measure of the quality effort, and they are best determined from an analysis of the costs of quality. Such an analysis provides:

- A method of assessing the effectiveness of the management of quality
- A means of determining problem areas, opportunities, savings, and action priorities

Cost of quality is also an important communication tool. Crosby demonstrated what a powerful tool it could be to raise awareness of the importance of quality. He referred to the measure as the "price of nonconformance" and argued that organizations choose to pay for poor quality. Many organizations will have true quality-related costs as high as 15%–20% of their sales revenue, and effective quality improvement programs can reduce this substantially, thus making a direct contribution to profits. Many businesses have started to compare the cost of quality with the cost of goods sold. This can better reflect the potential margin recovery that the organization is entitled to.

To identify, understand, and reap the cost benefits of quality improvement activities, an organization should include the following fundamental steps in its approach:

- Management commitment to finding the true costs of quality, both visible and hidden.
- A quality costing system to identify, report, and analyze quality-related cost. In the development of the costing system, decisions need to be made as to how deep a review is needed. Usually a Pareto approach is first taken to address the areas with the largest cost impact.
- A quality-related cost management team responsible for direction and coordination of the quality costing system.
- The inclusion of quality-costing training to enable everyone to understand the financial implications of quality improvement.

- The presentation of significant costs of quality to all personnel to promote the approach and identify areas for improvement.
- The introduction of schemes to achieve the maximum participation of all employees.

Some businesses are now evolving into a cost of poor execution (COPE) model. This incorporates both losses due to the organization's products and services and the internal systems losses via the "hidden factory."

The quality cost system, once established, should become dynamic and have a positive impact on the achievement of the organization's mission, goals, and objectives.

5. INTERNAL AUDITS TO IDENTIFY IMPROVEMENT OPPORTUNITIES

A *quality audit* is defined as "a systematic and independent examination to determine whether quality activities and related results comply with planned arrangements and whether these arrangements are implemented effectively and are suitable to achieve objectives."[1] An audit of a quality management system is carried out to ensure that actual practices conform to the documented procedures.

There should be a schedule for carrying out audits, with different activities requiring different frequencies based on their importance to the organization. An audit should not be conducted with the sole aim of revealing defects or irregularities—audits are for establishing the facts rather than finding faults. Audits do indicate necessary improvement and corrective actions, but they must also determine whether processes are effective and whether responsibilities have been correctly assigned.

The basic steps involved in conducting an audit are as follows:

1. Initiation and preparation, which includes defining the audit scope and objectives, assigning the resources (lead and support auditors), and developing an audit plan and checklists
2. Performance of the audit, which includes briefing concerned personnel and conducting the collection, evaluation, verification, and recording of information
3. Reporting, which includes developing an audit report and briefing concerned personnel on the audit results
4. Completion, which includes evaluating any corrective action taken as a result of the audit and closing out the audit process

The assessment of a quality system against a standard or set of requirements by the organization's own employees is known as a *first-party assessment* or *internal audit*.[2]

Beginning with a review of historical performance, management may identify activities, products, or projects that have resulted in high costs, customer complaints, performance concerns, chronic failure, unsatisfactory production levels, and delivery issues. The areas having the greatest impact on achieving the operational goals and objectives are the highest priority for the audit function to evaluate.[3]

If an external customer makes an assessment of a supplier, against either its own or a national or international standard, a *second-party audit* has been conducted.

An assessment by an independent organization that is not connected with any contract between the customer and the supplier but is acceptable to them both is an independent *third-party audit*. This type of audit can result in some form of certification or registration, such as ISO 9001 certification, provided by the assessing organization.

When an organization emphasizes process improvement and enhancing customer satisfaction, the audit process becomes one of the most important process improvement tools.

6. PROBLEM-SOLVING PROCESS

There is a difference between "fixing" a problem and "solving" a problem. Fixing the problem, though it may be necessary to provide immediate relief, does not guarantee the problem will not recur. This can also be viewed as a form of containment. Injecting a medicine to relieve a symptom does not imply that the underlying cause has been cured. Of course, many everyday problems can be easily fixed without taking elaborate steps, for example, squirting oil on a squeaky door hinge. In time, of course, the hinge may dry out and squeak again.

More complex problems fall into two broad categories: a problem related to a deficiency or failure of some kind (e.g., a sensor failed to signal an error) and a problem of discovering something new (e.g., seeking a drug that will cure a rare disease). This section deals with the former type of problem—instances where a nonconformance has occurred and the true or root cause is not immediately obvious.

> *If you always do what you have always done, you will always get what you always got.*
>
> Anonymous

Problem-Solving Model

Numerous models exist for problem solving, each with a series of steps; some are very simple and others are more complex. A seven-step model is shown in Figure 7.2 and described as follows:

1. Understand and define the problem
2. Collect, analyze, and prioritize data about the problem symptoms; determine the root cause(s) of the most significant symptoms
3. Identify possible solutions
4. Select the best solution
5. Develop an action plan
6. Implement the solution
7. Evaluate the effectiveness of the solution in solving the problem

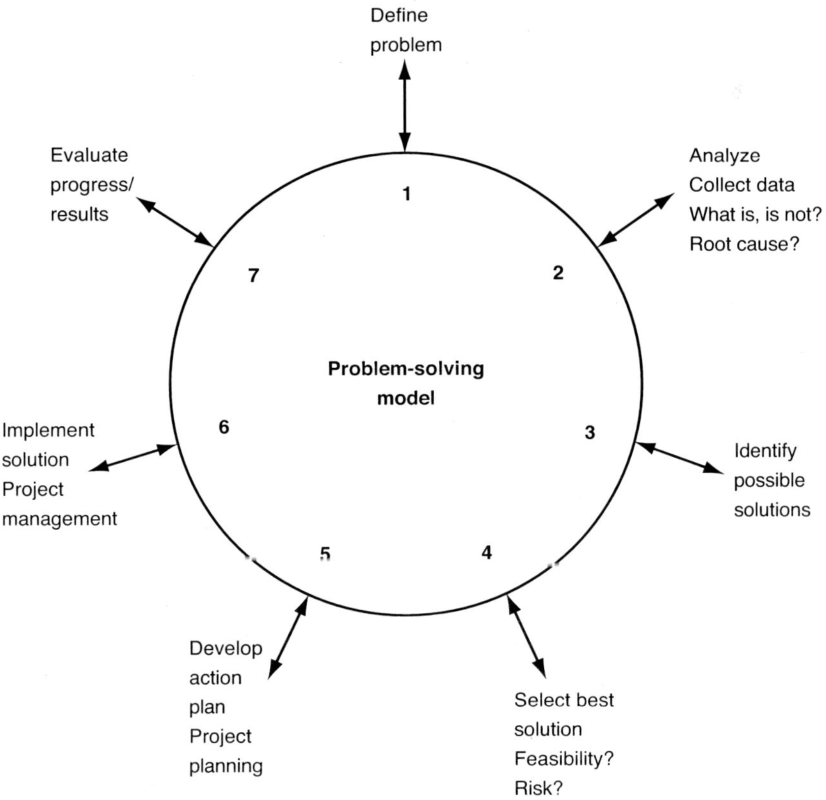

Figure 7.2 Problem-solving model.

1. Define the Problem

It is usually relatively simple to list the symptoms of a problem. Unfortunately, identifying the symptoms is often where problem analysis stops and selecting a solution takes over. This can result in missing the real cause, the *root cause,* and applying an inappropriate solution. The outcome can be that the problem was never solved and thus resurfaces again later—or in a worst-case scenario, the patient dies as a result of the problem.

> *For there are few things as useless—if not as dangerous—as the right answer to the wrong question.*
>
> Peter E. Ducker, *The Practice of Management*

Not all problems require a multistep process to resolve. If your morning newspaper is not lying in your driveway, as it usually is, you call the newspaper distribution office and they rush the paper to you. No need for you to analyze why the carrier missed the delivery. It's missing, you call, and it's delivered. Annoying, yes, but not a complex problem.

Useful questions to ask in explaining the problem are the following:

- What "it" is—what are we trying to explain?
- Where was "it" observed?
- Is "it" a real or an assumed problem?
- How did "it" become a problem?
- When did "it" occur?
- Has "it" been a problem before, how long ago, and what was done at the time?
- Is "it" a technical or nontechnical problem?
- What is unsatisfactory about the present situation?
- What are the observed symptoms? How often do these symptoms occur?
- What could have occurred, but didn't?
- Who or what is impacted/affected by the present situation?
- How widely spread is the problem?
- How serious is the problem according to those affected?
- What previous actions have already been taken to solve this occurrence of "it"?
- Is the cause of the problem truly known or merely suspect?

Additional ways to redefine the problem may be assisted by:

- Reversing the problem (turn it around, look at "it" from upside down, back to front) to get a different perspective
- Breaking a set (does "it" occur in the whole product line, or just in certain products?)

Using information from these questions, develop a written problem statement and the desired results. State why the problem is important to solve.

2. Analyze and Find the Root Cause

I keep six honest serving men
(They taught me all I know);
Their names are What and Why and When
And How and Where and Who.

Rudyard Kipling

A symptom is an observable phenomenon arising from and accompanying a defect.
A cause is an identified reason for the presence of a defect or problem.

Anonymous

Collect data to help identify potential causes. Some of the techniques and tools that are useful include:

- Brainstorming (see earlier in chapter)
- Cause-and-effect diagram (Chapter 9)
- Force-field analysis diagram (Chapter 9)
- Flowchart (Chapter 9)

Identify the most likely causes. Useful tools include:

- "Five Whys" (don't stop at five if more will be better) (Chapter 9)
- Pareto chart (prioritizing the potential causes) (Chapter 9)
- Reality check (Is the problem statement still valid?)

3. Identify Possible Solutions

Create a list of possible solutions. Creativity tools that may be useful include:

- Brainstorming (see earlier in chapter)
- What-is/what-is-not chart (Appendix C)[4]
- Mind mapping (Appendix C)
- Analogies (Appendix C)

4. Select the Best Solution

Reduce the number of alternatives from which to choose in three substeps:

- Use a paired-choice decision matrix to identify a small number of best solutions.
- Subject each of the two to five selections made in the previous substep to the following:
  - —Feasibility analysis (Do we have the resources to pursue this solution? Does this solution fit the organization's strategy? etc.)
  - —Risk analysis (What is the organization's exposure to risk if this solution is chosen?)
- Develop final selection criteria (up to six) and assign weights to criteria ("1"—low, "5"—highest). Apply weights to each criterion within each solution alternative. The solution having the highest total weight is the choice.

5. Develop an Action Plan

In all but very simple solutions, a project to implement the solution must be planned and managed. Figures 7.3a and 7.3b provide a sample form for action planning. A more complex problem solution may require more sophisticated project management methodology and tools.

Problem addressed:	Plan no.:	
	Date initiated:	
	Date needed:	
	Approval:	
Solution description:	Team (L):	
	Team:	

Major outcomes/objectives desired/required:

Scope (Where will the solution/implementation be applied? What limitations?):

By what criteria/measures will completion and success of project be measured?

Assumptions made, which may impact project (resources, circumstances outside this project):

Describe the overall approach to be taken:

When should the project be started to meet the date needed/wanted?

Estimate the resources required (time and money):

Outline the tentative major steps to be taken, a projected start and complete date for each step, and the person to be responsible for each step. (Use the back to sketch your timeline.)

Figure 7.3a Action plan form (front).

ACTION PLAN IMPLEMENTATION SCHEDULE

Step no.	Activity/Task/Event description	Responsibility	Start date	End date	Est. hours	Est. cost
				Totals =		

Figure 7.3b Action plan form (back).

6. Implement the Solution

Follow the plan.

7. Track and Measure Progress, Evaluate Results

Track the progress of the solution implementation against the action plan implementation schedule. Make necessary adjustments to achieve the solution objectives.

Evaluate accomplishment of outputs at completion of implementation. Evaluate outcomes of the solution after an appropriate period of time has elapsed. Ask the following questions:

- Has the problem been successfully eliminated?
- Is the process in which the problem occurred now stable?
- Has the solution produced a positive payback?
- Have steps been taken to ensure the problem will not recur?
- Have other processes where a similar problem might occur been examined, and has preventive action been taken?
- Have the lessons learned from experience with this problem been documented and made accessible for future training and problem-solving use?

Additional Root Cause Considerations in Dealing with Performance Problems

Table 7.1 summarizes actions to consider. An "X" in a column indicates the focus of potential action to be taken. A situation might involve both a knowledge/skill deficiency and a problem with the task. The task problem should be resolved first so that any training efforts are not wasted. Then ask:

- Does the performer have time to do the job well? (The job may need to be redesigned or the work better organized so the worker is not overburdened. Fix the job, not the worker.)
- Does the performer know what is supposed to be done? (Provide instruction and performance feedback.)
- Has the performer ever done the job correctly? (Refresh instruction and provide performance feedback.)
- Can the performer do the job if his or her life depended on it? (Change the consequences for performing the job to increase correct performance. Provide positive performance feedback.)
- Does the worker's supervisor have the requisite skills to fix the task and provide appropriate feedback and positive consequences? (If not, train the supervisor.)

Table 7.1 Distinguishing between performance and skill/knowledge issues.

Relative to Target Population (TP)	J	T	F	C
Does TP have time to do job well?	X	X		
Does TP have proper facilities in which to work?	X			
Does TP have the proper tools to do the work?	X			
Does TP have proper procedures, instructions, job aids?	X			
Does TP know what they are supposed to do?		X	X	
Has TP ever done the job correctly?		X	X	
Could TP do the job properly if their lives depended on it?		X		X
If TP could do the job in an exemplary way, would they?				X
Are there more negative than positive consequences in doing the job?				X
Does TP know when they are not performing as supervisor expects?			X	
Do supervisors of TP have requisite knowledge/skills?		X	X	X

Source: Reprinted with permission of R. T. Westcott & Associates.

Note: J = job satisfaction, T = training solution, F = feedback solution, C = consequences solution.

Benefits of Applying a Good Problem-Solving Process

Some of the benefits of a well-executed problem-solving process are:

- The right problem gets solved
- Future waste is saved because the problem does not recur
- Successful use of the problem-solving method fosters further use of the method
- It provides a basis for evaluating the effectiveness of not only the problem solution but also the methodology used

Decision Making

Problem solving and *decision making* are often combined in the same phrase. Though there are decisions to be made in the problem-solving process, such as how to define the problem and which solution is best, the decision-making process is generally considered distinct from problem solving. One differentiation is that decision making may be applied at three levels and time frames:

- Long-term, strategic-type decisions (three- to five-year or longer period)

- Tactical decisions made to translate strategic decisions into functional requirements (within a year)
- Operational decisions concerning the day-to-day running of the business

7. TOTAL QUALITY MANAGEMENT (TQM)

Total quality management (TQM) is an approach to quality management that emphasizes a thorough understanding by all members of an organization of the needs and desires of the ultimate product/service recipient, a viewpoint of wishing to provide world-class products/services to internal and external customers, and a knowledge of how to use specific data-related techniques and process improvement tools to assess and improve the quality of all organizational outputs.

CONCLUSION

The inherent tendency of many managers and professionals is often to leap from an inadequate definition of a problem to selection of an inappropriate or wrong solution. Because of this, increased emphasis is needed on *root cause analysis*—the core of problem solving.

NOTES

1. ASQ/ANSI/ISO 19011-2011 *Guidelines for auditing management systems*, 2011.
2. The term "audit" is gradually being replaced by the term "assessment" in relation to management systems, where the emphasis is less on strict conformance to specifications and more on the effectiveness of the management process. Accredited ISO 9000 registrars "assess" quality management systems prior to granting a certificate. The Baldrige Performance Excellence Program uses volunteer "assessors" to conduct "assessments" of organizations applying for the award.
3. G. Dennis Beecroft, Grace L. Duffy, and John W. Moran, eds., *The Executive Guide to Improvement and Change* (Milwaukee, WI: ASQ Quality Press, 2003), 163.
4. Charles H. Kepner and Benjamin B. Tregoe, *New Rational Manager: An Updated Edition for a New World* (Princeton, NJ: Kepner-Tregoe, 1997).

ADDITIONAL RESOURCES

ABS Consulting—Lee N. Vanden Heuvel, Donald K. Lorenzo, Randal L. Montgomery, Walter E. Hanson, and James R. Rooney. *Root Cause Analysis Handbook.* Milwaukee, WI: ASQ Quality Press, 2008.

Andersen, Bjørn, and Tom Fagerhaug. *The ASQ Pocket Guide to Root Cause Analysis.* Milwaukee, WI: ASQ Quality Press, 2013.

———. *Root Cause Analysis: Simplified Tools and Techniques.* 2nd ed. Milwaukee, WI: ASQ Quality Press, 2006.

Arter, Dennis R. *Quality Audits for Improved Performance.* 3rd ed. Milwaukee, WI: ASQ Quality Press, 2003.

Duffy, Grace L., ed. *The ASQ Quality Improvement Pocket Guide.* Milwaukee, WI: ASQ Quality Press, 2013.

Kepner, Charles H., and Benjamin B. Tregoe. *New Rational Manager: An Updated Edition for a New World.* Princeton, NJ: Kepner-Tregoe, 1997.

Okes, Duke. *Root Cause Analysis: The Core of Problem Solving and Corrective Action.* Milwaukee, WI: ASQ Quality Press, 2009.

Russell, J. P. *The ASQ Auditing Handbook.* 4th ed. Milwaukee, WI: ASQ Quality Press, 2013.

Westcott, Russell T., ed. *The Certified Manager of Quality/Organizational Excellence Handbook.* 4th ed. Milwaukee, WI: ASQ Quality Press, 2014.

Wood, Douglas C., ed. *Principles of Quality Costs; Financial Measures for Strategic Implementation of Quality Management.* 4th ed. Milwaukee, WI: ASQ Quality Press, 2013.

Chapter 8
B. Process Improvement

WHAT IS PROCESS IMPROVEMENT?

Process improvement means making things better, not just fighting fires or managing crises. It means setting aside the customary practice of blaming people for problems or failures. It is a way of looking at how better work can be done.

Taking a problem-solving approach by simply trying to fix what's broken may never uncover the root cause of the difficulty. Trying to fix the problem frequently does not change the underlying process that created the problem. Efforts to "fix" things may actually make them worse.

However, employing a proven process improvement methodology means learning what causes things to happen in a process and using this knowledge to reduce variation, remove activities that contribute no value to the product or service, and improve customer satisfaction. As an ongoing practice, an organization supports a cycle of process improvement teams to continually examine all the factors affecting processes: the materials used; the methods and machines used to transform materials into products or concepts into services; and the knowledge, experience, skills, aptitude, and attitude of the people performing the work.

HOW DOES THE ORGANIZATION BENEFIT FROM PROCESS IMPROVEMENT?

A standardized process improvement methodology looks at how work is performed. When all of the affected participants are involved in a process improvement, they can collectively focus on eliminating waste—of money, people, materials, time, and opportunities. The ideal result is that jobs can be done more cheaply, more quickly, more easily, and, most important, more safely. Using total quality tools and methods reinforces teamwork. Using team members' collective knowledge, experience, and effort is a proven approach to improving processes; the whole becomes greater than the sum of its parts.

The following four techniques, each supported by tools, may be used to contribute to the improvement effort:

1. Six Sigma
2. Lean
3. Benchmarking
4. Incremental and breakthrough approaches

1. SIX SIGMA

> Identify key six sigma concepts and tools, including the different roles and responsibilities of green belts and black belts, typical project types that are appropriate for six sigma techniques, and the DMAIC phases: design, measure, analyze, improve, and control. (Understand)
>
> **CQIA BoK 2014 III.B.1.**

Six Sigma is a methodology that mainly focuses on identifying and reducing variation in a process. The primary metric of Six Sigma is the sigma level or defect per million opportunities (DPMO). In Six Sigma, the higher the sigma level the better the process output, which translates into fewer errors, lower operating costs, lower risks, improved performance, and better use of resources.

Six Sigma is a continuous process improvement methodology that facilitates near perfection in the organization's processes. It considers not only the average performance but also the variability of what a business presents to the customer. This variation is often the cause of what is considered the "hidden factory," or the penalty for not getting it right the first time. For example, in public health activities, it consists of rework costs to reprocess forms before delivery to the client, scrap costs, recovery from a bad client experience, concessions for late service or paperwork deliveries, and write-offs to assuage offended clients or stakeholders.

When realizing that Six Sigma methods address the impact from defects in a process, consider how a defect should be defined in work activities, particularly on the local level. In general, a defect may be described as anything that results in customer dissatisfaction. A defect can also be defined as a product's or service's nonfulfillment of an intended requirement or reasonable expectation for use, including safety considerations.

If deployed properly, Six Sigma will create a structure to validate the right resources working on activities that will meet or exceed clients' or stakeholders' needs, reduce direct expense costs from, and provide a framework for measuring and monitoring those efforts. This is also the answer to the question "What should Six Sigma do for me?" If used correctly, Six Sigma will:

1. Create an infrastructure for managing improvement efforts and focus resources on those efforts
2. Ensure those improvement efforts are aligned with client and stakeholder needs
3. Develop a measurement system to monitor the impact of improvement efforts

Due to the importance of these outcomes, department leadership must be heavily involved in validating the benefit to the client and the organization, ensuring strategic linkage to the mission and vision, and visibly demonstrating commitment to projects. Without this level of support, process change agents will not gain the traction that is expected and the Six Sigma program will likely be unsuccessful.

The DMAIC Methodology

Improvement teams use the DMAIC methodology to root out and eliminate the causes of defects through the following planning and implementation phases:

D: Define a problem or improvement opportunity

M: Measure the existing process performance

A: Analyze the process to determine the root causes of poor performance; determine whether the process can be improved or should be redesigned

I: Improve the process by attacking root causes

C: Control the improved process to hold the gains

Table 8.1 describes the main responsibilities of Master Black Belts, Black Belts, and other team positions in a Six Sigma and Lean-Six Sigma organization.

Table 8.1 Six Sigma and Lean-Six Sigma roles, responsibilities, and characteristics.

Traditional Title	Characteristics and Responsibilities
Project Champion	• Dedicated to see it implemented • Absolute belief it is the right thing to do • Perseverance and stamina
Project Sponsor	• Believes in the concept/idea • Sound business acumen • Willing to take risk and responsibility for outcomes • Authority to approve needed resources • Upper management will listen to her or him
Process Owner	• Is a team member • Takes ownership of the project when it is complete • Is responsible for maintaining the project's gains • Removes barriers for Black Belts
Master Black Belt	• Expert on Six Sigma tools and concepts • Trains Black Belts and ensures proper application of methodology and tools • Coaches/mentors Black and Green Belts • Works high-level projects and those which impact multiple divisions or business units • Assists champions and process owners with project selection, management and Six Sigma administration

(continued)

Table 8.1 Six Sigma and Lean-Six Sigma roles, responsibilities, and characteristics. *(continued)*

Traditional Title	Characteristics and Responsibilities
Black Belt	• Leads, executes and completes DMAIC projects • Teaches team members the Six Sigma methodology and tools • Assists in identifying project opportunities and refining project details and scope • Reports progress to the project champions and process owners • Transfers knowledge to other Black Belts and the organization • Mentors Green Belts
Green Belt	• Committed to the team's mission and objectives • Capable of developing process maps, applying basic quality tools, creating charts, and engaging in basic statistical analysis • Experienced in planning, organizing, staffing, controlling, and directing • Capable of creating and maintaining channels that enable members to do their work • Capable of gaining the respect of team members; a role model • Is firm, fair, and factual in dealing with a team of diverse individuals • Facilitates discussion without dominating • Actively listens • Empowers team members to the extent possible within the organization's culture • Supports all team members equally • Respects each team member's individuality
Yellow Belt	• Willing to commit to the purpose of the team • Understands lean and Six Sigma tools and concepts • Able to express ideas, opinions, suggestions in a nonthreatening manner • Capable of listening attentively to other team members • Receptive to new ideas and suggestions • Able to engage in analysis of Lean-Six Sigma tools and concepts • Even-tempered, able to handle stress and cope with problems openly • Competent in one or more fields of expertise needed by the team • Favorable performance record • Willing to function as a team member and forfeit "star" status

Source: Modified by permission from R. Bialek, G. L. Duffy, and J. W. Moran, *The Public Health Quality Improvement Handbook* (Milwaukee, WI: ASQ Quality Press, 2009), 232–233.

Figure 8.1 gives an overview of the activities performed during each of the DMAIC steps in the continuous improvement Six Sigma cycle. The DMAIC steps are as follows:

1. *Define.* In this phase, the defect and the scope of the effort are determined. Project champions typically partner with a Master Black Belt to develop the intended outcome and criteria under which the Black Belt will operate. The project champion, the team leader, and the Black Belt should work closely to define the defect, determine the client and organizational impact, assign target dates, assign resources, and set goals for the project, all of which are documented in a project charter, which becomes the "contract" with the Black Belt. This contract must

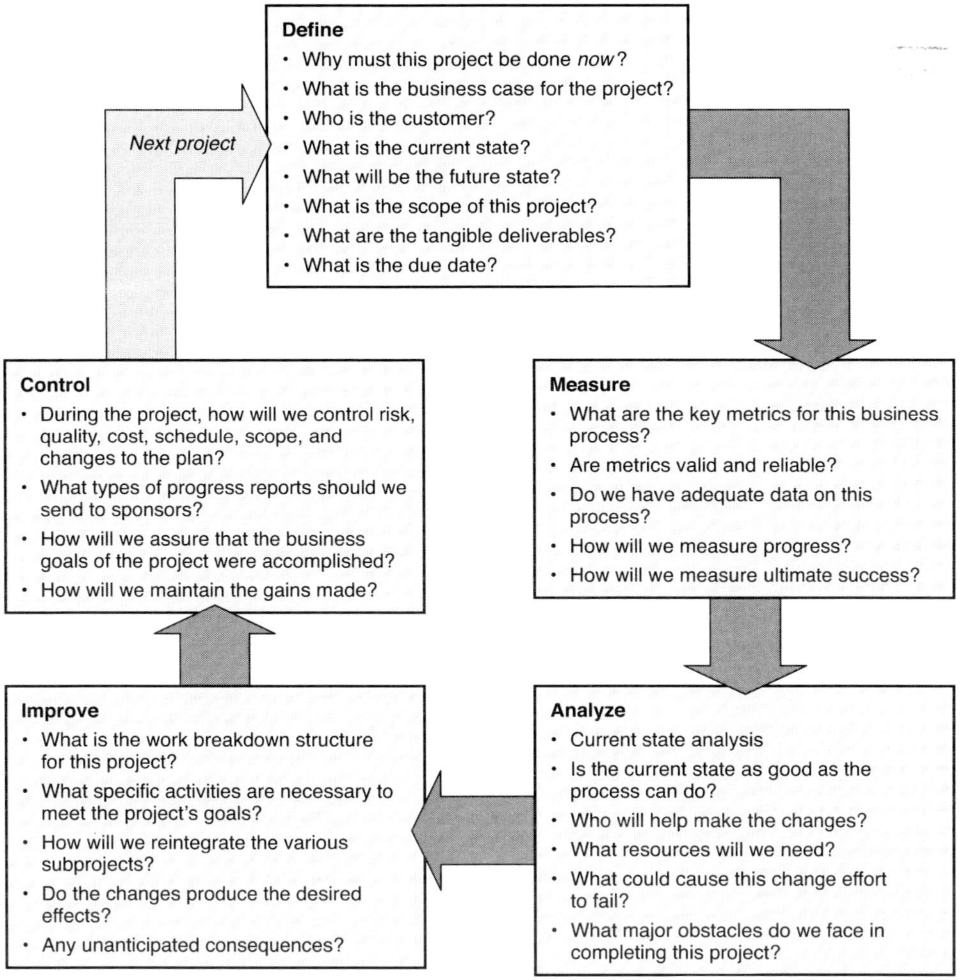

Figure 8.1 The Six Sigma project DMAIC cycle.

Source: Reproduced by permission from R. Bialek, G. L. Duffy, and J. W. Moran, *The Public Health Quality Improvement Handbook* (Milwaukee, WI: ASQ Quality Press, 2009), 226.

ensure alignment with organizational strategy to avoid any disconnects with the project goals and the overall organization. Once the contract is complete, a Black Belt begins using tools such as a process map and a cause-and-effect diagram to uncover the specifics of an issue and get to the root cause of the defects (see Chapter 9).

2. *Measure.* In this phase, the Six Sigma resource determines the baseline performance of the process, validates that the measurement system in place is accurate, verifies the cost of quality (Chapter 7)—the cost of not doing it right the first time—and makes an assessment of capability. This is the performance level of the process against customer requirements or expectations.

The question is, how *capable* is the process in meeting customers' needs? Statistically speaking, *sigma* is a term indicating to what extent a process varies from perfection. The quantity of units processed divided into the number of defects actually occurring, multiplied by one million results in *defects per million*. Adding a 1.5 sigma shift in the mean results in the following defects per million:

—1 sigma = 690,000 defects per million

—2 sigma = 308,000 defects per million

—3 sigma = 66,800 defects per mission

—4 sigma = 6,210 defects per million

—5 sigma = 230 defects per million

—6 sigma = 3.4 defects per million

Identifying whether the organization's process is capable of meeting customer requirements is the first checkpoint, or stagegate, where the determination to continue the effort is made. Some of the tools to employ are customer surveys, complaint data analysis, a Pareto chart, and run or control charts (Chapter 9).

Figure 8.2 is an example from a consolidated call center supporting a large county health department. The department's leadership met with a broad base of community stakeholders, clients, and service partners to learn of their priority needs for using the call center. Prompt response time was a major external customer requirement, identified in the statement "I consistently wait too long to speak with a call center representative."

Additionally, a significant internal customer comment was "Why are the monthly administrative costs suddenly higher than the last three months?" These two statements, when associated with the major functions of the health department, prompted leadership to identify

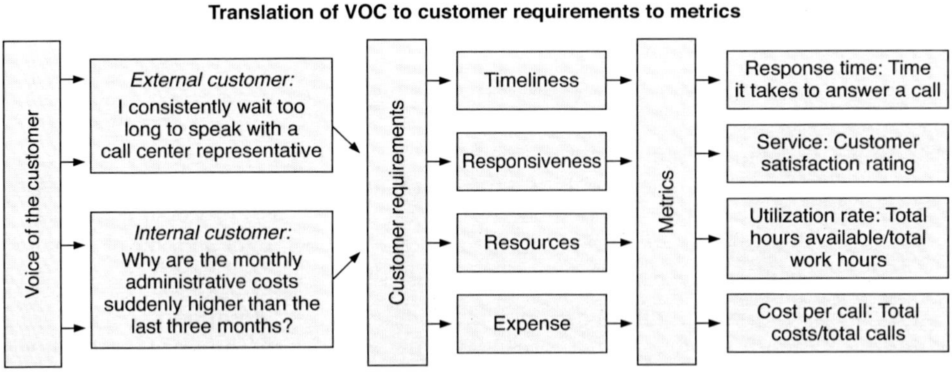

Figure 8.2 Performance metrics developed from customer requirements.

Source: Reproduced by permission from R. Bialek, G. L. Duffy, and J. W. Moran, *The Public Health Quality Improvement Handbook* (Milwaukee, WI: ASQ Quality Press, 2009), 227.

four measurement categories: response time, service, utilization rate, and cost per call.

3. *Analyze.* This phase is where a technical expert, the Black Belt, works with the team to scrub the data collected to uncover the root cause(s) of the defect. Process subject matter experts are also key to this phase of the process. Once the potential factors have been isolated, the team uses statistical, or hypothesis, testing to prove conclusively that the factor is indeed causing or contributing to the problem. Expect completed graphical analysis before any statistical testing is undertaken, and question any analysis that lacks statistical analysis backing it up.
4. *Improve.* When the team knows what is causing the problem, it can predict what the performance of the process would be if the identified issues were fixed. A number of different approaches for identifying possible solutions may be used. Setting performance expectations is crucial, as it facilitates the evaluation of the multiple solution sets, which should be documented in a decision matrix, to allow side-by-side comparison of the proposed solutions and the expected performance. This is the final point to halt the project prior to further investment and irreversible and costly changes to the process.
5. *Control.* After implementation in the Improve phase, this final phase ensures that the solution is integrated into daily operation and that it truly improves the process. Tools that may be employed are control charts, dashboards or balanced scorecards, and updated process effectiveness. Statistical proof must demand that post-implementation performance is better than it was and that it is in statistical process control. This ensures that if the process fails again, the process owner will know when and how to react to the situation. Another important practice that should be promoted across other areas of the organization is "standardization" of the solution. For example, if a solution is found in one location and the organization has three similar processes, the other processes should gain the benefit of the improvement project as well.

Six Sigma provides the framework to ask the right questions, depending on the process and desired outcome. Understanding the power of how a defect affects a process, operation, or practice is critical to success with any Six Sigma initiative. The DMAIC sequence is effective for processes that can benefit from corrective action or simple improvement. More complex redesign efforts, such as a total redesign of a process, are better addressed by a Six Sigma advanced approach called Design for Six Sigma (DFSS).

DFSS is a data-driven strategy for designing products and processes. It is an integral part of a Six Sigma quality initiative. DFSS consists of a series of five interconnected phases: Define, Measure, Analyze, Design, and Verify.

Six Sigma methods share similarities with other evidence-based (quantitative) projects, specifically the measure and analysis functionality of DMAIC methodology. This systemized approach complements and also challenges current paradigms that relate to the development of system-wide operations and procedures. DMAIC may also be crucial when larger supply chain partnerships seek to synchronize common initiatives.

Six Sigma is a very data-driven methodology. Implementing Six Sigma will cause significant demands for data collection and reporting. In addition, technology can provide significant cost savings by reducing variability through automation of receptive work processes.

Expanding data and information use and the associated technology growth may create friction between existing technology plans and the new needs being created to support projects (low-level data needs), control plans (low- and mid-level measures), and scorecards (high-level measures). Plan a way to prioritize these data needs. It should be a balance between the more strategic or structural needs for the high-level scorecards supporting the management system and the low- to midlevel needs of the DMAIC methodology.[1]

2. LEAN

> Identify lean tools that are used to reduce waste, including set-up and cycle-time reduction, pull systems (kanban), kaizen, just-in-time (JIT), 5S, and value stream mapping. (Understand)
>
> **CQIA BoK 2014 III.B.2.**

What Is Lean?

Originally, lean was a manufacturing philosophy to shorten the lead time between a customer order and the shipment of the parts ordered by eliminating all forms of waste. Lean helps firms in the reduction of costs, cycle times, and non-value-added activities, thus resulting in a more competitive, agile, and market-responsive company.

Lean concepts are now applicable beyond just the shop floor. All types of organizations have realized great benefit by implementing lean techniques in office functions, as well as in service firms such as banks, hospitals, restaurants, and so on. In this context, the practice is known as "lean enterprise."

A definition of lean, used by the Manufacturing Extension Partnership (of NIST/MEP, part of the US Department of Commerce), is "a systematic approach in identifying and eliminating waste (non-value-added activities) through continuous improvement by flowing the product at the pull of the customer in pursuit of perfection." Lean focuses on value-added expenditure of resources from the customers' viewpoint. In summary, give the customers:

- What they want
- When they want it
- Where they want it
- In the quantities and varieties they want

A planned, systematic implementation of lean leads to improved quality, better cash flow, increased sales, greater productivity and throughput, improved morale, and higher profits. Many of the concepts in total quality management (TQM) and team-based continuous improvement are also common to the implementation of lean strategies.[2]

The "Building Blocks" of Lean

The tools and techniques used in the introduction, sustaining, and improvement of the lean system are sometimes referred to as the lean building blocks (see Figure 8.3). These building blocks make up the "house of lean." Many of these building blocks are interconnected and can be implemented in tandem; for example, 5S (workplace organization and standardization), visual controls, point-of-use storage, standardized work, streamlined layout, and autonomous maintenance (part of total productive maintenance) can all be constituents of a planned implementation effort.

The building blocks include:

1. 5S: a system for workplace organization and standardization. This technique comprises five steps that all start with the letter S in Japanese (seiri, seiton, seison, seiketsu, and shitsuke). These five terms are loosely translated in English as *sort, set in order, shine, standardize,* and *sustain.*
2. Visual controls: the placement in plain view of all tooling, parts, production activities, and indicators so everyone involved can understand the status of the system at a glance.
3. Streamlined layout: plant layout designed according to optimum operational sequence.

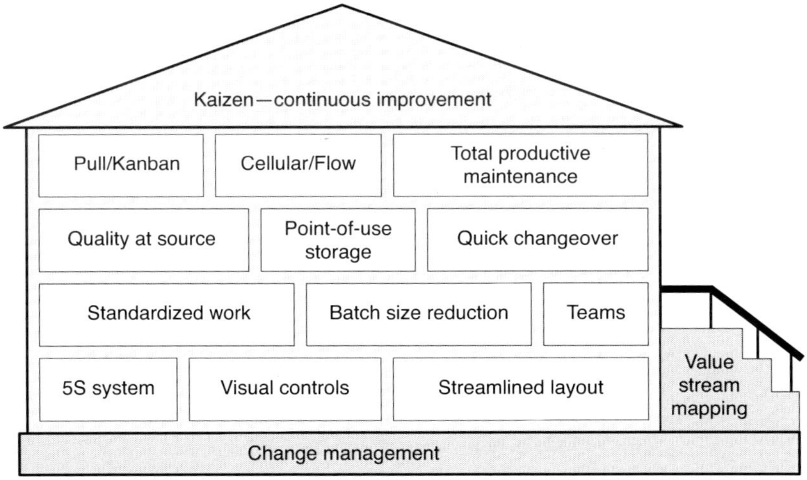

Figure 8.3 "House of Lean" (based on an NIST/MEP model).

Source: Reproduced by permission from G. D. Beecroft, G. L. Duffy, and J. W. Moran, *The Executive Guide to Improvement and Change* (Milwaukee, WI: ASQ Quality Press, 2003), 134.

4. Standardized work: consistent performance of a task, according to prescribed methods, without waste, and focused on human movement (ergonomics).
5. Batch size reduction: the best batch size is one-piece flow, or make one and move one. If one-piece flow is not appropriate, reduce the batch to the smallest size possible.
6. Teams: in the lean environment, the emphasis is on working in teams, whether it is an improvement team or a daily work team.
7. Quality at the source: the operators perform inspection and process control so they can ensure that they are passing along product that is of acceptable quality.
8. Point-of-use storage: raw material, parts, information, tooling, work standards, procedures, and so on, are stored where needed.
9. Quick changeover: the ability to change tooling and fixtures rapidly (usually in minutes) so multiple products in smaller batches can be run on the same equipment. This concept is also referred to as single minute exchange of die (SMED) or setup reduction.
10. Pull/Kanban: a system of sending delivery signals from downstream to upstream activities where the upstream supplier does not produce until the downstream customer signals the need ("kanban" system).
11. Cellular/Flow: physically linking and arranging manual and machine process steps into the most efficient combination to maximize value-added content while minimizing waste; the aim is single-piece flow.
12. Total productive maintenance: a lean equipment maintenance strategy for maximizing overall equipment effectiveness.

Besides these building blocks, other equally important concepts or techniques in lean include value stream mapping (VSM), just-in-time (JIT), error-proofing ("poka-yoke"), autonomation ("jidoka"), continuous improvement ("kaizen"), kaizen blitz for breakthrough improvements, and change management. Lean is a never-ending journey leaving room to continuously improve.

JIT is a practice whereby lean organizations seek to match rate of customer demand to rate of production, to operate all processes at a pace that mirrors customer requirements.

Cycle time is the average time for one part or service to be completed, from the beginning of a process to the end of a process.[3] Reducing the time to provide a part or service to the customer serves to increase customer satisfaction as well as improve productivity or throughput and achieve a more cost-effective production process.

Lean will not work if it is viewed as merely a project, or as a single-instance solution, or as a means for downsizing. It works best if deployed as a never-ending philosophy of continuous improvement. Lean should be considered a growth strategy. When improvements have been sustained, the remaining resources can be redeployed toward new business. Many firms have appointed and empowered lean champions to successfully implement their lean transformations. These champions help others as mentors, trainers, group facilitators, and communicators and act as the drivers of continuous improvements; they also serve as planners, evaluators, and cheerleaders celebrating each success. They also help in standardizing at the higher levels of performance as lean is implemented so as not to slip back to less effective practices.

How to Start the Lean Journey

The starting point of a lean initiative could be any one of the following:

1. VSM: charting a set of specific actions required to take a product family from raw material to finished goods per customer demand, concentrating on information management and physical transformation tasks. Outputs of VSM are a firm understanding of *takt time*, flowcharts (a *current state map* and a *future state map*), and an *implementation plan* to get from the current to the future state. Using VSM can drastically reduce the lead time so that it is closer to the actual value-added processing time, typically in a short duration such as 12 months, by attacking the identified bottlenecks and constraints. The implementation plan acts as the guide for doing so. Bottlenecks addressed could be long setup times, unreliable equipment, unacceptable first-pass yield, high work in process inventories, and so on. A typical current state map and future state map, drawn using different icons, are presented in Figures 8.4 and 8.5.

   In the current state map (Figure 8.4), the requirements from the customer and the requirements to the supplier, plus internal scheduling

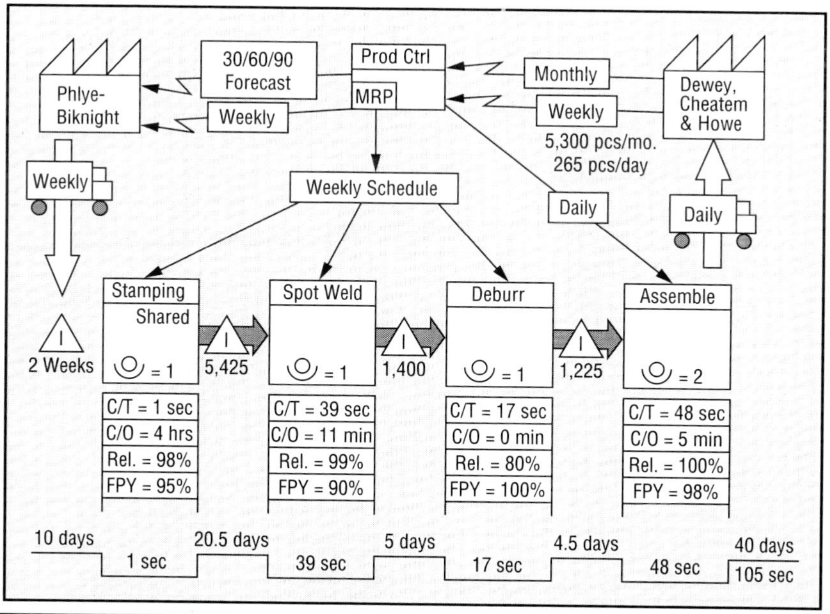

Figure 8.4 Current state map.

Source: Reproduced by permission from G. D. Beecroft, G. L. Duffy, and J. W. Moran, *The Executive Guide to Improvement and Change* (Milwaukee, WI: ASQ Quality Press, 2003), 136.

communications, are drawn at the top: "the information flow." In the center are the material flows from purchased product to finished goods. And at the bottom are data boxes with the lead time (40 days in this example) and the actual processing time (only 105 seconds).

In the future state map (Figure 8.5), the plan is to reduce the lead time to 7 days and the processing time by a few seconds to 91 seconds. The road map (or implementation plan) to get to the future state is not shown, but it can be as simple a project management tool as a Gantt chart showing the duration of the project. The timely implementation of the kaizens (represented by starbursts) identified on the future state map is the key.

2. Lean baseline assessment: using interviews, informal flowcharting, process observations, and analysis of reliable data, an "as is" situational report can be generated from which would flow the lean improvement plan based on the identified "gaps."
3. "Massive" training in lean to a critical mass of employees in "teach-do" cycles. Lean implementation should continue immediately after the training.
4. The "basic" building blocks: 5S, visual controls, streamlined layout, point-of-use storage, standardized work, and so on. Build on these

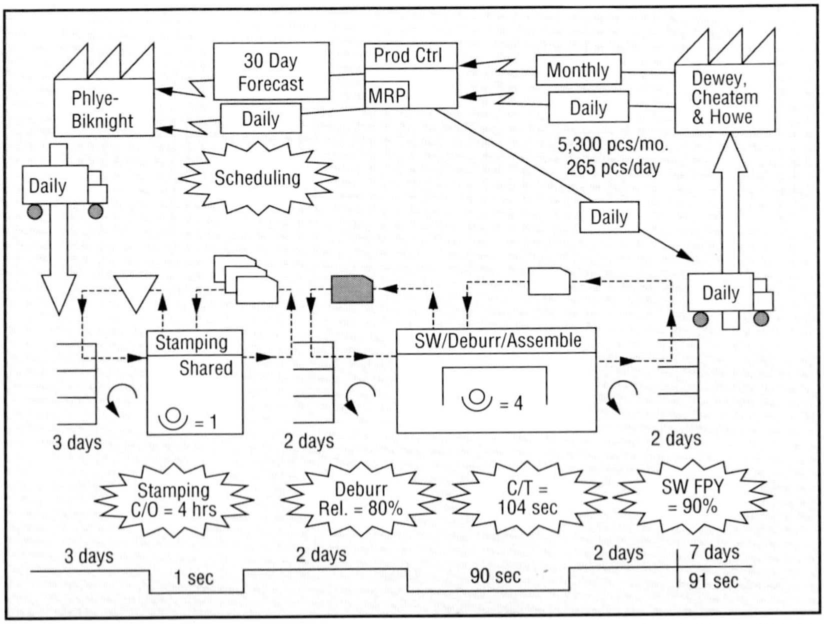

Figure 8.5 Future state map.

Source: Reproduced by permission from G. D. Beecroft, G. L. Duffy, and J. W. Moran, *The Executive Guide to Improvement and Change* (Milwaukee, WI: ASQ Quality Press, 2003), 136.

with the higher-level tools and techniques, finally achieving flow of production based on customer "pull."

5. Pilot project: choose a bottleneck or constraint area in which to do breakthrough lean improvement (use the kaizen blitz approach) and then, with the lessons learned, expand lean implementation to other areas.
6. Change management: align the company's strategies and workforce goals, and then change the culture from the traditional "push" production to lean "pull." This should eventually result in a philosophical change in people's daily work life.
7. Analysis of the internal overall equipment effectiveness (OEE) and the OEE losses: a Pareto of these losses will identify the "biggest bang for the buck" and indicate where to start the lean journey.[4]

A principal reason for improving processes is to remove waste. If an activity consumes resource time or capital but does not add value, it is wasteful and should be eliminated. The idea is to eliminate as many of these wastes as possible in daily work activities. Removing waste makes additional time and resources available for higher-priority objectives of the department. Table 8.2 explains the eight types of waste.

Waste occurs in a clearly visible form as well as an invisible form. Following are examples of visible and invisible waste:[5]

Examples of Visible Waste

- Out-of-spec incoming material: invoice from supplier has incorrect pricing; aluminum sheets are wrong size
- Scrap: holes drilled in wrong place; shoe soles improperly attached
- Downtime: school bus not operating; process 4 cannot begin because of backlog at process 3
- Product rework: failed electrical continuity test; customer number not coded on invoice

Examples of Invisible Waste

- Inefficient setups: jig requires frequent retightening; incoming orders not sorted correctly for data entry
- Queue times of work-in-process: assembly line not balanced to eliminate bottlenecks (constraints); inefficient loading-zone protocol slows school bus unloading, causing late classes
- Unnecessary motion: assembly materials located out of easy reach; need to bring each completed order to dispatch desk
- Wait time of people and machines: utility crew (three workers and truck) waiting until parked auto can be removed from work area; planes late in arriving due to inadequate scheduling of available terminal gates

Table 8.2 Eight types of waste.

Waste	Description	Example
Overprocessing	Spending more time than necessary to produce the product or service	Combining client survey instruments into one form rather than developing specific instruments for each program
Transportation handling	Unnecessary movement of materials or double handling	Department vehicles stored in a central facility, requiring constant movement of vehicles to and from other high-traffic locations
Unnecessary motion	Extra steps taken by employees and equipment to accommodate inefficient process layouts	Laboratory testing equipment stored in cabinets far from specialists' work area
Unnecessary inventory	Any inventory that is not directly required for the current client's order	Overestimating vaccination support materials, requiring additional locked storage cages, inventory counting, and reconciliation
Waiting	Periods of inactivity in a downstream process that occur because an upstream activity does not produce or deliver on time	Paperwork waiting for management signature or review
Defects	Errors produced during a service transaction or while developing a product; damage to equipment	Ineffective scripts for initial intake applications or unclear directions for filling out required forms
Overproduction	Items produced in excess quantity and before the customer needs them	Too many dated client information collection sheets prepared at beginning of shift
People	Not fully utilizing people's abilities (mental, creative, skills, experience, and so on); under- or overutilization of resources can also include waste created by safety issues impacting the human involvement within processes	Poor job design, ineffective process design within business functions, lack of empowerment, and maintaining a staffing complement not in balance with workload demand

Source: Reproduced by permission from G. L. Duffy, *Modular Kaizen* (Milwaukee, WI: ASQ Quality Press, 2014), 87.

- Inventory: obsolete material returned from distributor's annual clean-out is placed in inventory anticipating possibility of a future sale; to take advantage of quantity discounts, a yearly supply of paper bags is ordered and stored
- Movement of material (work-in-process and finished goods): in a function-oriented plant layout, work-in-process has to be moved from

15 to 950 feet to next operation; stacks of files are constantly being moved about to gain access to filing cabinets and machines

- Overproduction: because customers usually order the same item again, overrun is produced to place in inventory "just in case"; "extras" are made at earlier operations in case they are needed in subsequent operations
- Engineering changes: problems in production necessitate engineering changes; failure to clearly review customer requirements causes changes
- Unneeded reports: a report initiated five years ago is still produced each week even though the need was eliminated four years ago; a hard-copy report duplicates information available on a computer screen
- Meetings that add no value: a morning production meeting is held each day whether or not there is a need (coffee and Danish are served); 15 people attend a staff meeting each week at which one of the two hours is used to solve a problem usually involving less than one-fifth of the attendees
- Management processes that take too long or have no value: all requisitions (even for paper clips) must be signed by a manager; a "memo to file" must be prepared for every decision made between one department and another

A huge example of waste:

> Years ago, a division of a well-recognized conglomerate reengineered its manufacturing processes. The division built a new plant and installed all-new processes. Integral to the new process design was a sophisticated system for handling material to and from each workstation. In theory, the material conveyor system would allow a vast reduction in workspace heretofore taken up with buffer inventories in the old plant. Improved cycle time, inventory cost reduction, and smaller plant space were the touted advantages. The responsibility for designing the handling system was delegated to the equipment supplier's engineers, with very little company oversight.
>
> Unfortunately, the system was poorly planned before the expensive handling equipment was ordered and installed. Within less than two months of operation, the plant was hopelessly mired in piles of work-in-process and buffer stocks stacked under and between machines—so much so that trailer trucks were rented to store overflowing materials in the parking lot. After that short period of operation, the plant closed for a major reengineering with serious loss of business and financial impacts. Management was replaced.
>
> The lessons learned were the need to better understand the processes, especially the constraints involved; to avoid becoming enamored with state-of-the-art machinery and promises from suppliers; and to involve the people who will operate the system in the process design—and never delegate the whole project responsibility to a supplier.

3. BENCHMARKING

> Define benchmarking and describe how it can be used to develop and support best practices. (Understand)
>
> **CQIA 2014 III.B.3.**

Benchmarking is an evaluation technique in which an organization compares its own performance for a specific process with the "best practice" performance of a recognized leader in a comparable process. The evaluation helps the initiating organization identify shortcomings and establishes a baseline or standard against which to measure its progress in the development and maintenance of a quality assurance program.

Several different approaches to benchmarking include:

- Competitive—comparing with direct competitors, locally, nationally, or worldwide
- Functional—comparing with companies that have similar processes in the same function but outside one's industry
- Performance—comparing pricing, technical quality, features, and other quality or performance characteristics
- Process—comparing work processes such as billing, order entry, or employee training
- Strategic—comparing how companies compete and examining winning strategies that have led to a competitive advantage and market success

The basic steps involved in benchmarking are as follows:

1. Identify what is to be benchmarked. Be specific in deciding what the team wants to benchmark.
2. Decide which organizations/functions to benchmark. The comparison should be conducted not only against peers, if feasible, but also against recognized leading organizations with similar functions.
3. Determine the data collection method and collect data. Keep the data collection process simple. There is no one right way to benchmark. It is important to look outward, be innovative, and search for new and different ways to improve the process under study.
4. Contact a peer in the benchmark organization. Explain the purpose of the benchmarking study and what information is desired. Give assurance that confidential information will not be requested during the benchmarking process.
5. Mutually arrange the benchmarking event. During the benchmarking visit, inquire about the peer's organization: what it does, why it does it,

how it measures and/or evaluates the process under scrutiny and what its performance measures are, what has worked well, and what has not been successful.

6. After the visit, determine whether what the team learned from benchmarking can be applied to improve the organization's process. Are there new and different ways to solve the problem or improve the process? Are there other solutions to the problem that the team has overlooked? It's important to keep an open mind about new and perhaps radically different ways of doing things.

There are several caveats to consider, such as, has the initiating organization:

- Established benchmarking as an ongoing process?
- Made every attempt to bring a targeted process to be benchmarked to the highest level possible, before going outside?
- Carefully selected and trained its benchmarking team, prior to contacting a potential benchmarking organization?
- Successfully located a willing benchmarking partner-organization?
- Customized its benchmarking objectives, plans, and process to conduct the benchmarking study in accordance with mutually agreed-on protocols and terms?
- Prepared the team to share appropriate aspects of its process during the onsite benchmarking study?
- Clearly identified how the findings and lessons learned from conducting the benchmarking study will be shared after the study within the organization?
- Prepared itself to institute the next benchmarking study for another internal process?

4. INCREMENTAL AND BREAKTHROUGH IMPROVEMENT

> Describe and distinguish between these two types of improvements, the steps required for each, and the type of situation in which either type would be expected. (Understand)
>
> **CQIA BoK 2014 III.B.4.**

There are two fundamental philosophies relative to improvement. Improvement may be achieved on a gradual basis, taking one small step at a time. A dramatically different concept is practiced by proponents of breakthrough improvement, a "throw out the old and start anew" approach frequently referred to as *process reengineering*. Both approaches have proven to be effective depending on the circumstances, such as the size of the organization, the degree of urgency for change, the degree of acceptability within the organization's culture, the receptivity to the relative risks involved, the ability to absorb implementation costs, and the availability of competent people to effect the change.

Incremental Improvement

The following is an example of incremental improvement:

> A team is formed in the order fulfillment department of a magazine publisher to find ways to reduce the processing time for new subscriptions. The team will likely be seeking small steps it can take to improve the processing time. When a change is implemented and an improvement is confirmed, the team may meet again to see whether it can make further time reductions.

This incremental improvement approach may be in use throughout an organization.

Masaaki Imai made popular the practice of *kaizen*,[6] a strategy for making improvements in quality in all business areas. Kaizen focuses on implementing small, gradual changes over a long time period. When the strategy is fully utilized, everyone in the organization participates. Kaizen is driven by a basic belief that when quality becomes ingrained in the organization's culture and people, the quality of products and services will follow. Key factors are the initiation of operating practices that lead to the uncovering of waste and non-value-added steps, the total involvement of everyone in the organization, extensive training in the concepts and tools for improvement, and a management that is committed to and supportive of improvement as an integral part of the organization's strategy. In a serious problem situation, an intensified approach may be used, called a *kaizen blitz*. For example:

> MedElec, a manufacturer of switches used in medical diagnostic equipment, was faced with the potential of losing its six largest customers. The threat, due to mounting numbers of missed delivery dates, caused significant delays in the entire supply chain. Employing a facilitator, MedElec initiated a five-day kaizen blitz, with representatives from every department and management. The objective of the session was to find and implement ways to not only shorten the delivery cycle but also prevent any future late deliveries. Ultimately, the goal was to initiate an unconditional guarantee policy for on-time shipments to the company's customers.
>
> Following extensive training, the team members gathered and analyzed performance data, pinpointed the root causes of delays, and prioritized the problem areas. First dealing with those problems for which solutions could be immediately implemented, they next systematically addressed each remaining problem in order of priority. For each solution, a careful review ensured that no additional problems would be created once the solution was initiated. The team then took the solutions and began change implementation in their work areas.

The following steps, which follow a Plan-Do-Check-Act (PDCA) sequence, are typically taken in incremental improvement:

1. Select the process or subprocess to be process mapped
2. Define the process
   a. Inputs to the process, including suppliers
   b. Outputs from the process
   c. Users/customers to whom outputs are directed
   d. Requirements of users/customers
   e. Constraints (such as standards, regulations, and policies)
3. Map the main flow without exceptions
4. Add the decision points and alternative paths
5. Add the check/inspection points and alternative paths
6. Analyze the process flow to identify
   a. Non-value-added steps
   b. Redundancies
   c. Bottlenecks
   d. Inefficiencies
   e. Deficiencies
7. Prioritize problems
   a. Quantify the results of each problem
   b. Identify the impact each problem has on the overall process
   c. Subject the problems to Pareto analysis to identify the most important problem
8. Redo the map to remove a primary problem
9. Do a desktop walk-through with persons who are involved with the process
10. Modify the process map as needed (and modifications will be needed!)
11. Review changes and obtain approvals
12. Institute changes
13. Review results of changes
14. Make needed changes to documented procedures
15. Repeat the process for the next-most-important problem area

The individuals responsible for the process may make incremental improvements. However, depending on organizational policies and procedures, appropriate approvals may be required. Also, there should be concern for interactions with other processes that take place before and after the process being changed. More typically, a team from the work group involved initiates incremental changes. If the organization has a suggestion system in place, care must be taken to ensure that conflict of interest does not result.

Breakthrough Improvement

Taken to its extreme, breakthrough improvement may encompass totally reengineering an entire organization.[7] This usually means literally ignoring how the organization is structured and how it currently produces and delivers its products and services. It's a "start from a clean sheet of paper" approach. The subject of much criticism and a number of notable failures, this "whole organization" approach has gained a negative reputation. Unfortunately, many organizations grabbed at this approach as a way to drastically cut costs, most significantly by reducing the number of employees. In those organizations with a quest to cut back (on everything), the basic tenets of the reengineering approach were either ignored or sublimated.

The most important factors to consider include the need for:

- Careful understanding of the organization's culture and management's commitment to change (especially when positions are threatened)
- A well-communicated policy and plan for the disposition of people displaced by the changes
- A well-communicated plan for the transition (e.g., whether the changes just mean more work for the employees left behind)
- Means for dealing with the psychological trauma inherent in downsizing (such as the guilt felt about being a survivor, the loss of friends, and the anger of terminated or transferred employees)
- Means for addressing the potential for sabotage, intentional or unintentional (such as lethargy, loss of interest in the job, retaliation, a careless attitude, etc.)

Given the small number of real successes in totally reengineering an entire company all at once, as proposed by Hammer and Champy,[8] a more limited approach has emerged, typically called *process reengineering*. Using process reengineering, a team examines a given process, such as complaint handling. It may take a macro look at how complaints are now handled, just to gain a sense of the situation. Then, starting with a clean sheet of paper (and perhaps based on information gained from benchmarking), the members of the team devise a new (and hopefully better) process approach without just fixing how the present process operates. The resultant process design is a *breakthrough*. Achievement of the breakthrough presumes that the team participants are able to shed their biases and their ingrained notions of how things have always been done. For example:

> State University realizes that its student enrollment process is cumbersome to administer and frustrating for new students. A cross-functional process improvement team is formed with a charter to "completely overhaul" the enrollment process.

The team members undergo training in the concepts of process reengineering and the tools they may need. Up front, they identify the primary subprocesses that must be considered: student applications (review, selection, and notification), payment processing, student loans, new student orientation, class assignments, dormitory assignments, special requirements (security issues, dietary needs, and disability accommodations), document completion, data entry, data processing, and report preparation. They then generate a macro-level process flowchart showing the interaction of these subprocesses. A brainstorming session, followed by a multivoting activity, uncovers a host of ideas on how some of the subprocesses can be improved and a priority for addressing the ideas and how the ideas can be prioritized.

As the team progresses, it becomes apparent that almost all of the data required to initiate student enrollment can be captured on a single document prepared by the expectant enrollee in machine-readable format. From this document, students selected for enrollment can be sent a bar-coded identification card that can be used throughout the enrollment process and subsequently for ongoing transactions throughout the academic year. Upon arrival on enrollment day, the student presents the bar-coded card to a computer terminal that generates a printout of the student's class and dormitory assignments and any special requirements. The equipment needed to handle the enrollment-day processing is "on loan" from other university processes, such as the cafeteria and the school store.

This major breakthrough reduces the number of administrators needed to staff tables on enrollment day. It also eliminates the long wait times in lines and the crowding for forms and places to fill out the forms. Essentially, the only table requiring staff, assuming a well-designed system, is one to handle student requests for assignment changes.

The team drafts a process map of the new student enrollment process, in detail, and drafts an implementation plan. The plans are submitted to the appropriate officials, modifications are made as needed, and approval is obtained. The major breakthrough results in reduced processing time, greater accuracy, and substantial reduction in student complaints.

Certain generic steps are usually involved in initiating breakthrough improvements:

1. Ensure that there is a strong, committed leader supporting the initiative.
2. Form a high-level, cross-functional steering committee.
3. Create a macro-level process map for the entire organization.
4. Select one of the major processes to be reengineered.
5. Form a cross-functional reengineering team.
6. Examine customers' requirements and wants in detail.
7. Look at and understand the current process from the customer's perspective (its function, its performance, and critical concerns), but not in finite detail.
8. Brainstorm ways to respond to customers' needs. Think outside the box.

9. Create breakthrough process redesign (assuming that the process is still needed!):
   a. Design to include as few people as possible in the performance of the process.
   b. Identify and question all assumptions and eliminate as many as possible.
   c. Eliminate non-value-added steps.
   d. Integrate steps and simplify everything possible.
   e. Incorporate the advantages of information technology wherever feasible.
   f. Prepare a new vision statement.
   g. Plan how to communicate the new vision and news of the process redesign.
   h. Determine how to achieve performers' "buy-in" of new process design.
   i. Determine how to get management to see the wisdom of dismantling the old process design.
   j. Determine how the inevitable displacement of people (new work procedures, job elimination, transfers, and downsizing) will be addressed.
10. Test-drive the new process design with a portion of the business and with one or two customers who can be counted on for collaboration and feedback.
11. Collect feedback from the selected customers, the involved employees, management, and other affected stakeholders (such as the union, suppliers, and stockholders).
12. Modify the process redesign as needed and communicate the changes.
13. Plan a controlled rollout of the process redesign.
14. Implement the rollout plan.
15. Evaluate the effectiveness of the redesigned process continuously at every stage.
    a. Assess assimilation of the changes by workforce and management.
       - Individual acceptance of changes (technical and social).
       - Understanding of need for displacement of people (reassignments and terminations).
       - Changes to managerial and supervisory roles and status (redistribution of responsibilities and authority).
       - Changes to compensation, training, development, and other human support systems.

b. Assess the impact of the changes on customers (e.g., did the redesign accomplish what the customers needed and wanted?).

c. Assess the impact of the changes on other stakeholders (e.g., did the redesign achieve its intended purpose with minimum negative consequences?).

5. ESTABLISHING CONTINUOUS PROCESS IMPROVEMENT CYCLES

A continuous process improvement cycle is an action or series of actions taken as the result of an organized and planned effort and aimed at continually improving an organization's processes. The organization commits to an ongoing cycle of continuous improvement, taking the principal processes in order of importance, ultimately revisiting each such process as it appears again in the rotation.

An essential first step in getting started on process improvement is when senior management makes it a strategic organizational goal. The importance of process improvement must be communicated from the top. Leaders need to foster an organizational environment in which a process improvement can thrive and people regularly use quality improvement–related techniques and tools. Further, information has been developed to provide teams with a step-by-step approach for their process improvement efforts. The focus is on improving a process over the long term, not just patching up procedures and work routines as problems occur. Managers need to start thinking about the following:

- What processes should be selected for improvement, and when?
- What resources will be required?
- Who are the right people to work on improving a selected process?
- What's the best way to learn more about the selected process?
- How should the task of improving a process be initiated?
- Upon completion, how can the lessons learned help to institutionalize the improved process and support upcoming process improvements in the cycle?

Figure 8.6 is a basic process improvement model. The basic model has two parts:

- Steps 1–7 represent the process simplification part, in which the team begins process improvement activities
- Depending on the stability and capability of the process, the team may continue on to step 8 or go directly to step 14

The PDCA cycle, also known as the Plan-Do-Study-Act (PDSA) cycle (Figure 8.7), which consists of steps 8–14, flows from the process simplification segment. Using all 14 steps of the model will increase an organization's process knowledge, broaden decision-making options, and enhance the likelihood of satisfactory long-term results.

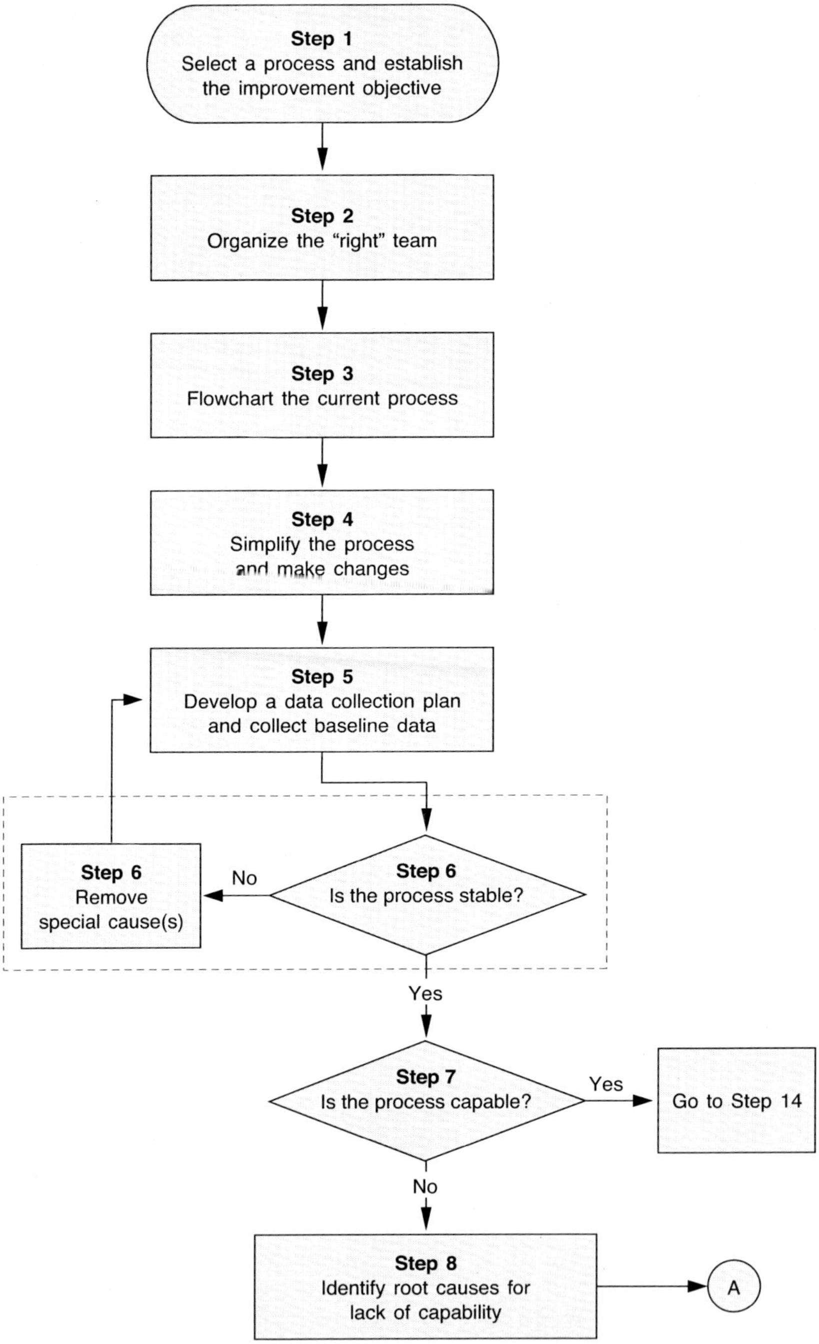

Figure 8.6 Basic process improvement model.

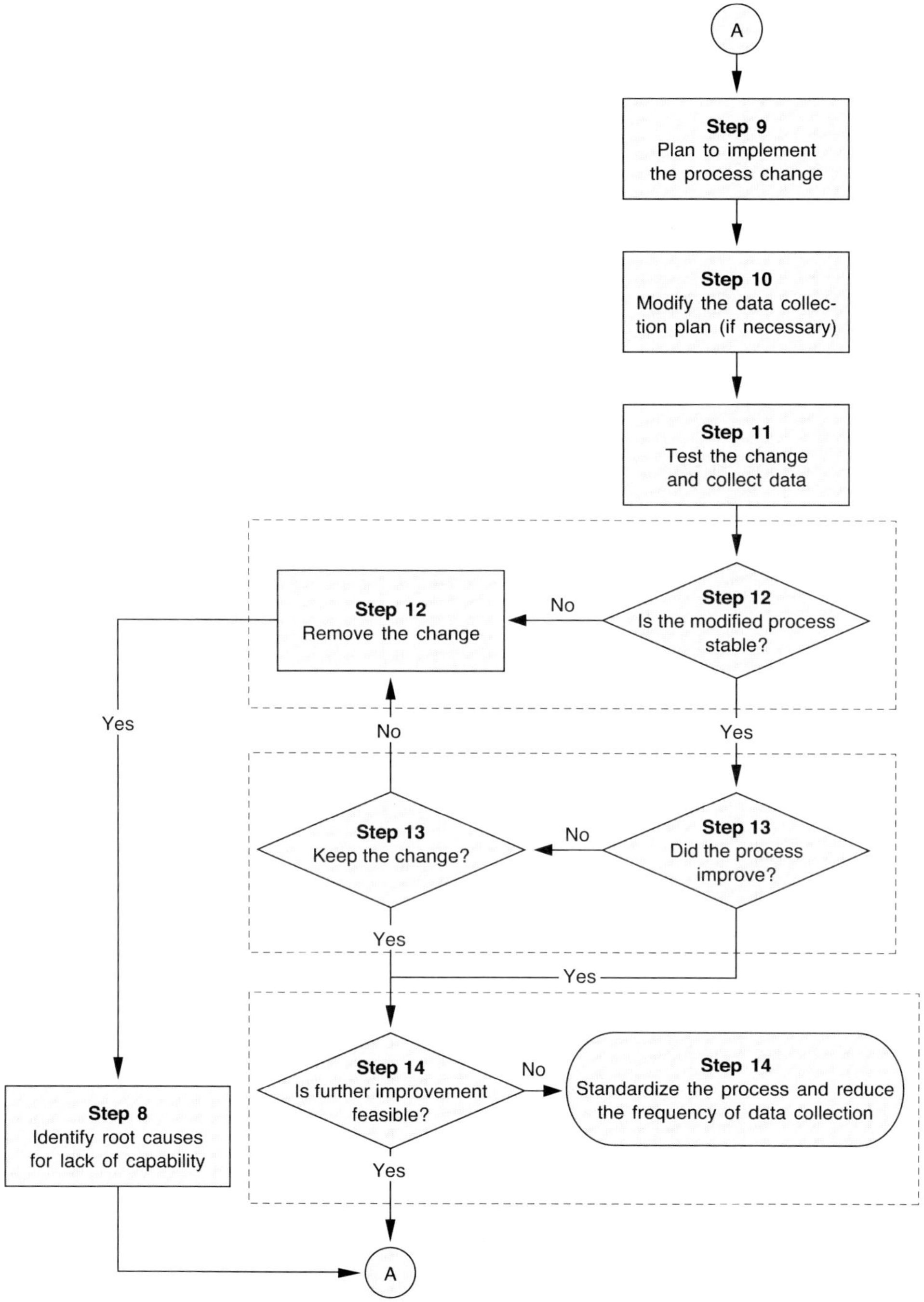

Figure 8.6 Basic process improvement model. *(continued)*

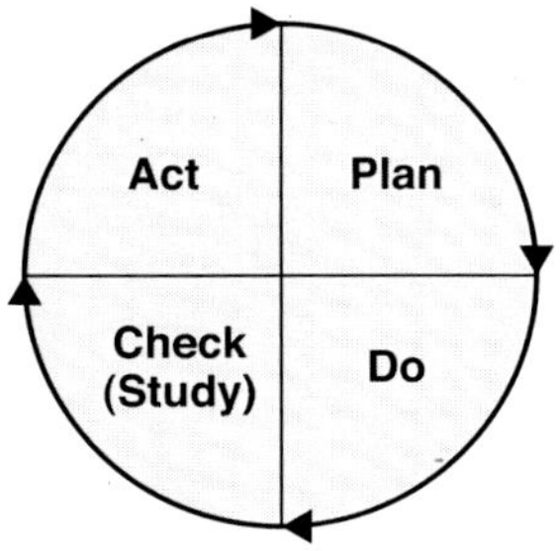

Figure 8.7 Plan-Do-Check/Study-Act cycle.

Possible actions for the PDCA cycle are as follows:

Plan

- Select project
- Define problem and aim or intent
- Clarify/understand
- Set targets/schedules
- Inform and register the project
- Solve/come up with most suitable recommendation

Do

- Record/observe/collect data
- Examine/prioritize/analyze
- Justify/evaluate cost
- Investigate/determine most likely solutions
- Test and verify/determine cost and benefits
- Develop/test most likely causes

Check (Study)

- Consolidate ideas
- Select next project
- Seek approval from management

Act

- Plan installation/implementation plan
- Install/implement approved project/training
- Maintain/standardize

The following is an overview of what may be involved in each step in the model:

Step 1: Select the process to be improved and establish a well-defined process improvement objective. The objective may be established by the team or may come from other interested parties, such as customers or management.

Step 2: Organize a team to improve the process. This involves selecting the "right" people to serve on the team; identifying the resources available for the improvement effort, such as people, time, money, and materials; setting reporting requirements; and determining the team's level of authority. These elements may be formalized in a written charter.

Step 3: Define the current process using a flowchart. This tool is used to generate a step-by-step map of the activities, actions, and decisions that occur between the starting and stopping points of the process.

Step 4: Simplify the process by removing redundant or unnecessary activities. People may have seen the process on paper in its entirety for the first time in step 3. This can be a real eye-opener that prepares them to take these first steps in improving the process.

Step 5: Develop a plan for collecting data and then collect baseline data. Ensure that the data evaluation process is verified for accuracy. These data will be used as the yardstick for comparison later in the model. This begins the evaluation of the process against the process improvement objective established in step 1. The flowchart from step 3 helps the team determine who should collect data and where in the process data should be collected.

Step 6: Assess whether the process is stable. The team creates a control chart or run chart out of the data collected in step 5 to gain a better understanding of what is happening in the process. The follow-up actions of the team are dictated by whether special cause variation is found in the process.

Step 7: Assess whether the process is capable. The team plots a histogram to compare the data collected in step 5 against the process improvement objective established in step 1. Usually the process simplification actions in step 4 are not enough to make the process capable of meeting the objective, and the team will have to continue on to step 8 in search of root causes. Even if the data indicate that the process is meeting the objective, the team should consider whether it is feasible to improve the process further before going on to step 14.

Step 8: Identify the root causes that prevent the process from meeting the objective. The team begins the PDCA cycle here, using the cause-and-effect diagram or brainstorming tools to generate possible reasons that the process fails to meet the desired objective.

Step 9: Develop a plan for implementing a change based on the possible reasons for the process's inability to meet the objective set for it. These root causes were identified in step 8. The planned improvement involves revising the steps in the simplified flowchart created after changes were made in step 4.

Step 10: Modify the data collection plan developed in step 5, if necessary.

Step 11: Test the changed process and collect data.

Step 12: Assess whether the changed process is stable. As in step 6, the team uses a control chart or run chart to determine process stability. If the process is stable, the team can move on to step 13; if not, the team must return the process to its former state and plan another change.

Step 13: Assess whether the change improved the process. Using the data collected in step 11 and a histogram, the team determines whether the process is closer to meeting the process improvement objective established in step 1. If the objective is met, the team can progress to step 14; if not, the team must decide whether to keep or discard the change.

Step 14: Determine whether additional process improvements are feasible. The team is faced with this decision following process simplification in step 7 and again after initiating an improvement in steps 8–13. In step 14, the team has the choice of embarking on continuous process improvement by reentering the model at step 9 or simply monitoring the performance of the process until further improvement is indicated.

Additional Suggestions

Selecting the Process

When an organization initially undertakes process improvement efforts, senior management may identify problem areas and nominate the first processes to be investigated. Later, processes with potential for improvement may be identified at any organizational level by any employee, with the approval of his or her immediate supervisor.

The following considerations are important in selecting processes for improvement:

- Total quality is predicated on understanding what is important to the customer. Every work unit, whether large or small, has both internal and external customers. Hence, the starting point in selecting a process for improvement is to obtain information from customers about their satisfaction or dissatisfaction with the products or services produced by the organization.
- It's best to start on a small scale. Once people can handle improving a simple process, they can work on more complicated ones.
- The selected process should occur often enough to be observed and documented. The team should be able to complete at least one

improvement cycle within 30–90 days; otherwise its members may lose interest.

- The process boundaries have to be determined. These are the starting and stopping points of the process that provide the framework within which the team will conduct its process improvement efforts. It is crucial to make sure that the steps involved in meeting the process improvement objective are located inside the boundaries.
- A Pareto analysis can help the team identify one or more factors or problems that occur frequently and can be investigated by the team. This analysis would be based on some preliminary data collected by the team. After the organization members have some experience working with the basic process improvement model, processes can be selected that have been performing poorly or that offer a potentially high payback in improving organizational performance. The former category might include processes that are routinely accomplished in a less-than-satisfactory manner. The latter category includes critical processes, such as internal auditing, corrective and preventive action, and cost reductions. In each case, it's best to move from the simple to the complicated and from the better-performing to the worst-performing processes.
- Because the process improvement initiative is ongoing, an effort should be made to not overuse team members by assigning them to consecutive improvement projects. It is essential that as many of the organization's employees participate in the process improvement cycle as is feasible. A team member rotation practice will help avoid personnel burnout.

Establishing the Process Improvement Objective

Once a process is selected, a well-defined process improvement objective needs to be established. The definition of the objective should answer the question *What improvement do we want to accomplish by using a process improvement methodology?*

The process improvement objective is frequently formulated by listening to internal and external customers. The team can use interviews or written surveys to identify target values to use as objectives for improving the product or service produced by the process.

Identifying a problem associated with the process helps define the process improvement objective. The people working in the process can identify activities that take too long, involve too many work hours, include redundant or unnecessary steps, or are subject to frequent breakdowns or other delays. But this is not just a problem-solving exercise; this is process improvement. Problems are symptoms of process failure, and it is the root cause deficiencies in the process that must be identified and corrected.

For an improvement effort to be successful, the team must start with a clear definition of what the problem is and what is expected from the process improvement. For example:

> An organization's internal audit activity has found only three deviations from process requirements in the last six audits. The team knows

from experience that there are many day-to-day problems that should be detected by the internal audit process. The team defines the problem as "an internal audit process that is not functioning to its full potential." In beginning to formulate a process improvement objective, the initial words could be "Improve the internal audit process so it will routinely find day-to-day process deviations." A time frame, measures, and so forth, will then be added.

A team formulating a process improvement objective may find it helpful to proceed by:

- Writing a description of the process that starts, "The process by which we . . . "
- Specifying the objectives of the process improvement effort (see Table 8.3 for guidelines for setting objectives the S.M.A.R.T. W.A.Y.)

If a team is achieving little improvement in its efforts, periodic review of clearly stated process improvement objectives will keep the team's work focused.

Organize the "Right" Team

Once the process has been selected and the boundaries established, the next criti cal step is selecting the "right" team to improve it. The right team consists of a good representation of people who work inside the boundaries of the process and have an intimate knowledge of the way it works.

Teams consisting of five to seven members seem to function most effectively. Though larger teams are not uncommon, studies have shown that teams with more than seven members may have trouble reaching consensus and achieving objectives.

The team leader may be chosen in any of several ways. The department head or process owner may appoint a knowledgeable individual to lead the team, or the process owner may opt to fill the position personally. Also, the team members may elect the team leader from their own ranks during the first meeting. Any of these methods of selecting a leader is acceptable.

Table 8.3 Setting objectives the S.M.A.R.T. W.A.Y.

S	Focus on *specific* needs and opportunities
M	Establish a *measurement* for each objective
A	Be sure objectives are *achievable* as well as challenging
R	Set stretch objectives that are also *realistic*
T	Indicate a *time* frame for each objective
W	Ensure that every objective is *worth* doing
A	*Assign* responsibility for each objective
Y	Ensure that all objectives stated will *yield* desired return

The team leader has the following responsibilities:

- Schedule and run the team's meetings.
  - Come to an understanding with the supervisor or whoever formed or chartered the team on the following:
    - The team's decision-making authority. The team may only be able to make recommendations based on its data collection and analysis efforts, or it may be able to implement and test changes without prior approval.
    - The time limit for the team to complete the improvement actions.
- Determine how the team's results and recommendations will be communicated up through the organization.
- Arrange for the resources—money, material, equipment, training, additional people, and so on—that the team will need to do the job.
- Decide how much time the team will devote to process improvement. Sometimes, improving a process is important enough to require a full-time effort by team members for a short period. At other times, the improvement team's work is best conducted at intervals of one- or two-hour segments.

Team members are selected by the team leader or the individual who formed the team. Members may have various skills, pay levels, or supervisory status. Depending on the nature of the process, they may come from different departments, divisions, work centers, or offices. The key factor is that the people selected for the team should be closely involved in the process that is being improved.

Being a team member carries certain obligations. Members are responsible for carrying out all team-related work assignments, such as data collection, data analysis, presentation development, sharing of knowledge, and participation in team discussions and decisions. Ideally, when actual process workers are on a team, they approach these responsibilities as an opportunity to improve the way their jobs are done rather than as extra work. (Many of the points made in this section about teams have been further amplified in Chapters 4–6.)

Team Charter

A *charter* is a document that describes the boundaries, expected results, and resources to be used by a process improvement team. A charter is usually provided by the individual or group who formed the team. Sometimes the process owner or the team members develop the charter. A charter is always required for a team working on a process that crosses departmental lines. A charter may not be necessary for a team that is improving a process found solely within a single work unit.

A charter should identify the following:

- The process to be improved
- Time constraints, when applicable
- The process improvement objectives

- The team's decision-making authority
- The team leader
- The resources to be provided
- The team members
- Reporting requirements

Other information pertinent to the improvement effort may also be included, such as the name of the process owner, the recommended frequency of meetings, or any other elements deemed necessary by those chartering the team.

Flowchart the Current Process

Before a team can improve a process, the members must understand how it works. The most useful tool for studying the current process is a flowchart. To develop an accurate flowchart, the team assigns one or more members to observe the flow of work through the process. It may be necessary for the observers to follow the flow of activity through the process several times before they can completely see and chart (map) what actually occurs. This record of where actions are taken, decisions are made, inspections are performed, and approvals are required becomes the "as is" flowchart. For some organizations, it may be the first accurate and complete picture of the process from beginning to end.

As the team participants start work on this first flowchart, they need to be careful to depict what is really happening in the process. They don't want to fall into the trap of flowcharting how people think the process is working, how they would like it to work, or how an instruction or manual says it should work. Only an "as is" flowchart that displays the process as it is actually working today can reveal the improvements that may be needed. When teams work on processes that cross departmental lines, they will have to talk to people at all levels across the organization who are involved in or affected by the process they are working on. It is even more important to get an accurate picture of those cross-functional processes than of those where boundaries are inside a work unit or office. The goal of this step is for the team to fully understand the process before making any attempt to change it. Changing a process before it is fully understood can cause more problems than already exist.

The team can further define the current situation by answering these questions:

- Does the flowchart show exactly how things are done now?
- If not, what needs to be added or modified to make it an "as is" picture of the process?
- Have the workers involved in the process contributed their knowledge of the process steps and their sequence?
- Are other members of the organization involved in the process, perhaps as customers? What do they have to say about how it really works?
- After gathering this information, is it necessary to rewrite the process improvement objectives (step 1)?

Simplify the Process and Make Improvements

The team has described the current process by developing an "as is" flowchart. Reviewing this depiction of how the process really works helps team members spot problems in the process flow. They may locate steps or decision points that are redundant. They may find that the process contains unnecessary inspections. They may discover procedures that were installed in the past in an attempt to mistake-proof the process after errors or failures were experienced. All of these consume scarce resources. Besides identifying areas where resources are being wasted, the team may find a weak link in the process that it can strengthen by adding one or more steps.

But before stepping in to make changes in the process based on this preliminary review of the "as is" flowchart, the team should answer the following questions for each process step:

- Can this step be done in parallel with other steps, rather than in its present sequence?
- Does this step have to be completed before another can be started, or can two or more steps be performed at the same time?
- What would happen if this step were eliminated? Would the output of the process remain the same? Would the output be unacceptable because it is incomplete or has too many defects?
- Would eliminating this step achieve the process improvement objective?
- Is the step being performed by the appropriate person or function?
- Is the step a work-around because of poor training or a safety net inserted to prevent recurrence of a failure?
- Is the step a single repeated action, or is it part of a rework loop that can be eliminated?
- Does the step add value to the product or service produced by the process?

If the answers to these questions indicate waste, the team should consider doing away with the step. If a step or decision block can be removed without degrading the process, the team may be recovering resources that can be used elsewhere.

Eliminating redundant or unnecessary steps decreases cycle time. Only part of the time it takes to complete most processes is productive time; the rest is delay. Delay consists of waiting for someone to take action, waiting for a part or document to be received, and similar unproductive activities. Consequently, removing a step that causes delay reduces cycle time by decreasing the total time it takes to complete the process.

After making preliminary changes in the process, the team should create a tentative flowchart of the simplified process. Then the team does a reality check:

> Can the simplified process produce products or services acceptable to customers and in compliance with applicable existing standards and regulations?

If the answer is yes, and the team has the authority to make changes, it should institute the simplified flowchart as the new standard process. Should the team require permission to make the recommended changes, a comparison of the simplified flowchart with the original flowchart can become the centerpiece of a briefing to those in a position to grant approval.

At this point, the people working in the process must be trained using the new flowchart of the simplified process. It is vital to ensure that they understand and adhere to the new way of doing business. Otherwise, the process can rapidly revert to the way it was before the improvement team started work.

Develop a Data Collection Plan and Collect Baseline Data

The earlier steps (1–4) took the team through a process simplification phase of process improvement. In this phase, all decisions were based on experience, qualitative knowledge of the process, and perceptions of the best way to operate.

For the remaining steps in the basic process improvement model, the team will be using a more scientific approach. From this point on the steps rely on statistical data that, when collected and analyzed, are used to make decisions about the process. In step 5, the team develops a data collection plan.

The process improvement objective established in step 1 is based on customers' expectations and needs regarding the product or service produced by the process. When the team develops a data collection plan, it must first identify the characteristic of the product or service that has to be changed in order to meet the objective. For example:

> A local coffeehouse prepares coffee and sells it to patrons. The coffee is brewed in a separate urn in the kitchen and then transferred to an urn in the front of the store. Lately, customers have been complaining that the coffee is cold when it's received.
>
> A team formed to improve this situation developed a process improvement objective that the coffee would be delivered to customers at a temperature between 109°F and 111°F. The team members then looked at their simplified flowchart to identify individual steps where measurements should be taken.
>
> Some members of the team thought that the water temperature should be measured as the water is boiled, prior to the actual brewing of the coffee. Others thought that such a measurement might be easy to obtain, and even potentially change, but would not help them understand why cold coffee was given to customers.

The key to this step of the model is to use process knowledge and common sense in determining where to take measurements. The team should ask: Will the data collected at this point help us decide what to do to improve the process?

The team in the example investigated the process further and opted to measure the temperature of the coffee just after it was poured into the urn at the front of the shop.

Once the team determined what data to collect—and why, how, where, and when to collect it—it had the rudiments of a data collection plan. To implement the data collection plan, the team developed a data collection guide. This guide must include explicit directions on how and when to use it. The team should try to make it as user friendly as possible.

The team can collect baseline data when, and only when, the data collection plan is in place, the data collection guide has been developed, and the data collectors have been trained in the procedure to use.

Is the Process Stable?

The team analyzes the baseline data collected in step 5. Two tools that are useful in this analysis are a control chart or a run chart. Both of these tools organize the data and allow the team to make sense of the data. They are explained in Chapter 9, "Quality Improvement Tools."

Variables control charts are better at revealing whether a process is stable and its future performance predictable. However, even if a team begins with the simpler run chart, it can convert it to a control chart with a little extra work. A control chart is important because it helps the team identify special cause variations in the process.

Whenever an individual or a team repeats a sequence of actions, there will be some variation in the process. Let's look at an example:

> Think about the amount of time it took to get up in the morning, get dressed, and leave the house for work during the past four weeks. Although the average time may have been 28 minutes, no two days were exactly the same. On one occasion it may have taken 48 minutes to get out of the house.

This is where a control chart or a run chart can help analyze the data. Control charts, and to a lesser extent run charts, display variation and unusual patterns such as runs, trends, and cycles. Data that are outside the computed control limits, or unusual patterns in the graphic display of data on a run chart, may signal the presence of special cause variation that should be investigated. Returning to the example:

> Investigation revealed that a delay was experienced by an early morning phone call from a child who is in college. The data provided a signal of special cause variation in the getting-off-to-work process.

But what if over a period of 10 days a series of times is recorded that averages 48 minutes? Inquiry reveals that the getting-off-to-work process now includes making breakfast for a son and daughter. This is not just a variation—the data indicate that the process has been changed.

Though this example portrays an obvious change in the process, subtle changes often occur without the knowledge of workers. These minor changes produce enough variation to be evident when the data are analyzed. If special cause variation is found in the process, the team is obligated to find the cause before moving on to the next step in the model. Depending on the nature of the special cause, the team may act to remove it, take note of it but take no action, or change something in the process:

- When special cause variation reduces the effectiveness and efficiency of the process, the team must investigate the root cause and take action to remove it.
- If it is determined that the special cause was temporary in nature, no action may be required beyond understanding the reason for it. In the

current example, the early phone call caused a variation in the data that was easily explained and required no further action.

- Occasionally, special cause variation actually signals a need for improvement in the process to bring it closer to the process improvement objective. When that happens, the team may want to incorporate the change permanently.

If the team fails to investigate a signal of special cause variation and continues with its improvement activities, the process may be neither stable nor predictable when fully implemented, thus preventing the team from achieving the process improvement objective.

Is the Process Capable?

Once the process has been stabilized, the data collected in step 5 are used again. This time the team plots the individual data points to produce a type of bar graph called a histogram. This tool is explained in Chapter 9, "Quality Improvement Tools."

To prepare the histogram, the team superimposes the target value for the process on the bar graph. The target value was established in step 1 as the process improvement objective.

If there are upper and/or lower specification limits for the process, the team should plot them as well. (Note: Specification limits are not the upper and lower control limits used in control charts.)

Once the data, the target value, and the specification limits (if applicable) are plotted, the team can determine whether the process is capable. The following questions can be used to guide the team's thinking:

- Are there any unusual patterns in the plotted data? Does the histogram have multiple tall peaks and steep valleys? This may be an indication that other processes are influencing the process the team is investigating.
- Do all of the data points fall inside the upper and lower specification limits (if applicable)? If not, the process is not capable.
- If all of the data points fall within the specification limits, are the points grouped closely enough to the target value? This is a judgment call by the team. Even when the process is capable, the team may not be satisfied with the results it produces. If that's the case, the team may elect to continue trying to improve the process by entering step 8 of the basic process improvement model.
- If there are no specification limits for the process, does the shape of the histogram approximate a bell curve? After examining the shape created by plotting the data on the histogram, the team has to decide whether the shape is satisfactory and whether the data points are close enough to the target value. These are subjective decisions. If the team is satisfied with both the shape and the clustering of data points, it can choose to standardize the simplified process or to continue through the steps of the basic process improvement model.

From here to the end of the basic process improvement model, the team will use the scientific methodology of the PDCA cycle for conducting process improvement.

The team will plan a change, conduct a test and collect data, evaluate the test results to find out whether the process improved, and decide whether to standardize or continue to improve the process. The PDCA cycle is just that—a cycle. There are no limitations on how many times the team can attempt to improve the process incrementally.

Identify the Root Causes for Lack of Capability

Steps 1–7 of the model are concerned with gaining an understanding of the process and documenting it. In step 8, the team begins the PDCA cycle by identifying the root causes for the lack of process capability.

The data the team has looked at so far measure the output of the process. To improve the process, the team must find what causes the product or service to be unsatisfactory. The team uses a cause-and-effect diagram to begin to identify root causes. This tool is explained in Chapter 9, "Quality Improvement Tools."

Once the team identifies possible root causes, it must then collect data to determine how much these causes actually affect the results. Team members are often surprised to find that the data do not substantiate their predictions or perceptions as to root causes.

The team can use a Pareto chart to show the relative importance of the causes it has identified. This tool is also explained in Chapter 9, "Quality Improvement Tools."

Plan to Implement the Process Change

Step 9 begins the "plan" phase of the PDCA cycle. Step 10 completes this phase.

After considering the possible root causes identified in step 8, the team picks one to work on. The team then develops a plan to implement a change in the process to reduce or eliminate the root cause.

The major features of the plan include changing the simplified flowchart created in step 4 and making all of the preparations required to implement the change.

The team can use the following list of questions as a guide in developing the plan:

- What steps in the process will be changed?
- Are there any risks associated with the proposed change?
- What will the change cost? (The cost includes not only money but time, number of people, materials used, customer perceptions, and other factors.)
- Which workers or customers will be affected by the change?
- Who is responsible for implementing the change?
- What has to be done to implement the change?
- Where and when will the change be implemented?
- How will the implementation be controlled?
- At what steps in the process will measurements be taken?
- How will data be collected?
- Is a small-scale test necessary prior to full implementation of the change?

- How long will the test last?
- What risks are involved, and how will they be addressed?
- What is the probability of success?
- Is there a downside to the proposed change?

Once the improvement plan is formulated, the team makes the planned changes in the process, if empowered by the team charter to do so. Otherwise, the team presents the improvement plan to the process owner or other individual who formed the team, to obtain approval to implement the change.

Review and Modify the Data Collection Plan

The data collection plan was originally developed in step 5. Because the process is going to change when the planned improvement is instituted, the team must now review the original plan to ensure that it is still capable of providing the data the team needs to assess process performance. If the determination is made that the data collection plan should be modified, the team considers the same thinking and methodologies as in step 5.

Test the Change (Also Known as Verification)

Step 11 is the "do" phase of the PDCA cycle. If feasible, the change should be implemented on a limited basis before it is applied to the entire organization, sometimes referred to as a pilot test or trial run. For example, the changed process could be instituted in a single office or work center while the rest of the organization continues to use the old process. If the organization is working on a shift basis, the changed process could be tried on one shift while the other shifts continue as before. Whatever method the team applies, the goals are to prove the effectiveness of the change, avoid widespread failure, and maintain organization-wide support.

In some situations, a small-scale test is not feasible. If that is the case, the team will have to inform everyone involved of the nature and expected effects of the change and conduct training adequate to support a full-scale test.

The information that the team developed in step 9 provides the outline for the test plan. During the test, it is important to collect appropriate data so that the results of the change can be evaluated. The team will have to take the following actions in conducting the test to determine whether the change actually results in process improvement:

- Finalize the test plan
- Prepare the data collection sheets
- Train everyone involved in the test
- Distribute the data collection sheets
- Change the process and run it to test the improvement
- Collect and collate the data

Check: Is the Modified Process Stable?

Steps 12 and 13 together constitute the "check" phase of the PDCA cycle.

The team has modified the process based on the improvement plan and conducted a test. During the test of the new procedure, data were collected. The team determines whether the expected results were achieved.

The approach in this step is identical to that of step 6. The team uses the data it has collected to check the process for stability by preparing a control chart or run chart. Because the process has changed, it is appropriate to recompute the control limits for the control chart using the new data.

If the data collected in step 11 show that process performance is worse, the team must return to step 8 and try again to improve the process. The process must be stable before the team goes on to the next step.

Check: Did the Process Improve?

Step 13 completes the "check" phase of the PDCA cycle. The procedures are similar to those in step 7.

This is a good place for the team members to identify any differences between the way they planned the process improvement and the way it was executed.

The following questions will guide the team in checking the test results:

- Did the change in the process eliminate the root cause of the problem? Whether the answer is yes or no, describe what occurred.
- Are the data taken in step 11 closer to the process improvement objective than the baseline data collected in step 5? The answer indicates how much or how little the process has improved.
- Were the expected results achieved? If not, the team should analyze the data further to find out why process performance improved less than expected or even became worse.
- Were there any problems with the plan? The team needs to review the planned improvement as well as the execution of the data collection effort.

Standardize the Process and Reduce the Frequency of Data Collection

Step 14 is the "act" phase of the PDCA cycle. In this step, the team makes some important decisions. First, the team must decide whether to implement the change on a full-scale basis. In making this decision, the following questions need asking and answering:

- Is the process stable?
- Is the process capable?
- Do the results satisfy customers, internal and/or external?
- Are the necessary resources available?
- Does the team have authorization?

If the answers are yes, the changed process can be installed as the new standard process.

Second, the team must decide what to do next. Even when everything is in place for implementing and standardizing the process, the team still has to choose between two courses of action:

- *Identifying possibilities for making further process changes.* Assuming that resources are available and approval is given, the team may choose to continue trying to improve the process by reentering the PDCA cycle at step 9.
- *Standardizing the changed process without further efforts to improve it.* If this decision is made, the team is still involved—documenting the changes, monitoring process performance, and institutionalizing the process improvement.

To standardize the changed process, the team initiates changes in documentation involving procedures, instructions, manuals, and other related issues. Training will have to be developed and provided to make sure everyone is using the new standard process correctly.

The team continues to use the data collection plan developed in step 11 but significantly reduces the frequency of data collection by process workers. There are no hard-and-fast rules on how often to collect data at this stage, but, as a rule of thumb, the team can try reducing collection to a quarter of what is called for in the data collection plan. The team can then adjust the frequency of measurement as necessary. The point is that enough data must be collected to enable the team to monitor the performance of the process.

The team must periodically assess whether the process remains stable and capable. To do this, the data collected in step 14 should be entered into the control chart or run chart and histogram developed in steps 12 and 13, respectively.

Whichever course of action the team pursues, it should complete one last task: documenting the lessons learned during the process improvement effort and making it available to others within the organization. This documentation should include satisfactory outputs from the improvement effort and, if applicable, plans for assessment of the long-term outcomes from the improvement project.

The process improvement project is complete. The team's work is recognized and rewarded. The team is disbanded.

NOTES

1. Ron Bialek, Grace L. Duffy, and John W. Moran, *The Public Health Quality Improvement Handbook* (Milwaukee, WI: ASQ Quality Press, 2009).
2. G. Dennis Beecroft, Grace L. Duffy, and John W. Moran, eds., *The Executive Guide to Improvement and Change* (Milwaukee, WI: ASQ Quality Press, 2003).
3. Anthony Manos and Chad Vincent, eds., *The Lean Handbook* (Milwaukee, WI: ASQ Quality Press, 2012).
4. Beecroft, Duffy, and Moran, *The Executive Guide to Improvement and Change.*
5. Russell T. Westcott, ed., *The Certified Manager of Quality/Organizational Excellence,* 4th ed. (Milwaukee, WI: ASQ Quality Press, 2014).
6. M. Imai, *Kaizen: The Key to Japan's Competitive Success* (New York: McGraw-Hill, 1986).
7. Popularized by M. Hammer and J. Champy in *Reengineering the Corporation: A Manifesto for Business Revolution* (New York: HarperBusiness, 1993).
8. Hammer and Champy, *Reengineering the Corporation.*

Chapter 9
C. Quality Improvement Tools

Select, interpret, and apply the seven basic quality tools:

1. Flowcharts
2. Histograms
3. Pareto charts
4. Scatter diagrams
5. Cause and effect diagrams
6. Check sheets
7. Control charts

Describe and interpret basic control chart concepts, including centerlines, control limits, out-of-control conditions. (Apply)

CQIA BoK 2014 III.C.

A *tool* is a device used to help accomplish the purpose of a technique. Quality improvement tools are numeric and graphic devices used to help individuals and teams work with, understand, and improve processes.[1]

Walter Shewhart and W. Edwards Deming began developing the initial quality improvement tools in the 1930s and 1940s. This development resulted in better understanding of processes and led to the expansion of the use of these tools. In the 1950s, the Japanese began to learn and apply the statistical quality control tools and thinking taught by Kaoru Ishikawa, head of the Union of Japanese Scientists and Engineers (JUSE). These tools were further expanded by the Japanese in the 1960s with the introduction of the following seven classic quality control tools:[2]

1. Flowcharts
2. Histograms
3. Pareto charts

4. Scatter diagrams
5. Cause-and-effect diagrams (fishbone or Ishikawa diagram)
6. Check sheets
7. Control charts (formerly run charts)

In 1976, the Japanese Society for Quality Control Technique Development proposed the following seven new tools for quality improvement:

1. Relations diagram (interrelationship digraph)
2. Affinity diagram (Chapter 7)
3. Systematic diagram (tree diagram)
4. Matrix diagram
5. Matrix data analysis
6. Process decision program chart (PDPC)
7. Arrow diagram

At the beginning of a process improvement project, it's important to understand the current state or condition of the process. Check sheets, flowcharts, and histograms are useful for acquiring and displaying basic data for this purpose. Control charts can be used to determine whether the process is in control. If there is a possibility of interrelated factors, scatter diagrams may be used to test for correlations between two sets of variables.

Once a problem has been defined using the methods described, various approaches can be used to find solutions. Of the seven basic tools, the fishbone diagram works very well for teams seeking the most likely root cause for a problem. Once the causes are identified, they can be prioritized and displayed in a Pareto diagram to help determine which problem should be addressed first.

The following information describes many of the basic quality improvement tools and how they are used. The tools are discussed in alphabetical order, not in any order of preference.[3]

ARROW DIAGRAM

The *arrow diagramming* method establishes a sequenced plan and a tool for monitoring progress. It may be represented graphically by either a horizontal or vertical structure connecting the planned activities or events. Another name for this chart is *activity network diagram* (AND).

The arrow diagram method can be used to:

- Implement plans for new product development and its follow-up
- Develop product improvement plans and follow-up activities
- Establish daily plans for experimental trials and follow-up activities

- Establish daily plans for increases in production and their follow-up activities
- Synchronize the preceding plans for quality control activities
- Develop plans for a facility move and for monitoring follow-up
- Implement a periodic facility maintenance plan and its follow-up
- Analyze a manufacturing process and draw up plans for improved efficiency
- Plan and follow up quality control inspections and diagnostic tests
- Plan and follow up quality control conferences and quality control circle conferences
- Plan an office move or furniture rearrangement for improved personnel communication
- Establish a better process for moving a supplies request form through the office for signatures

Figure 9.1 shows the interdependencies of steps for a systems project.

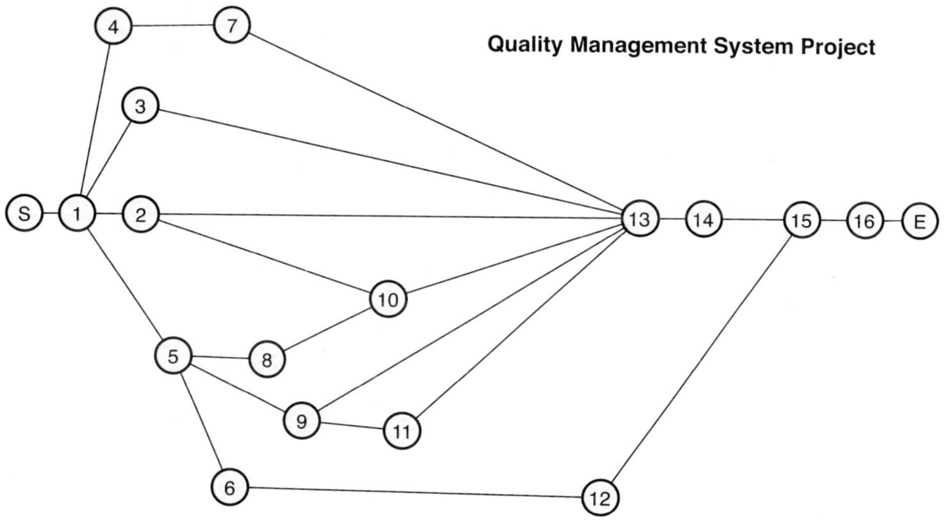

Figure 9.1 Arrow diagram.

BAR CHART

A *bar chart* is a graphic display of data in the form of a "bar" showing the number of units (e.g., frequency) in each category. Different types of bar charts (histograms, Pareto charts, etc.) are described in this chapter.

CAUSE-AND-EFFECT DIAGRAM

The cause-and-effect diagram graphically illustrates the relationship between a given outcome and all the factors that influence the outcome. It is sometimes called the *Ishikawa diagram* (after its creator, Kaoru Ishikawa) or the *fishbone diagram* (due to its shape). This type of diagram displays the factors that are thought to affect a particular output or outcome in a system. The factors are often shown as groupings of related subfactors that act in concert to form the overall effect of the group. The diagram helps show the relationship of the parts (and subparts) to the whole by:

- Determining the factors that cause a positive or negative outcome (or effect)
- Focusing on a specific issue without resorting to complaints and irrelevant discussion
- Determining the root causes of a given effect
- Identifying areas where there is a lack of data

Although both individuals and teams can use the cause-and-effect diagram, it is probably most effectively used with a group of people. A typical approach is one in which the team leader draws the fishbone diagram on a whiteboard, states the main problem, and asks for assistance from the group to determine the main causes, which are subsequently drawn on the board as the "main bones." The team assists by making suggestions, and eventually the entire cause-and-effect diagram is filled out. Then team discussion takes place to decide which are the most likely root causes of the problem. Figure 9.2 shows the completed diagram resulting from a team's initial effort to identify potential causes for poor photocopy quality.

The cause-and-effect diagram is used for identifying potential causes of a problem or issue in an orderly way. It can help answer questions such as "Why has

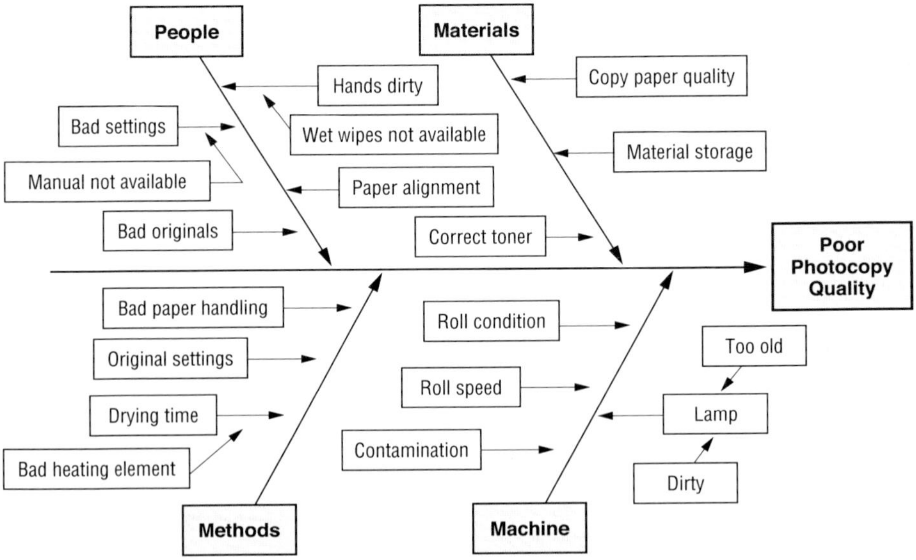

Figure 9.2 Cause-and-effect diagram.

membership in the organization decreased?" "Why isn't mail being answered on time?" and "Why is the shipping process suddenly producing so many defects?" It is also used for summarizing major causes into categories.

The basic steps involved in creating a cause-and-effect diagram are as follows:

1. Draw a long horizontal line with a box at the far right end of the line.
2. Indicate in the box what effect, output, or improvement goal is to be addressed. The effect can be positive (an objective) or negative (a problem). When possible, use a positive effect instead of a negative one as the effect to be discussed. Focusing on problems can produce finger-pointing, whereas focusing on desired outcomes fosters pride and ownership of productive areas. The resulting positive atmosphere will enhance the group's creativity.
3. Draw four diagonal lines emanating from the horizontal line. Terminate each diagonal line with a box.
4. Label the boxes on the diagonal lines to show four categories of potential major causes (Men/Women, Machines, Methods, and Materials or, alternatively, Policies, Procedures, People, and Plant). Other categories may be used if desired.
5. On each of the four diagonal lines, draw smaller horizontal lines (smaller "bones") to represent subcategories and indicate on these lines information that is thought to be related to the cause. Draw as many lines as are needed, making sure that the information is legible. Encourage idea generating to identify the factors and subfactors within each major category.
6. Use the diagram as a discussion tool to better understand how to proceed with process improvement efforts. The diagram can also be used to communicate the many potential causes of quality that impact the effect/output/improvement goal. Look for factors that appear repeatedly and list them. Also, list those factors that have a significant effect, based on the data available. Keep in mind that the location of a cause in your diagram is not an indicator of its importance. A subfactor may be the root cause of all the problems. It may be appropriate to collect more data on a factor that has not been previously identified

Cause-and-effect diagrams can be used at varying levels of specificity and can be applied at a number of different times in process improvement efforts. They are very effective in summarizing and describing a process and the factors impacting the output of that process. Use this tool when it fits with a particular process improvement effort. It is possible to have a number of cause-and-effect diagrams depicting various aspects of the team's process improvement efforts.

CHECK SHEET

A *check sheet* is a form used to record the frequency of specific events during a data collection period. It is a simple form that can be used to collect data in an organized manner and easily convert the data into readily useful information. The most straightforward way to use a check sheet is simply to make a list of items (actions, events, defects, behaviors, etc.) expected to appear in a process and make a checkmark beside each item when it does appear. This type of data collection can be used for almost anything, from checking off the occurrence of particular types of defects to counting expected items (e.g., the number of times the telephone rings before it is answered). Check sheets can be directly related to histograms to provide a direct visualization of the information collected. Figure 9.3 shows the frequency of reasons for undelivered letters over a one-week period.

Various innovations in check sheets are possible. Consider, for example, using a map of the United States as a check sheet. The concept for this check sheet is for the user to simply mark on the map the location of each sale made. The map becomes a very effective graphic presentation of where sales are the strongest. Another name for this type of check sheet is a *measles chart.*

A check sheet may be used to:

- Collect data with minimal effort
- Convert raw data into useful information
- Translate perceptions of what is happening into what is actually happening

The basic steps involved in creating a check sheet are as follows:

1. Clarify the measurement objectives. Ask questions such as "What is the problem?" "Why should data be collected?" "Who will use the information being collected?" and "Who will collect the data?"
2. Create a form for collecting data. Determine the specific things that will be measured and write them down the left side of the check sheet.

Reasons for Undelivered Letters

<table>
<tr><th>Type of Defect</th><th>April 23</th><th>April 24</th><th>April 25</th><th>April 26</th><th>April 27</th><th>Total Defects</th></tr>
<tr><td>Illegible address</td><td>||||| |||||
										</td><td>							</td><td>									
							</td><td>									
			</td><td>									
</td><td>71</td></tr>
<tr><td>Wrong state</td><td>						</td><td>		</td><td>				</td><td>					</td><td>					</td><td>22</td></tr>
<tr><td>Wrong zip code</td><td>									
									</td><td>					</td><td>									
		</td><td>									
	</td><td>									</td><td>59</td></tr>
<tr><td>Bad office symbol</td><td>|||</td><td>|||||</td><td>|</td><td>|||</td><td>||||</td><td>16</td></tr>
<tr><td>Total Defects</td><td>50</td><td>19</td><td>36</td><td>34</td><td>29</td><td>168</td></tr>
</table>

Figure 9.3 Check sheet.

Determine the time or place being measured and write this across the top of the columns.

3. Label the measure for which data will be collected (event, action, defect, etc.).
4. Collect the data by making a checkmark next to each occurrence directly on the check sheet as it happens.
5. Tally the data by totaling the number of occurrences for each category being observed and measured.
6. Summarize the data from the check sheet, using a Pareto chart or a histogram.

A check sheet is not the same as a checklist, the latter being what you would create before going to purchase groceries or packing an auto before a trip.

CONTROL CHART

A *control chart* is used to measure sequential or time-related process performance and variability. The control chart is probably the best known, most useful, and most difficult-to-understand quality tool. It is a sophisticated tool of quality improvement.

A control chart is a line chart (run chart) with control limits. It is based on the work of Drs. Shewhart and Deming. Control charts are statistically based. The underlying concept is that processes have statistical variation. One must assess this variation to determine whether a process is operating between the expected boundaries or whether something has happened that has caused the process to go "out of control." Control limits are mathematically constructed at three standard deviations above and below the average. Extensive research by Dr. Shewhart indicated that 99.73% of common cause variation would fall within upper and lower limits established at three times the standard deviation of the process (plus and minus, respectively).

Data are collected by repeated samples and are charted. From the graphic presentation of the data on the control chart, one can observe variation and investigate to determine whether the variation is due to normal, inherent events (common causes) or is produced by unique events (special causes).

A typical control chart contains a centerline that represents the average value (mean) of the quality characteristic corresponding to the in-control state. Two other horizontal lines, called the *upper control limit* (UCL) and the *lower control limit* (LCL), are also drawn. These control limits are chosen so that when the process is in control, nearly all of the sample points will fall between them. As long as the points plot within the control limits, the process is assumed to be in control (stable), and no action is necessary. A point that plots outside the control limits is interpreted as evidence that the process may be out of control, and investigation and corrective action could be required to find and eliminate the causes responsible for this occurrence. The control points are connected with straight lines for easy visualization. Even if all the points plot inside the control limits, if over several consecutive time intervals they display in a repetitive upward or downward trend, or other nonrandom manner, this is an indication that the process may be

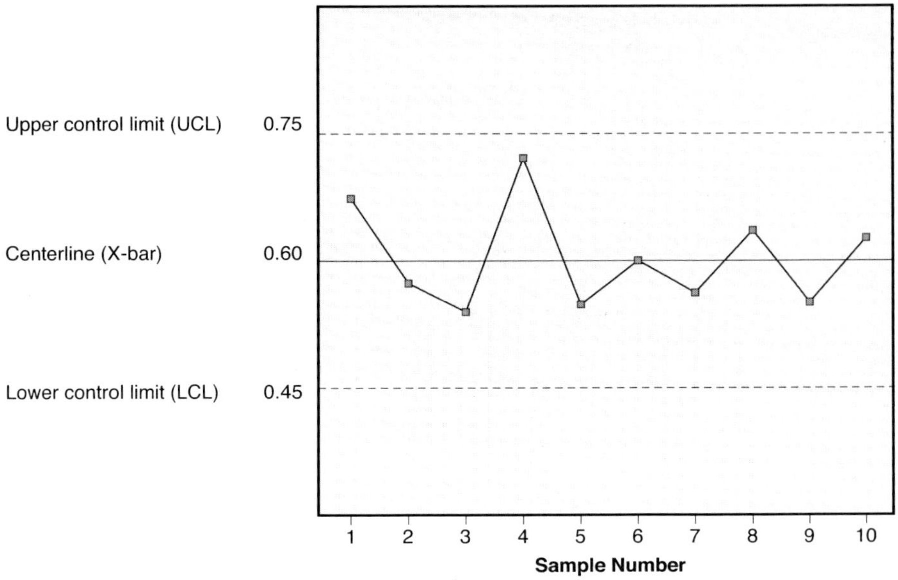

Figure 9.4 Control chart (process in control).

out of control. Figure 9.4 shows points representing the variable measurement taken for each of 10 items.

Note that upper and lower control limits are *not* specification limits. Specification limits are based on product or customer requirements. Control limits have a mathematical relationship to the process outputs.

Compare the ongoing current process data with these three plotted lines and look for out-of-control signals:

- If the data fluctuate within the limits, it is the result of common causes within the process and the process is in control.
- If one of the data points falls outside the control limits, it could be the result of special causes and can indicate that the process is out of control and that corrective action may be needed after a thorough investigation of the cause.
- A run of eight points on one side of the centerline indicates a shift in the process output and needs investigation.
- Two of three consecutive points outside the two-sigma warning limits but still inside the control limits could indicate a process shift.
- A trend of seven points in a row upward or downward may be a result of gradual deterioration in the process.

This is not an inclusive list of out-of-control warning signals but rather a few examples. Refer to a textbook on statistical process control for a full list of possible out-of-control signals.[4]

There are several types of control charts, but all have the same basic structure. The two main categories of control charts are those that display attribute data and those that display variables data.

Attribute Data

The attribute data category of control charts displays data that result from counting the number of occurrences or items in a single category of similar items or occurrences. These "count" data may be expressed as pass/fail, yes/no, or presence/absence of a defect. Charting the proportion of failed items results in the ability to observe whether a process is in control or out of control.

Variable Data

The variable data category of control charts displays values resulting from the measurement of a continuous variable. Examples of variable data are elapsed time, temperature, and radiation dose. (For more information and an explanation of these chart types and their characteristics, refer to publications addressing statistics used in the quality profession.)

Use control charts to:

- Display and understand variation in a process
- Help the investigator determine when actual events fall outside specified tolerance limits (control limits) and become outliers that are out of control
- Determine whether quality improvement efforts have made a statistically significant difference to a key quality indicator
- Monitor a process output (such as cost or a quality characteristic) to determine whether special causes of variation have occurred in the process
- Determine how capable the current process is of meeting specifications, if specification limits exist, and of allowing for improvements in the process

The benefits of control charts are that they:

- Help organizations identify and understand variation and how to control it
- Help identify special causes of variation and changes in performance
- Keep organizations from trying to fix a process that is varying randomly within control limits (i.e., no special causes are present)
- Assist in the diagnosis of process problems
- Determine whether process improvements are having the desired effects

A control chart may indicate an out-of-control condition either when one or more points fall beyond the control limits or when the plotted points exhibit some nonrandom pattern.

DESIGN OF EXPERIMENTS

Design of experiments (DOE) provides a structured way to characterize processes. A multifunctional team analyzes a process and identifies key characteristics, or factors, that most impact the quality of the end item. Using DOE, the team runs a limited number of tests, and data are collected and analyzed. The results indicate which factors contribute the most to final quality and also define the parameter settings for those factors. Now, rather than tweaking or tampering with the system, managers have the profound knowledge of their processes that allows them to build quality in, starting at the earliest stages of design. This allows management to determine that equitable requirement trade-offs are made between the design and manufacturing processes during development.

FIVE WHYS

Five whys is a simple technique for getting at the root causes of a problem by asking "why" after each successive response, up to five times. Asking why is a favorite technique of the Japanese for discovering the root cause (or causes) of a problem. By asking the question "Why?" a number of times (five is only a suggested number), layer after layer of "symptoms" is peeled away to get to the heart of an issue. There is no way to know ahead of time exactly how many times the "why" question will be needed.

The five whys technique helps to:

- Identify the root cause(s) of a problem
- Show how the different causes of a problem might be related

The basic steps in using the five whys technique are as follows:

1. Describe the problem in very specific terms.
2. Ask why it happens.
3. Continue asking why until the root causes are identified. If the answer doesn't identify a root cause, ask why again. You'll know you've identified the root cause when asking why doesn't yield any more useful information. This may take more or fewer than five whys.
4. Always focus on the process aspects of a problem rather than the personalities involved. Finding scapegoats does not solve problems!

Multiple root causes may contribute to multiple symptoms. Figure 9.5 is an example of the use of five whys.

FLOWCHART

A *flowchart* is a graphic representation of the flow of a process. It is a useful way to examine how the various steps in a process relate to one another, to define the boundaries of the process, to identify and verify customer–supplier relationships in a process, to create common understanding of the process flow, to determine the current "best method" of performing the process, to find omissions, and to identify redundancy and unnecessary complexity.

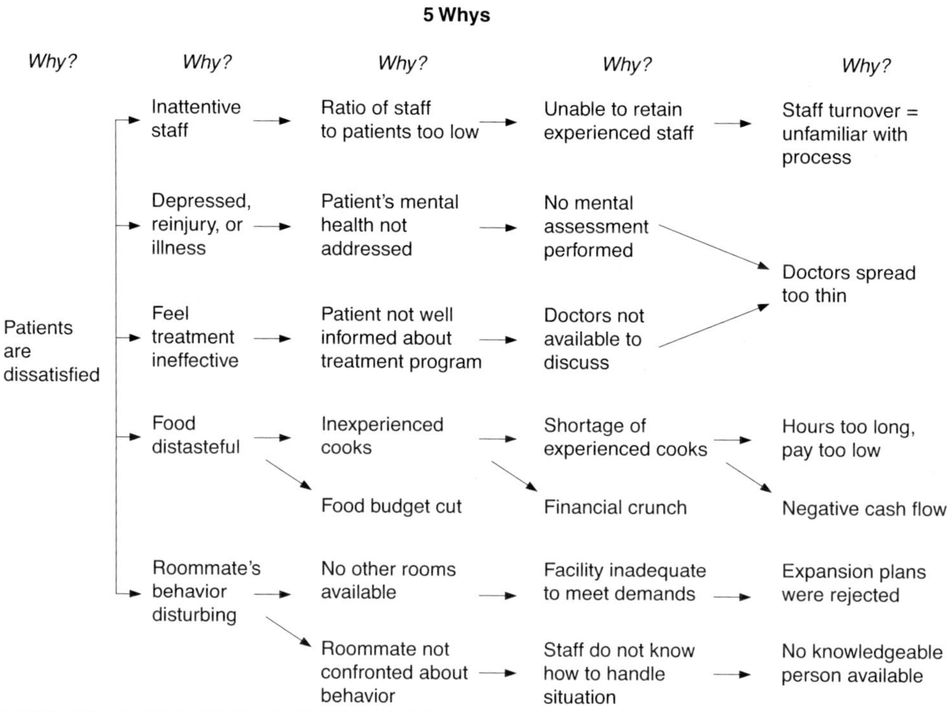

Figure 9.5 Five Whys example.

Source: Reproduced by permission from R. T. Westcott, ed., *The Certified Manager of Quality/Organizational Excellence Handbook*, 4th ed. (Milwaukee, WI: ASQ Quality Press, 2014), 344.

A flowchart displays the order of activities. An oblong symbol indicates the beginning or end of the process, boxes indicate action items, and diamonds indicate decision points.

Flowcharts can be used to:

- Identify and communicate the steps in a work process
- Identify areas that may be the source of a problem or determine improvement opportunities

A flowchart provides the visualization of a process by the use of symbols that represent different types of actions, activities, or situations. Figure 9.6 displays a typical flowchart that describes the simple process of getting a cup of coffee. The symbols used are connected with arrows to show the flow of information between steps in the process.

A flowchart may be used to document an existing process as it is presently performed, or it may be used to design a new or changed process. The basic steps for creating a flowchart are as follows:

1. Select the process to chart.
2. Determine whether to develop a high-level or detailed flowchart.
3. Define the boundaries of the selected process.

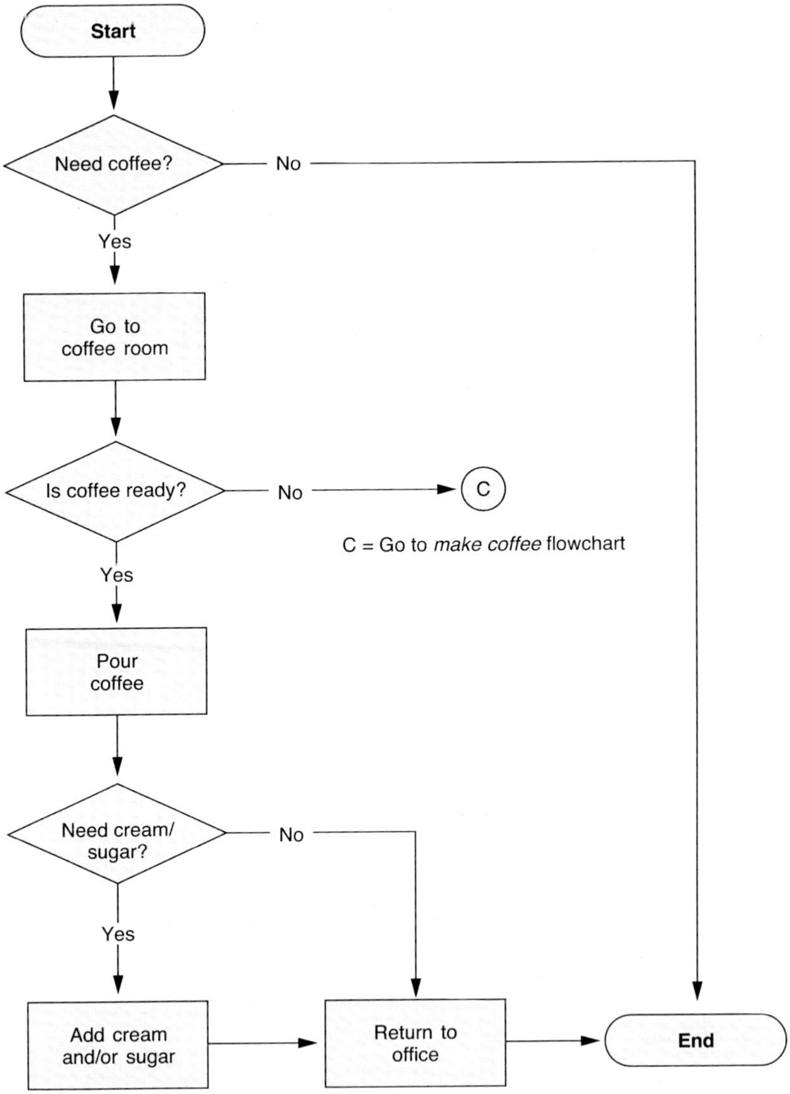

Figure 9.6 Morning coffee flowchart.

4. Identify the "start symbol" and place it on the top left corner of the page.
5. Identify the "finish symbol" and place it on the bottom right corner of the page.
6. Try to identify the easiest and most efficient way to go from the "start block" to the "finish block." Though this step isn't absolutely necessary, it does make it easier to do the next step.
7. Document each step in sequence, starting with the first (or last) step.
8. Use the appropriate symbol for each step (see Figure 9.7).

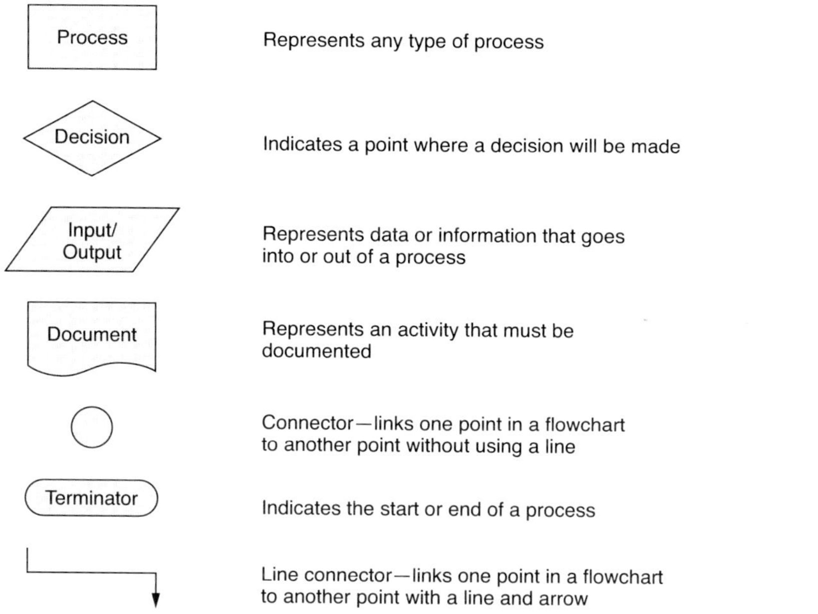

Figure 9.7 Basic flowchart symbols.

9. At each decision point, choose one branch and continue flowcharting that section of the process.
10. If a segment of the process is unfamiliar to everyone, make a note and continue flowcharting.
11. Repeat steps 6, 7, and 8 until that section of the process is complete. Go back and flowchart the other branches from the decision symbols.
12. Identify all the areas that hinder your process or add little or no value.
13. After the flowchart is complete and accurate for the present state, analyze it.
14. Construct a new flowchart that corrects the problems you identified in the previous chart, the future state.

Note: The steps of the process can be placed on index cards or sticky notes. This allows rearrangement of the diagram without erasing and redrawing and prevents ideas from being discarded simply because it's too much work to redraw the diagram.

A completed flowchart:

- Shows how the process is actually or will be performed
- Encourages communication between customers and suppliers
- Illustrates the relationship of various steps in a process
- Educates team members about all the steps within the process
- Can be used to train new employees involved in the process

- Shows who is involved in the process
- Helps set the boundaries of the process
- Identifies team members needed
- Shows where the process can be improved
- Is useful for data collection
- May identify immediate improvement opportunities

For an existing process, failure to document the *actual* process is an important pitfall that should be avoided. The failure to reflect reality may result from a variety of causes:

- The process is drawn as it was designed and not as it actually happens
- Team members are reluctant to draw parts of the process that might expose weaknesses in their areas
- Rework loops are seen as small and unimportant and are overlooked
- Team members truly do not know how the process operates

Two types of flowcharts are the following:

- *Process flowcharts* use symbols to represent the input from suppliers, the sequential work activities, the decisions to be made, and the output to the stakeholder
- *Deployment flowcharts* show the functions or people responsible for tasks as well as the flow of tasks in a process, sometimes called a *swim-lane chart* (Figure 9.8)

Flowcharting has been around for a very long time and is used by many organizations to gain vital process information. The reason for this is obvious. A flowchart can be customized to fit any need or purpose. For this reason, flowcharts are recognized as a very valuable quality improvement method. The term *process mapping* refers to flowcharting a process but adds several refinements.

FOCUS GROUP

The *focus group* is a customer-oriented approach for collecting information from a group of participants (10–12) who are strangers to one another. They meet to discuss and share ideas about a certain issue. Focus groups are a useful qualitative analysis tool for helping to understand the beliefs and perceptions of the population represented by the group. It is often used to obtain basic pros and cons, and suggestions prior to preparing questions for a planned survey.

A focus group may also be used internally with a group of employees to sound out likes and dislikes of a new process, product, or service design before scheduling an implementation. Likewise, a focus group could be used with supplier representatives or stockholders to collect data and information concerning a proposed change or issue.

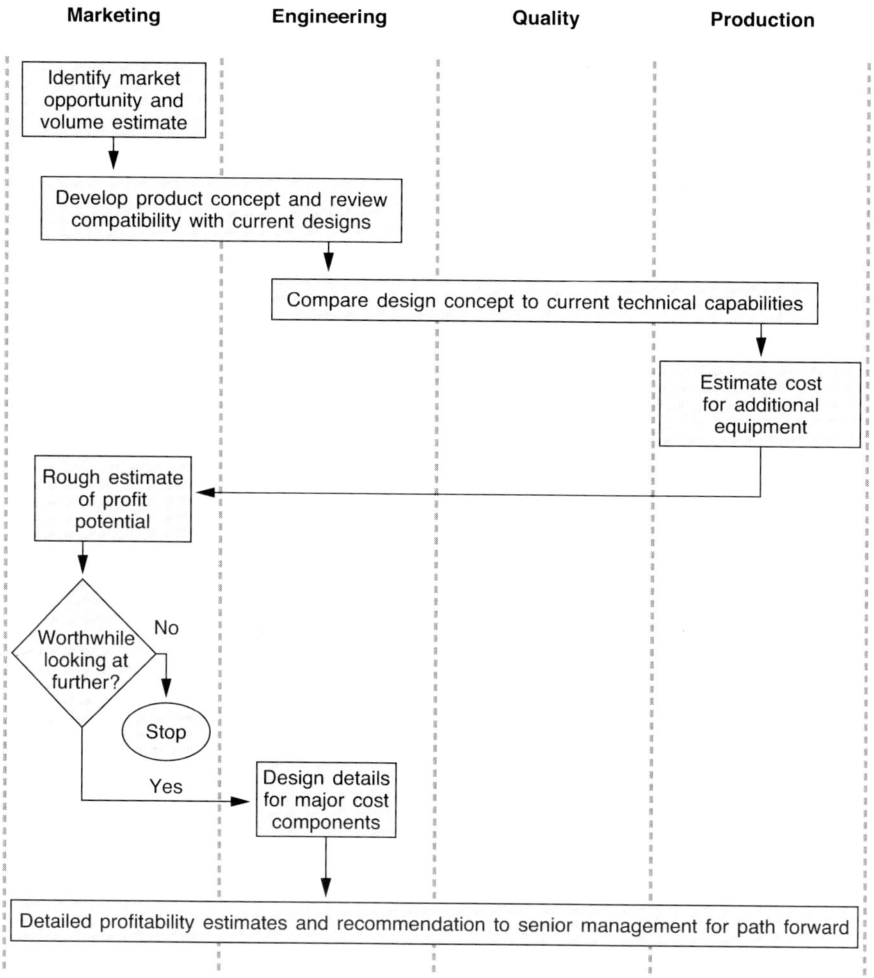

Figure 9.8 Deployment flowchart example (also called a swim-lane chart).

Source: Reproduced by permission from R. T. Westcott, ed., *The Certified Manager of Quality/Organizational Excellence Handbook*, 4th ed. (Milwaukee, WI: ASQ Quality Press, 2014), 317.

FORCE-FIELD ANALYSIS

Force-field analysis (FFA) is a tool that uses a creative process for encouraging agreement about all facets of a desired change. It is used for clarifying and strengthening the "driving forces" for change (e.g., what things are "driving" us toward school improvement?). It can also be used to identify obstacles, or "restraining forces," to change (e.g., what is "restraining" us from achieving increased test scores?). Finally, it can be used for encouraging agreement on the relative priority of factors on each side of the "plus/minus" sheet.

The basic steps involved in FFA are as follows:

1. Identify, discuss, and come to agreement with a group (usually five to seven people) on the current situation and the goal
2. Write this situation on a flip chart
3. Brainstorm the "driving" and "restraining" forces:
   — Driving forces are things (actions, skills, equipment, procedures, culture, people, etc.) that help move toward the goal
   — Restraining forces are things that can inhibit reaching the goal
4. Prioritize the driving and restraining forces
5. Discuss action strategies to eliminate the restraining forces and to capitalize on the driving forces

To create an FFA diagram, start by drawing a large letter "T" on a piece of paper. Write the issue and the ideal situation to be addressed at the top of the paper (see Figure 9.9). As a group, describe the ideal situation, and afterward write the resolution in the upper right-hand corner of the paper. Figure 9.9 depicts the discussion status before determining the resolution.

Have a facilitator work with the group to brainstorm forces leading to or preventing the ideal situation. These forces may be internal or external. List positive forces on the left side of the "T," and list forces restraining movement toward the ideal state on the right side of the "T."

As in any planning activity, the team should identify potential obstacles that could affect the successful completion of a task. It should identify both positive and negative forces affecting the task. Once all positive and negative forces are listed, prioritize the forces that need to be strengthened or identify the restraining

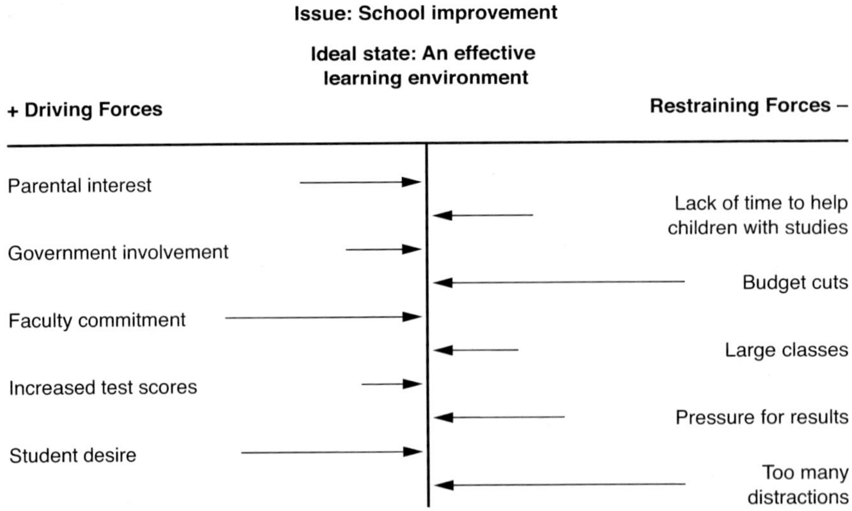

Figure 9.9 Force-field analysis diagram.

forces that need to be minimized to accomplish the goal—for instance, increased test scores. This provides a positive structure and removes the negative force of increased pressure on students to perform. The facilitator keeps discussion going among the participants until consensus is reached on each impediment to increasing student test scores. Arrow lines are used to indicate the relative priority of restraining and driving forces. Users of FFA often vary the length and/or thickness of the horizontal arrow lines to indicate the relative strength of each of the forces.

FFA encourages team members to raise questions and concerns throughout the process. These concerns and questions shouldn't be considered obstacles to successful planning that need to be rejected, but should instead be valued. The process of openly considering individual ideas encourages diversity in the planning process.

FFA is a powerful tool that encourages communication at all levels of management. By creating a structured environment for problem solving, it minimizes feelings of defensiveness. There is a feeling of openness about problem solving because all members of the group are focused on the issue rather than personal agendas. FFA inhibits hierarchical or traditional power structures that are likely to restrict the flow of creative ideas.

GANTT CHART

The *Gantt chart* is a combination matrix and horizontal bar chart used by project managers and others in planning and control to display planned work and targets as well as work that has been completed. A Gantt chart/action plan is a graphic representation of a project's schedule, showing the sequence of critical tasks in relation to time. For a small project, the chart indicates which tasks can be performed simultaneously. (A larger project may require an AND chart.)

The Gantt chart can be used for an entire project or for a key phase of a project. It allows a team to avoid unrealistic timetables and schedule expectations, helps identify and shorten tasks that act as bottlenecks, and focuses attention on the most critical tasks. By adding milestones (interim checkpoints) and completion indicators, the Gantt chart becomes a tool for ongoing monitoring of progress.

Gantt charts are most useful for planning and tracking entire projects or for scheduling and tracking the implementation phase of a planning or improvement effort. A Gantt chart is used to:

- Identify critical tasks or project components
- Identify the sequence of tasks that must be completed
- Identify any tasks that can be started simultaneously with another task
- Identify task durations
- Monitor progress
- Provide a concise view of the status of a project, especially to top management or others who may not be familiar with the project

Readers should refer to a project management text for further information. Most commercially available project management software will generate a Gantt chart/action plan similar to the example shown in Figure 9.10.

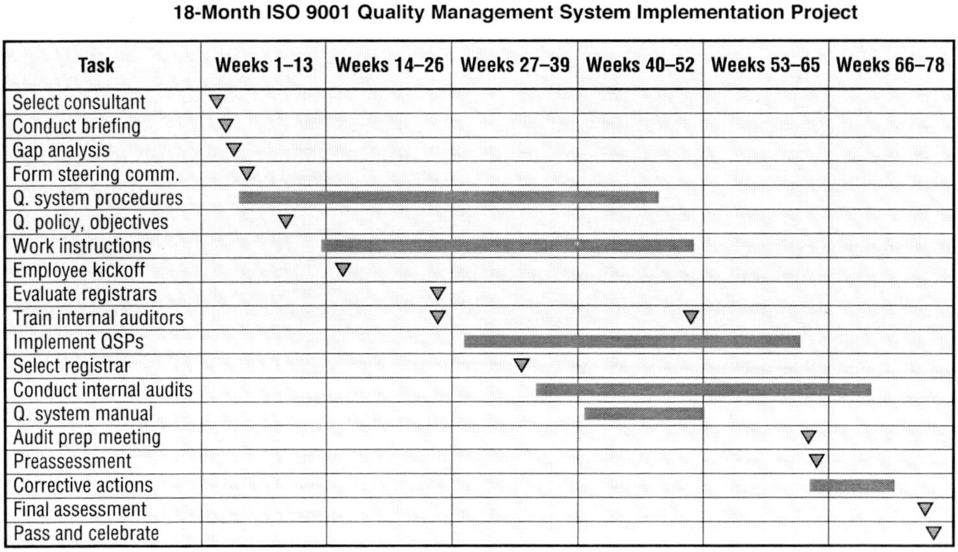

Figure 9.10 Gantt chart.

HISTOGRAM

A *histogram* is a graphic representation (bar chart) used to plot the frequency with which different values of a given variable occur. Histograms are used to examine existing patterns, identify the range of variables, and suggest a central tendency in variables.

An example would be to line up, by height, a group of people in a class. One person would be the tallest, one would be the shortest, and a cluster of people would be around an average height. Hence the term *normal distribution.* This tool helps identify the cause of problems in a process by the shape of the distribution as well as the width of the distribution.

The histogram evolved to meet the need to evaluate data that occur at a certain frequency. This is possible because it allows for a concise portrayal of information in a bar-graph format. This tool clearly portrays information on location, spread, and shape, which enables the user to perceive subtleties regarding the functioning of the physical process that is generating the data. It can also help suggest both the nature of and possible improvements for the physical mechanisms at work in the process. When combined with the concept of the normal curve and knowledge of a particular process, the histogram becomes an effective, practical working tool to use in the early stages of data analysis. A histogram may be interpreted by asking three questions:

- Is the process performing within specification limits?
- Does the process seem to exhibit wide variation?
- If action needs to be taken on the process, what action is appropriate?

The answers to these three questions lie in analyzing three characteristics of the histogram. How well is the histogram centered? The centering of the data provides information on the process aim about some mean or nominal value. How wide is the histogram? Looking at histogram width defines the variability of the process about the target value. What is the shape of the histogram? Remember that the data are expected to form a normal or bell-shaped curve. Any significant change or anomaly usually indicates that something is going on in the process that is causing the quality problem.

Figure 9.11 shows a histogram with an abnormal distribution. Histograms are constructed to examine characteristics of variation and provide an excellent visualization tool for varying data. The utility of histograms is in gaining a quick look at how the data collected from a process are distributed.

The basic steps involved in developing a histogram are as follows:

1. Determine the type of data you want to collect.
2. Be sure that the data are measurable (e.g., time, length, and speed).
3. Collect as many measurable data points as possible.
4. Collect data on one parameter at a time.
5. Count the total number of points you have collected.
6. Determine the number of intervals required.
7. Determine the range. To do this, subtract the smallest value in the data set from the largest. This value is the range of your data set.

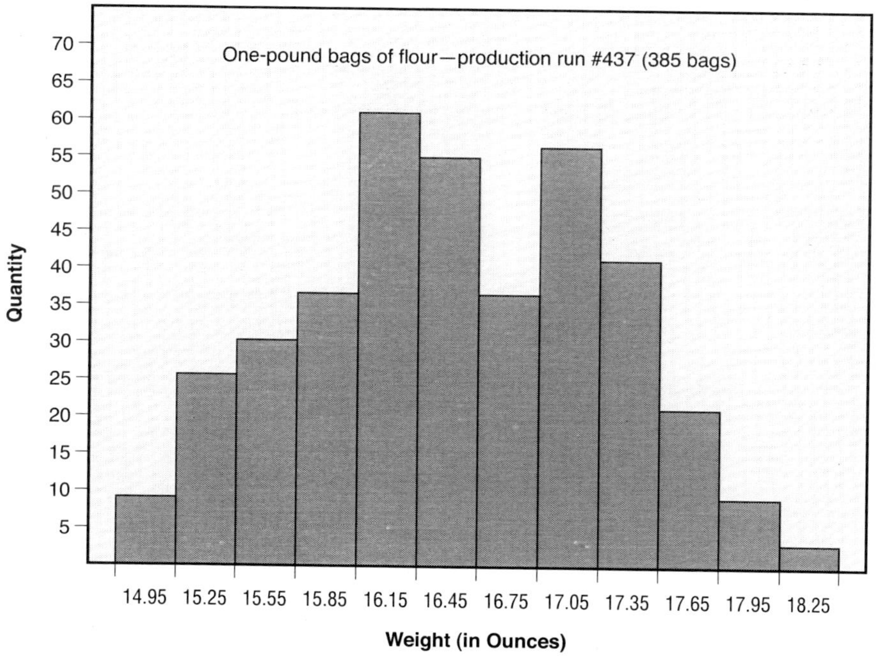

Figure 9.11 Histogram.

8. Determine the interval width. To do this, divide the range by the number of intervals.
9. Determine the starting point of each interval.
10. Draw horizontal (x) and vertical (y) axis lines.
11. Label the horizontal axis to indicate what is being displayed and mark the unit of measure (smallest to largest values).
12. Label the vertical axis to indicate what is being measured and mark the unit of measure (smallest to largest values).
13. Plot the data. Construct a vertical bar for each value, with the height corresponding to the frequency of occurrence of each value.

MATRIX ANALYSIS

The *matrix analysis* method quantifies and arranges matrix diagram data so that the information is easy to visualize and comprehend. The relationships between the elements shown in a matrix diagram are quantified by obtaining numerical data for intersecting cells.

The matrix data analysis method can be used to:

- Analyze production processes in which factors are complexly intertwined
- Analyze causes of nonconformities that involve a large volume of data
- Grasp the desired quality level indicated by the results of a market survey
- Classify sensory characteristics systematically
- Accomplish complex quality evaluations
- Analyze curvilinear data

MATRIX DIAGRAM

The *matrix diagram* clarifies problematic spots through multidimensional thinking. This method identifies corresponding elements involved in a problem situation or event. These elements are arranged in rows and columns on a chart that shows the presence or absence of relationships among collected pairs of elements.

Matrix diagrams can be used to:

- Establish ideas and concepts for the development and improvement of system products
- Achieve quality deployment in product materials
- Establish and strengthen the quality assurance system by linking certified levels of quality with various control functions
- Reinforce and improve the efficiency of the quality evaluation system
- Pursue the causes of nonconformities in the manufacturing process

- Establish strategies for the mix of products to send to market by evaluating the relationships between the products and market conditions
- Plan the allocation of resources (see the "Resource Allocation Matrix" subsection on page 158)

PARETO CHART

A *Pareto chart* is a graphic representation of the frequency with which certain events occur. It is a rank-order chart that displays the relative importance of variables in a data set and may be used to assign priorities regarding opportunities for improvement. Pareto charts are bar charts, prioritized in descending order from left to right, used to identify the vital few opportunities for improvement. It shows where to apply your initial effort to get the most gain.

Figure 9.12 is an example of a Pareto chart. The chart appears much the same as a histogram or bar chart. The bars are arranged in decreasing order of magnitude from left to right along the x-axis, excepting an "other" category. The fundamental use of the Pareto chart in quality improvement is the ordering of factors that contribute to a quality deficiency. The purpose of the chart is to identify which of the problems should be worked on first and how much of the total problem correcting one or more of the identified problems will solve. The Pareto chart is useful in summarizing information and in predicting how much of a problem can be corrected by attacking any specific part of the problem.

The tool is named after Vilfredo Pareto, an Italian sociologist and economist who invented this method of information presentation toward the end of the nineteenth century. The Pareto chart was derived from Pareto's 80/20 rule. Pareto noticed that 80% of the wealth in Italy was held by 20% of the people. Later, Joseph Juran, a leading quality expert, noticed that this rule could also be applied to the

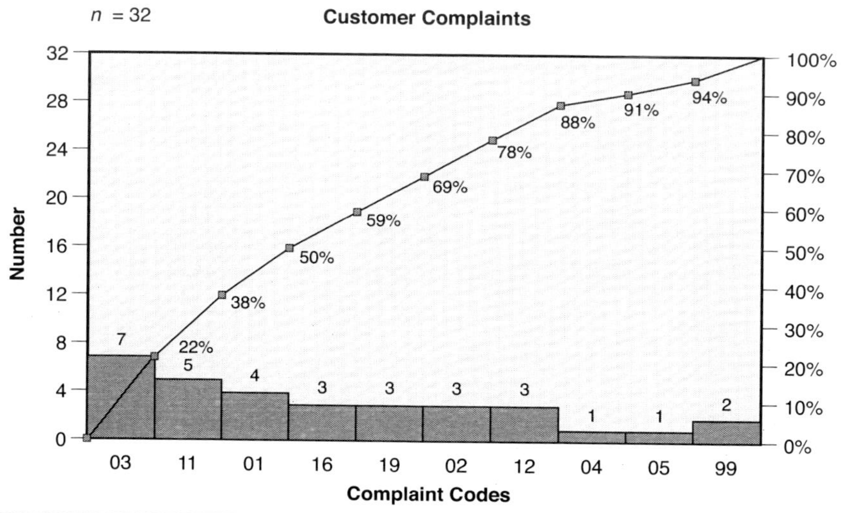

Figure 9.12 Pareto chart.

causes of defects: 80% of defects are due to only 20% of causes. Therefore, by minimizing 20% of the causes, we can eliminate 80% of the problems. The 20% of the problems are the "vital few," and the remaining problems are the "useful many." A Pareto chart can help organizations to:

- Separate the few major problems from the many possible problems in order to focus improvement efforts
- Arrange data according to priority or importance
- Determine which problems are the most important using data, not perception

The basic steps involved in constructing a Pareto chart are as follows:

1. Define the measurement scale for the potential causes. (This is usually the frequency of occurrence or cost.)
2. Define the time period during which to collect data about the potential causes (days, weeks, or as much time as is required to observe a significant number of occurrences).
3. Collect and tally data for each potential cause.
4. Label the horizontal (x) axis with all the possible root causes in descending order of value.
5. Label the measurement scale on the vertical (y) axis.
6. Draw one bar for each possible cause to represent the value of the measurement.
7. If desired, add a vertical (y) axis on the right side of the chart to represent cumulative percentage values.
8. Draw a line to show the cumulative percentage from left to right as each cause is added to the chart.

Pareto charts are used to:

- Identify the most important problems using different measurement scales
- Point out that "most frequent" may not always mean "most costly"
- Analyze different groups of data
- Measure the impact of changes made in the process before and after
- Break down broad causes into more specific parts

POKA-YOKE

The term *poka-yoke* is a hybrid word created by Japanese manufacturing engineer Shigeo Shingo. It comes from the words *yokeru* ("to avoid") and *poka* ("inadvertent error"). Hence, the combination word means "avoiding inadvertent errors." The term can be further anglicized as mistake-proofing, or making it impossible to do a task incorrectly. It involves creating processes that prevent the making of mistakes. As an example, if a part must fit into an assembly in only one orientation, the part is designed so that it is physically impossible to place the part in any other orientation.

PROCESS DECISION PROGRAM CHART

The *process decision program chart* (PDPC) method helps determine which processes to use to obtain the desired results by evaluating the progress of events and the variety of conceivable outcomes. Implementation plans do not always progress as anticipated. When problems, technical or otherwise, arise, solutions are frequently not apparent. The PDPC method, in response to these kinds of problems, anticipates possible outcomes and prepares countermeasures that will lead to the best possible solutions. Figure 9.13 charts the decisions needed to establish a cardiac treatment unit in a small, underfunded hospital. Where question marks are shown in the figure, estimates would be determined and inserted (e.g., costs, time, quantity).

The PDPC method can be used to:

- Establish an implementation plan for contingency management
- Establish an implementation plan for technology-development themes
- Establish a policy of forecasting and responding in advance to major events predicted in the system
- Implement countermeasures to minimize nonconformities in the manufacturing process
- Set up and select measures for process improvements

The PDPC diagram is a simple graphic tool that can be used to mitigate risk in virtually any undertaking.

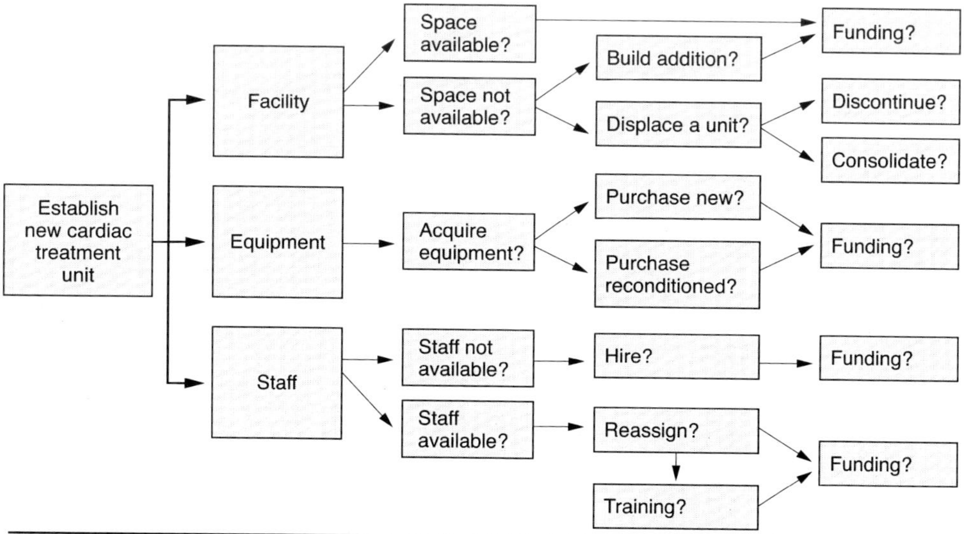

Figure 9.13 Process decision program chart (PDPC).

QUALITY FUNCTION DEPLOYMENT

Quality function deployment (QFD) is a planning process that uses multifunctional teams to transform the voice of the customer into design specifications. User requirements and preferences are defined and categorized as user attributes, which are then weighted based on their importance to the user. Users are then asked to compare how their requirements are being met now by a current product design versus a new design. QFD provides the design team with an understanding of customer desires (in clear-text language), forces the customer to prioritize those desires, and compares/benchmarks one design approach against another. Each customer attribute is then satisfied by at least one technical solution. Values for those technical solutions are determined and again rated among competing designs. Finally, the technical solutions are evaluated against each other to identify conflicts. A convenient form for viewing the ultimate product is the "house of quality" graphic, which should help the design team translate customer attribute information into firm operating or engineering goals as well as identify key manufacturing characteristics. Figure 9.14 shows the basic framework of the QFD matrix. QFD is also called the "house of quality" because of its resemblance to a house.

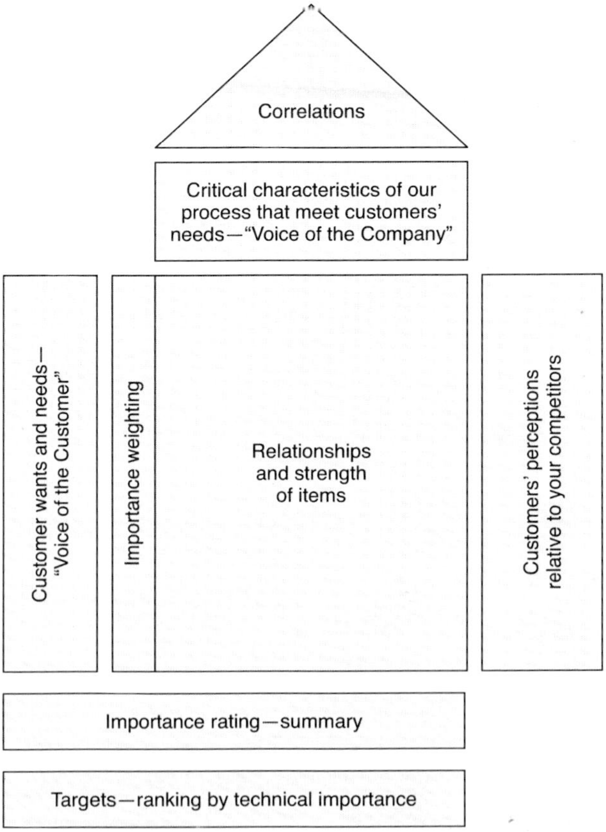

Figure 9.14 Quality function deployment (QFD) matrix or "house of quality."

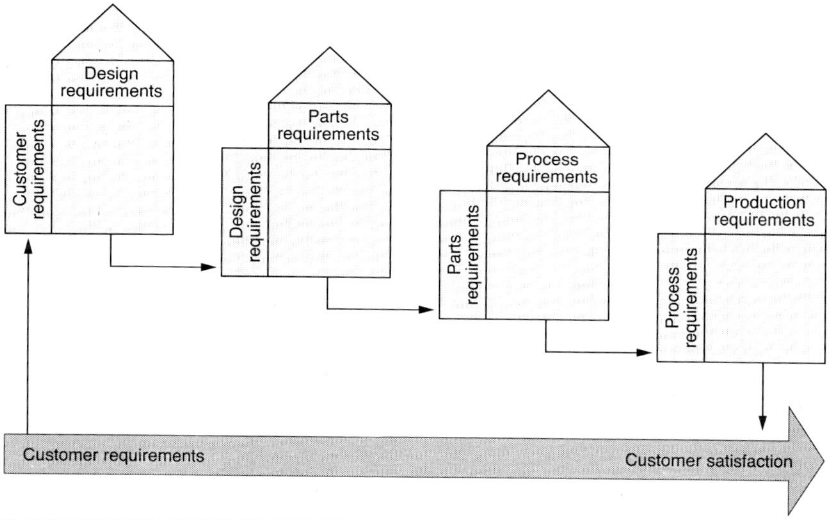

Figure 9.15 Voice of the customer deployment.
Source: Reproduced by permission from R. T. Westcott, ed., *The Certified Manager of Quality/Organizational Excellence Handbook*, 4th ed. (Milwaukee, WI: ASQ Quality Press, 2014), 459.

Supported by multiple additional matrices and data, the "voice of the customer" is cascaded throughout the organization. See Figure 9.15.

RELATIONS DIAGRAM (INTERRELATIONSHIP DIGRAPH)

The *relations diagramming* method is a technique developed to clarify intertwined causal relationships in a complex situation in order to find an appropriate solution.

Relations diagrams can be used to:

- Determine and develop quality assurance policies
- Establish promotional plans for total quality control introduction
- Design steps to counter market complaints
- Improve quality in the manufacturing process (especially in planning to eliminate latent defects)
- Promote quality control in purchased or ordered items
- Provide measures against troubles related to payment and process control
- Promote small group activities effectively
- Reform administrative and business departments

The digraph in Figure 9.16 shows some of the interrelating factors pertaining to ongoing and proposed projects.

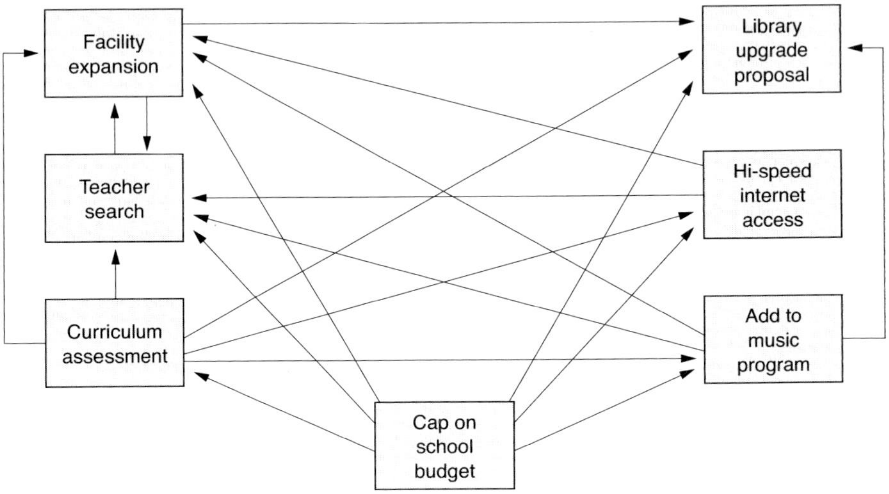

Figure 9.16 Interrelationship digraph.

RESOURCE ALLOCATION MATRIX

A matrix chart is useful in planning the allocation of resources (such as personnel, equipment, facilities, and funds). It is frequently used in planning larger projects. The matrix enables planners to see where potential conflicts may arise in utilizing resources for a project that are already committed to ongoing operations. Figure 9.17 shows a matrix for allocation of five types of personnel required for a project.

RUN CHART

A *run chart* is a line graph that shows data points plotted in the order in which they occur. This type of chart is used to reveal trends and shifts in a process over time, to show variation within a time period, and to identify decline or improvement in a process. It can be used to examine variables or attribute data.

The data must be collected in chronological or sequential order starting from any point. For best results, 25 or more samples must be taken to get an accurate run chart.

The chart in Figure 9.18 plots the average rod diameter of each of 10 lots of rods. A lot is one day's total run.

Run charts can help an organization to:

- Recognize patterns of performance in a process
- Document trends over time

Project Delta Team—Personnel Requirements—October through May
(Days)

Task	Data Entry Operator	Design Engineer	Systems Analyst	Computer Operator	Production Planner	Total
Build test data file	Nov. 15.0	Oct.–Nov. 5.5	Oct. 3.5	Oct. 6.25		30.25
Run desk check of data		Nov. 3.0	Nov. 2.0	Nov. 1.25		6.25
Modify test data	Dec. 1.5	Dec. 1.0	Dec. 1.0	Dec. 2.0		5.50
Run computer test				Dec. 8.0		8.00
Analyze test results		Dec.–Jan. 15.0	Dec.–Jan. 15.0	Dec.–Jan. 5.0		35.00
Make modifications		Jan.–Feb. 25.0	Jan.–Feb. 12.0	Jan.–Feb. 3.0		40.00
Prepare first month data	Mar. 6.0		Mar. 1.0	Mar. 3.0		10.00
Prepare second month data	Apr. 5.0		Apr. .5	Apr. 1.0		6.50
Prepare third month data	May 5.0		May .5	May .5		6.00
Run full-scale production				May 1.5	May .75	2.25
Analyze results		May 3.0				3.00
	32.5	52.5	35.5	31.5	.75	152.75

Figure 9.17 Resource allocation matrix.

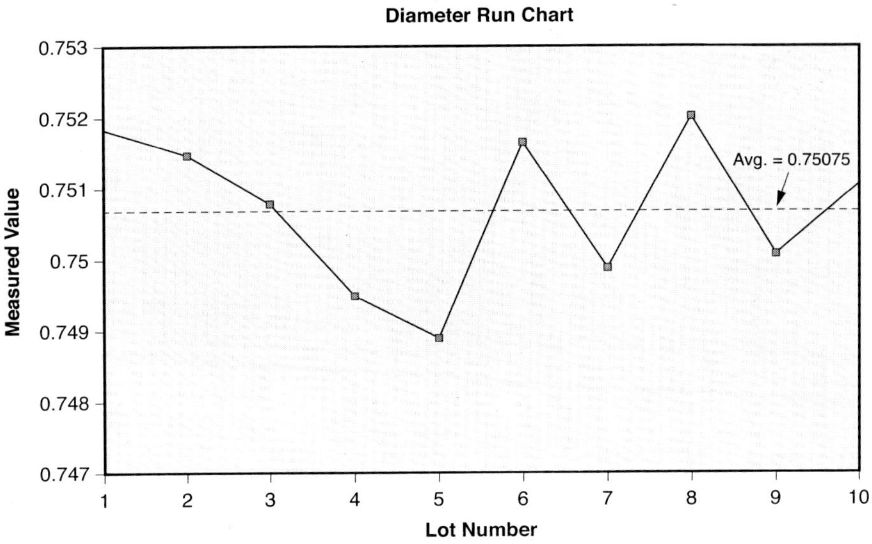

Figure 9.18 Run chart.

A run chart shows the history and pattern. Plot a point for each time a measurement is taken of variation. It is helpful to indicate on the chart whether up is good or down is good.

Run charts can be used to:

- Summarize occurrences of a particular situation
- Display measurement results over time
- Identify trends, fluctuations, or unusual events
- Determine common cause versus special cause variation

The basic steps involved in constructing a run chart are as follows:

1. Construct a horizontal (x) axis line and a vertical (y) axis line. The horizontal axis represents time, and the vertical axis represents the values of measurement or the frequency with which an event occurs.
2. Collect data for an appropriate number of time periods, in accordance with your data collection strategy.
3. Plot a point for each time a measurement is taken.
4. Connect the points with a line.
5. Identify questions that the data should answer about the process. Record any questions or observations that can be made as a result of the data.
6. Compute the average for subsequent blocks of time, or after a significant change has occurred.

Keeping in mind the process, interpret the chart. Possible signals that the process has significantly changed are:

- Six points in a row that steadily increase or decrease
- Nine points in a row that are on the same side of the average
- Other patterns such as significant shifts in levels, cyclical patterns, and bunching of data points

Run charts provide information that helps to:

- Identify trends in which more points are above or below the average. An equal number of points should lie above and below the average. When a larger number of points lie either above or below the average, this indicates that there has been an unusual event and that the average has changed. Such changes should be investigated.
- Identify trends in which several points steadily increase or decrease with no reversals. Neither pattern would be expected to happen based on random chance. This would likely indicate an important change and the need to investigate.
- Identify common and special cause variation within a process.

SCATTER DIAGRAM

A *scatter diagram* is a chart in which one variable is plotted against another to determine whether there is a correlation between the two variables. These diagrams are used to plot the distribution of information in two dimensions. Scatter diagrams are useful in rapidly screening for a relationship between two variables.

A scatter diagram shows the pattern of relationship between two variables that are thought to be related. For example, is there a relationship between outside temperature and cases of the common cold? As temperatures drop, do colds increase? The more closely the points hug a diagonal line, the more likely it is that there is a one-to-one relationship.

The purpose of the scatter diagram is to display what happens to one variable when another variable is changed. The diagram is used to test a theory that the two variables are related. The slope of the diagram indicates the type of relationship that exists.

Figure 9.19 shows a plot of two variables—in this example, predicted values versus observed values. As the predicted value increases, so does the actual measured value. These variables are said to be positively correlated; that is, if one increases, so does the other. The line plotted is a "regression" line, which shows the average linear relationship between the variables. If the line in a scatter diagram has a negative slope, the variables are negatively correlated; that is, when one increases, the other decreases, and vice versa. When no regression line can be plotted and the scatter diagram appears to simply be a ball of diffused points, the variables are said to be uncorrelated.

The utility of the scatter diagram for quality assessment lies in its measurement of variables in a process to see whether any two or more are correlated or

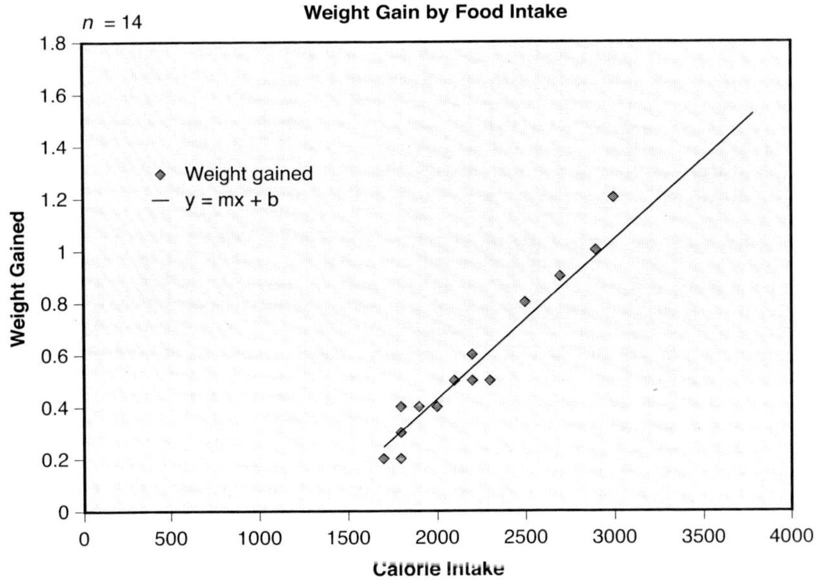

Figure 9.19 Scatter diagram.

uncorrelated. The specific utility of finding correlations is to infer causal relationships among variables and ultimately to find the root causes of problems.

The basic steps involved in constructing a scatter diagram are as follows:

1. Define the *x* variable on a graph-paper scatter diagram form. This variable is often thought of as the cause variable and is typically plotted on the horizontal axis.

2. Define the *y* variable on the diagram. This variable is often thought of as the effect variable and is typically plotted on the vertical axis.

3. Number the pairs of *x* and *y* variable measurements consecutively. Record each pair of measures for *x* and *y* in the appropriate columns. Make sure that the *x* measures and the corresponding *y* measures remain paired so that the data are accurate.

4. Plot the *x* and *y* data pairs on the diagram. Locate the *x* value on the horizontal axis, and then locate the *y* value on the vertical axis. Place a point on the graph where these two intersect.

5. Study the shape that is formed by the series of data points plotted. In general, conclusions can be made about the association between two variables (referred to as *x* and *y*) based on the shape of the scatter diagram. Scatter diagrams that display associations between two variables tend to look like elliptical spheres or even straight lines. Analysis patterns are:

   a. Scatter diagrams on which the plotted points appear in a circular fashion show little or no correlation between *x* and *y*.

b. Scatter diagrams on which the points form a pattern of increasing values for both variables show a positive correlation; as values of x increase, so do values of y. The more tightly the points are clustered in a linear fashion, the stronger the positive correlation, or the association between the two variables.

c. Scatter diagrams on which one variable increases in value while the second variable decreases in value show a negative correlation between x and y. Again, the more tightly the points are clustered in a linear fashion, the stronger the association between the two variables.

If there appears to be a relationship between two variables, they are said to be correlated. Both negative and positive correlations are useful for continuous process improvement.

Scatter diagrams show only that a relationship exists, not that one variable causes the other. Further analysis using advanced statistical techniques can quantify how strong the relationship is between two variables.

STRATIFICATION

A technique called *stratification* is often very useful in analyzing data in order to find improvement opportunities. Stratification helps analyze cases in which data actually mask the real facts. This often happens when the recorded data are from many sources but are treated as one number.

The basic idea in stratification is that data that are examined may be obtained from sources with different statistical characteristics. For example, consider that two different machines, such as a cutting machine and a polishing machine, may influence the measurement of the width of a particular part in a manufacturing assembly. Each machine will contribute to variations in the width of the final product, but with potentially different statistical variations.

Data on complaints may be recorded as a single figure (either rising or falling). However, that number is actually the sum total of complaints (including those, for example, about office staff, field nurses, and home health aides). Stratification breaks down single numbers into meaningful categories or classifications in order to focus corrective action.

TREE DIAGRAM

A *tree diagram* is a graphic representation of the separation of broad, general information into increasing levels of detail. The tool ensures that action plans remain visibly linked to overall goals, that actions flow logically from identified goals, and that the true level of a project's complexity will be fully understood. The goal to establish objectives for improving operations is diagrammed in Figure 9.20.

Tree diagrams are used in the quality planning process. The diagram begins with a generalized goal (the tree top) and then identifies progressively finer levels of actions (the branches) needed to accomplish the goal. As part of process improvement, it can be used to help identify root causes of trouble. The tool is especially useful in designing new products or services and in creating an implementation

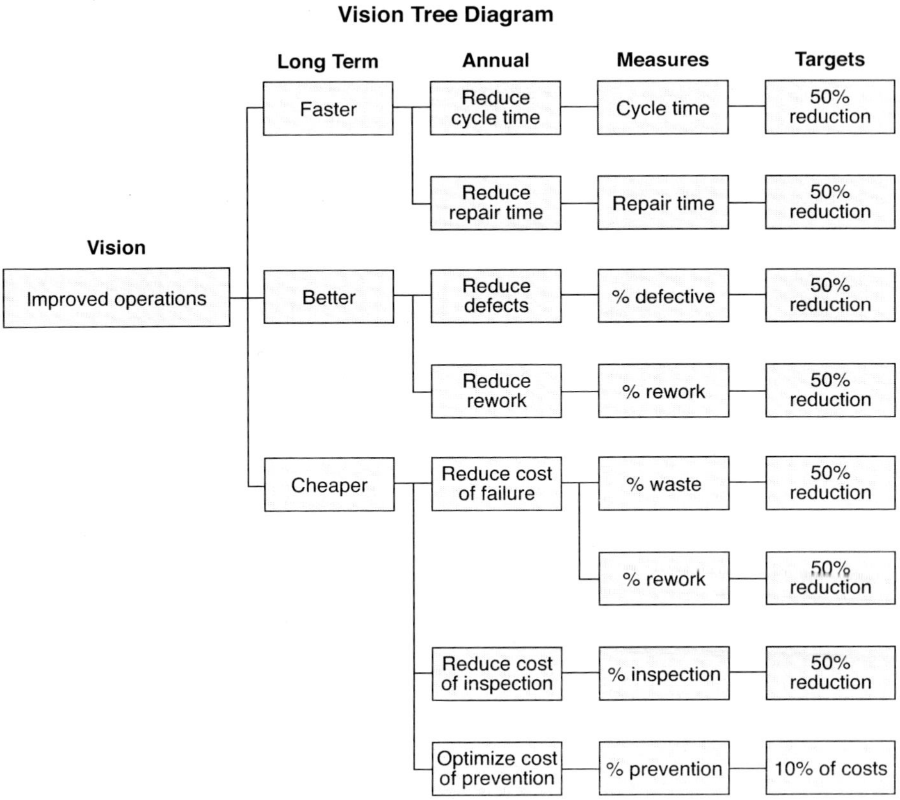

Figure 9.20 Tree diagram.

plan to remedy identified process problems. In order for the diagram to accurately reflect the project, it is essential that the team using it have a detailed understanding of the tasks required.

The steps involved in generating a tree diagram are as follows:

1. Identify the goal statement or primary objective. This should be a clear, action-oriented statement to which the entire team agrees. Such statements may come from the root cause/driver identified in an interrelationship digraph or from the headings of an affinity diagram. Write this goal on the extreme left or top of the chart (the diagram may be drawn from left to right or top to bottom).

2. Subdivide the goal statement into major secondary categories. These branches should represent goals, activities, or events that directly lead to the primary objective or that are directly required to achieve the overall goal. The team should continually ask, "What is required to meet this condition?" "What happens next?" and "What needs to be addressed?" Write the secondary categories to the right of the goal

statement. Using sticky notes at this stage makes later changes easier to accomplish.

3. Break each major heading into greater detail. As you move from left to right in the tree, the tasks and activities should become more and more specific. Stop the breakdown of each level once there are assignable tasks. If at some point the team does not have enough knowledge to continue, identify the individuals who can supply the information and continue the breakdown later with those individuals present.
4. Review the diagram for logic and completeness. Make sure that each subheading and path has a direct cause-and-effect relationship with the one before. Examine the paths to ensure that no obvious steps have been left out. Also ensure that the completion of listed actions will indeed lead to the anticipated results.

SUMMARY OF QUALITY IMPROVEMENT TOOLS AND TECHNIQUES

The quality improvement tools and techniques described in this chapter provide a simple yet powerful set of methodologies for collecting, analyzing, and visualizing information from different perspectives. The problem is the lack of use of the methodologies by organizations. An organization cannot solve its own problems without understanding the way these methodologies operate and how they can assist the organization in understanding and improving its processes.

Many of the tools and techniques mentioned in this chapter are discussed in greater depth in the reference materials cited in Appendix D.

NOTES

1. Some information in this section is adapted from US Department of the Navy, *Handbook for Basic Process Improvement* (available from ASQ, http://asq.org/gov/handbook-for-basic-process-improvement.html?shl=088779) and the *US Air Force Quality Institute Process Improvement Guide*, 2nd ed. (1994)
2. In more recent times, the seven basic tools are the cause-and-effect diagram, check sheet, control chart, flowchart, histogram, Pareto chart, and scatter diagram.
3. Additional information on quality tools may be gained from Grace L. Duffy, ed., *The ASQ Quality Improvement Pocket Guide* (Milwaukee, WI: ASQ Quality Press, 2013).
4. ASQ Statistics Division, *Improving Performance through Statistical Thinking* (Milwaukee, WI: ASQ Quality Press, 2000).

ADDITIONAL RESOURCES

Bauer, J. E., G. L. Duffy, and J. W. Moran. "Solve Problems with Open Communication." *Quality Progress*, July 2001, 160.

Beecroft, G. Dennis, Grace L. Duffy, and John W. Moran, eds. *The Executive Guide to Improvement and Change*. Milwaukee, WI: ASQ Quality Press, 2003.

Brassard, M., and D. Ritter. *The Memory Jogger 2: Tools for Continuous Improvement and Effective Planning*. 2nd ed. Salem, NH: GOAL/QPC, 2010.

Duffy, Grace L., ed. *The ASQ Quality Improvement Pocket Guide*. Milwaukee, WI: ASQ Quality Press, 2013.

Duffy, Grace L., John W. Moran, and William Riley. *Quality Function Deployment and Lean-Six Sigma Applications in Public Health*. Milwaukee, WI: ASQ Quality Press, 2010.

Wood, Douglas C., ed. *Principles of Quality Costs*. 4th ed. Milwaukee, WI: ASQ Quality Press, 2013.

Part IV

Customer-Supplier Relations

Chapter 10
A. Internal and External Customers and Suppliers

> Distinguish between internal and external customers and suppliers. Describe their impact on products, services, and processes, and identify strategies for working with them to make improvements. (Understand)
>
> **CQIA BoK 2014 IV.A.**

I do not consider a sale complete until the goods are worn out and the customer is still satisfied.

Leon Leonwood Bean, founder of L.L.Bean

There is only one boss—the customer. And he can fire everybody in the company from the chairman on down simply by spending his money somewhere else.

Sam Walton, founder of Wal-Mart

Anyone who thinks customers aren't important should try doing without them for 90 days.

Anonymous

1. INTERNAL AND EXTERNAL CUSTOMERS

Internal Customers

Internal customers are those customers within the organization. The term *next operation as customer* (NOAC) is often used to describe the relationship of internal provider to internal receiver.[1] Every function and work group in an organization is both a receiver of services and/or products from internal and/or external sources and a provider of services and/or products to internal and/or external customers. These interfaces between provider and receiver may be one to one, one to many, many to one, or many to many. Each receiver has needs and requirements.

Whether the delivered service or product meets the needs and requirements of the receiver, it impacts the effectiveness and quality of services and/or products to its customers, and so on. Following are some examples of internal customer situations:

- If A delivers part X to B one hour late, B may have to apply extra effort and cost to make up the time or else perpetuate the delay by delivering late to the next customer.
- Engineering designs a product based on a salesperson's understanding of the external customer's need. Production produces the product, expending resources. The external customer rejects the product because it fails to meet the customer's needs. The provider reengineers the product, and production makes a new one, which the customer accepts beyond the original required delivery date. The result is waste and possibly no further orders from this customer.
- Information technology (IT) delivers copies of a production cost report (which averages 50 pages of fine print per week) to six internal customers. IT has established elaborate quality control of the accuracy, timeliness, and physical quality of the report. However, of the six report receivers, only two still need information of this type. Neither finds the report directly usable for their current needs. Each has assigned clerical people to manually extract pertinent data for their specific use. All six admit that they diligently store the reports for the prescribed retention period. This is wasteful. Redesign the report.
- Production tickets, computer-printed on light card stock, are attached by removable tape to modules. When each module reaches the paint shop, it is given an acid bath, a rinse, high-temperature drying, painting, and high-temperature baking. Very few tickets survive intact and readable. The operation following the paint shop requires attaching other parts to the painted modules, based on information contained on the tickets. Operators depend on their experience to guess which goes with what. About 95% of the modules emerge from this process correctly, except when a product variation is ordered or when an experienced operator is absent. Change the process.

The steps to improve processes and services are as follows:

1. Identify internal customer interfaces (providers of services/products and receivers of their services/products)
2. Establish internal customers' service/product needs and requirements
3. Ensure that the internal customer requirements are consistent with and supportive of external customer requirements
4. Document service-level agreements between providers and receivers.[2]
5. Establish improvement goals and measurements
6. Implement systems for tracking and reporting performance and for supporting the continuous improvement of the process

Treatment of Internal Customers and the Effect on External Customers

Careless behavior of management (and management's systems) toward internal customers (poor tools and equipment, defective or late material from a previous operation, incorrect/incomplete instructions, illegible work orders or prints, circumvention of worker safety procedures and practices, unhealthy work environment, lack of interest in internal complaints, disregard for external customer feedback, etc.) may engender careless or indifferent treatment of external customers. Continued, this indifference can generate a downward spiral that could adversely affect an organization's business. Ignoring the needs of internal customers makes it very difficult to instill a desire to care for the needs of external customers.

In providing products or service to inter-company (I/C) buyers, such as delivering from one location to another, usually from a vertical integration perspective, there can be disregard and shoddy treatment. In these relationships and transactions with their I/C sister sites, aside from delivery and quality issues, there are often complex financial transaction processes established for which no customer actually pays. However, the whole business painfully absorbs the cost of these often large internal expenses.

So many organizations fail to learn, or ignore, the internal customers' needs and wonder why their management's exhortations fail to stimulate internal customers to care about what they do for external customers and how they do it. The surly and uncooperative sales representative, waitperson, housekeeping employee, healthcare provider, delivery person, and customer service representative often reflect a lack of caring for internal customers.

Organizations must work constantly to address the internal customers' lament: "How do you expect me to care about the next operator, or external customer, when no one cares whether I get what I need to do my job right?"

External Customers

External customers are those customers who are served by or who receive products from the supplier organization. There are many types of external customers.

1. Consumers/End Users

- *Retail buyer of products.* The retail buyer influences the design and usability of product features and accessories based on the volume purchased. Consumer product "watch" organizations warn purchasers of potential problems. For example:

  > In the late 1990s, a fake fat substance was introduced in a number of food products as a boon to weight-conscious people. These products didn't taste good and were found to have harmful side effects. Many consumers stopped buying the products.

  The factors important to this type of buyer, depending on the type of product, are reasonable price, ease of use, performance, safety, aesthetics, and durability. Other influences on product offerings include easy purchase process, installation, instructions for use, post-purchase service, warranty period, packaging, friendliness of seller's personnel, and brand name.

- *Discount buyer.* The discount buyer shops primarily for price, is more willing to accept less-well-known brands, and is willing to buy quantities in excess of immediate needs. These buyers have relatively little influence on the products, except for, perhaps, creating a market for off-brands, production surpluses, and discontinued items.
- *Employee buyer.* The employee buyer purchases the employer's products, usually at a deep discount. Often being familiar with or even a contributor to the products bought, this buyer can provide valuable feedback to the employer (both directly, through surveys, and indirectly, through volume and items purchased).
- *Service buyer.* Buyers of services (such as TV repair, dental work, and tax preparation) often buy by word-of-mouth. Word of good or poor service spreads rapidly and influences the continuance of the service provider's business.
- *Service user.* The captive service user (such as the user of electricity, gas, water, municipal services, and schools) generally has little choice from which supplier it receives services. Until competition is introduced, there is little incentive for providers to vary their services. Recent deregulation has resulted in a more competitive marketplace for some utilities.
- *Organization buyer.* Sometimes referred to as Business to Business (B2B). Buyers for organizations that use a product or service in the course of their business or activity can have a significant influence on the types of products offered them as well as on the organization from which they buy. Raw materials or devices that become part of a manufactured product are especially critical in sustaining quality and competitiveness for the buyer's organization (including performance, serviceability, price, ease of use, durability, simplicity of design, safety, and ease of disposal). Other factors include flexibility in delivery, discounts, allowances for returned material, extraordinary guarantees, and so forth.

  Factors that particularly pertain to purchased services are the reputation and credibility of the provider, range of services offered, degree of customization offered, timeliness, fee structure, and so forth.

2. Intermediate Customers

- *Wholesale buyer.* Wholesalers buy what they expect they can sell, typically buying in large quantities. They may have little direct influence on product design and manufacture, but they do influence the providers' production schedules, pricing policies, warehousing and delivery arrangements, return policies for unsold merchandise, and so forth.
- *Distributor.* Distributors are similar to wholesalers in some ways but differ in the fact that they may stock a wider variety of products from a wide range of producers. What they stock is directly influenced by their customers' demands and needs. Their customers' orders are often small and may consist of a mix of products. The distributors' forte is stocking thousands of catalog items that can be "picked" and shipped on short notice, at an attractive price. Customers seeking an industry

level of quality, at a good price and immediately available, mainly influence distributors stocking commodity-type items, such as sheet metal, construction materials, mineral products, and stationary items. "Blanket orders" for a yearly quantity delivered at specified intervals are prevalent for some materials.

- *Retail chain buyer.* Buyers for large retail chains, because of the size of their orders, place major demands on their providers, such as pricing concessions, very flexible deliveries, requirements that the providers assume warehousing costs for already-purchased products, special packaging requirements, no-cost return policy, and requirements that the providers be able to accept electronically sent orders.
- *Other volume buyers.* Government entities, educational institutions, healthcare organizations, transportation companies, public utilities, cruise lines, hotel chains, and restaurant chains all represent large-volume buyers that provide services to customers. Such organizations have regulations governing their services. Each requires a wide range of products, materials, and external services in delivering its services, much of which is transparent to the consumer. Each requires high quality, and each has tight limitations on what it can pay (e.g., based on appropriations, cost-control mandates, tariffs, or heavy competition). Each such buyer demands much for its money but may offer long-term contracts for fixed quantities. The buying organizations' internal customers frequently generate the influences on the products required.
- *Service providers.* The diversity of service providers buying products and services from other providers is mind-boggling. These buyers include plumbers, public accountants, dentists, doctors, building contractors, cleaning services, computer programmers, website designers, consultants, manufacturer's representatives, actors, and taxi drivers, among many others. This type of buyer, often self-employed, buys very small quantities, shops for value, buys only when the product or service is needed (when the buyer has a job, patient, or client), and relies on high quality of purchases to maintain customers' satisfaction. Influences on products or services for this type of buyer range from having the provider be able to furnish service and/or replacement parts for old or obsolete equipment, be able to supply extremely small quantities of an extremely large number of products (such as those supplied by a hardware store, construction materials depot, or medical products supply house), and have product knowledge that extends to knowing how the product is to be used.

A simplified hypothetical product/service flow through several types of customers for a consumer product sold via an internet web page follows:

a. A consumer (external customer) accesses the web through an external internet service provider (ISP).

b. The consumer searches for a particular book at the lowest price available, accessing various product sellers (the ISP is an external service provider to the various sellers).

c. The consumer selects a seller and places an order via the seller's web page.

d. The seller forwards the order to a selected publisher's order service (the seller is an external customer of the publisher).

e. The order service department of the publisher notifies the seller, which notifies the consumer that the book order has been placed.

f. The publisher's order service department forwards a "pick" order to the warehouse, which picks the book from inventory and sends it to shipping (the warehouse is an internal customer of the order service department, and shipping is an internal customer of the warehouse).

g. Shipping packages and sends the book via Package Delivery Service (PDS) directly to the consumer, notifying the publisher's order service and billing departments and the seller that shipment has taken place (PDS is a service provider to the publisher, and the billing department is an internal customer of shipping).

h. The publisher's billing department adds the shipment to the amount to be billed to the seller at month end.

i. PDS delivers the book to the consumer.

j. The seller bills the consumer (the consumer is an external customer of the seller's billing department).

With some exceptions (such as very small organizations), most organizations segment their customer base in order to better serve the needs of different types of customers. Providing one product or service to every type of customer is no longer feasible.

Henry Ford is reported to have said, "People can have the Model T in any color—so long as it's black." (Black was the only color of paint available that dried fast enough to allow Ford's assembly-line approach to work.)

Customers sharing particular wants or needs may be segmented by:

- Purchase volume
- Profitability (to the selling organization)
- Industry classification
- Geographic factors (such as municipalities, regions, states, countries, and continents)
- Demographic factors (such as age, income, marital status, education, and gender)
- Psychographic factors (such as values, beliefs, and attitudes)

An organization must decide whether it is interested in simply pursuing more customers (or contributors, in the case of a not-for-profit fund-raiser) or in targeting the right customers. It is not unusual for an organization, after segmenting its customer base, to find that it is not economically feasible to continue to serve a particular segment. Conversely, an organization may find that it is uniquely capable of further penetrating a particular market segment or may even discover a niche not presently served by other organizations.

Deploying the Voice of the Customer

In becoming a customer-focused organization, it is important that the requirements and expectations of the customer permeate every function within the organization. One tool for deploying (cascading) the voice of the customer (VOC) downward throughout the organization is *quality function deployment* (QFD). QFD consists of a series of interlocking matrices, outlined in Figure 10.1. In this example, customer requirements are aligned with internal design requirements, design requirements are aligned with parts requirements, parts requirements with process requirements, and process requirements with production requirements—to produce a product that meets the customer's requirements and expectations.

A *focus group* is a means for capturing insightful information about customers' expectations before a product or service is designed and launched as well as a means for gathering customers' satisfaction with products or services purchased.

Internal Suppliers

Internal suppliers are the "providers" discussed in the earlier section on internal customers. *Internal suppliers* include not only those providers directly involved in producing the products/services, but also those involved with support functions, such as tariff checkers in a trucking company, materials management and cost accounting functions in manufacturing, facility maintenance in a school, the pharmacy in a hospital, the motor pool in a government agency, and market research.

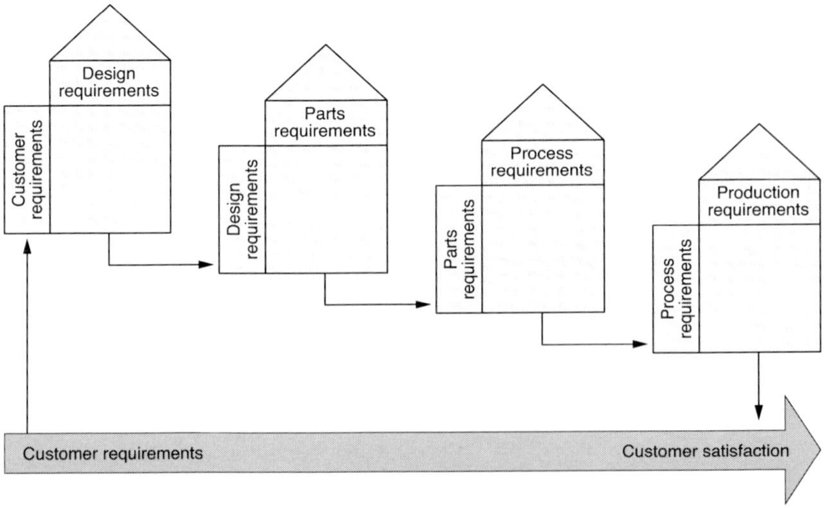

Figure 10.1 Voice of the customer deployed.

Source: Reproduced by permission from R. T. Westcott, ed., *The Certified Manager of Quality/Organizational Excellence Handbook*, 4th ed. (Milwaukee, WI: ASQ Quality Press, 2014), 459.

In many organizations, internal suppliers establish *service-level agreements* (SLAs) with their customers. These agreements, usually for primary processes or sub-processes, provide the requirements that must be met by the supplier and allow for quantitative measurement of results. Internal data processing and information technology groups have used SLAs for many years to mutually establish customer requirements and measure performance to requirements.[3]

External Suppliers

Communicating stated expectations and requirements between customer and supplier is frequently a problem. Because of the pressures to get and keep business, suppliers often accept poorly communicated requirements. Consider the ramifications of the following incoming phone call:

> "This is Acme. Joe, send me 150 more of those parts you sold me last week. Goodbye."

Exaggerated? Maybe, but it frequently happens like this. Look at the potential for error. The supplier may have more than one customer called "Acme." The caller's company received two shipments over the last seven working days that were for different products. Each shipment required a different delivery method: one was delivered by UPS, and the customer picked up the other. One order was for parts costing Joe's company $5 each to make. The other order was for parts costing $50 each to make. Though the parts look similar, the more expensive part was made to a more stringent aerospace specification. Does Joe's company take a guess as to what to make and ship for this telephone order? Unfortunately, the guess prevails all too often. Joe's past experience with the customer leads him to believe that the customer needs the more expensive part. The outcome will be either that the customer is satisfied to get what was expected or that the customer is frantic about having received the wrong parts and having to wait for the correct parts to be made and shipped. Unfortunately for Joe, the outcome is the latter. Joe's company has lost $7500 in material and manufacturing costs for the wrong parts, the cost of shipping, and the cost of upsetting scheduling in order to get the replacement parts produced and shipped on an emergency basis. Who's to blame? Joe's company assumes the burden of clarifying the customer's requirements, up front, and the consequences of not doing so.

Often, a smaller organization fears losing business by antagonizing a large customer, and perhaps major customer, with more extensive probing as to what the customer really needs. In some situations, this may mean asking the customer more about how and where the supplier's product will be used (usually imperative in medical device manufacturing). A commonly used international standard for quality management systems requires reviewing contracts and clarifying customers' requirements before accepting an order. Larger organizations may establish and manage certain purchasing processes through long-term agreements (LTAs).

Given the ambiguous call Joe received, Joe's company should have a policy of confirming the order in writing (i.e., by e-mail) to request customer approval before accepting the order. Short of that, Joe should have called back with what he understood to be the requirement and to get an oral confirmation.

Many organizations are changing their approach to their external suppliers from the traditional adversarial relationship to a collaborative relationship. In past times, a supplier (more often called a "vendor") was considered an entity beneath the status of the buying organization. The customer's "purchasing agent" of old would seek to pressure vendors until the lowest price was obtained. Often the buying organization was significantly larger than the vendor's organization and wielded the power of offering potentially large orders. Price and delivery were the primary drivers in the vendor selection process. If quality became a problem, an order was canceled and another vendor was selected.

Increasingly, buying and selling organizations are forming quasi-partnerships and alliances to collaborate on improving the buyer–seller relationship as well as the quality of the products or services being purchased. Buying organizations have been able to substantially reduce the number of suppliers for any given product or service and cut costs through improved quality. It is not uncommon now for the buying organization to assist a supplier with training to use quality tools, material handling and stocking practices, and so forth. In this collaboration, the buying organization expects that the established quality and service levels will be consistent with its needs, that the supplier's practices will be continually improved, and that lower prices will result. The supplier often receives assurance of longer-term contracts, assistance in making improvements, and sometimes certification as a preferred supplier.

NOTES

1. Concept initiated by Dr. Kaoru Ishikawa.
2. R. T. Westcott, "Quality Level Agreements for Clarity of Expectations," in *Stepping Up to ISO 9004:2000* (Chico, CA: Paton Press, 2003), appendix C.
3. R. T. Westcott, ed., "Quality-Level Agreement," in *CMQ/OE Handbook* (Milwaukee, WI: ASQ Quality Press, 2014), 437–438.

ADDITIONAL RESOURCES

Allen, D., and T. R. Rao. *Analysis of Customer Satisfaction Data.* Milwaukee, WI: ASQ Quality Press, 2000.

Barlow, J., and C. Moller. *A Complaint Is a Gift.* San Francisco: Berrett-Koehler Publishers, 1996.

Chaplin, Ed, and John Terninko. *Customer Driven Healthcare: QFD for Process Improvement and Cost Reduction.* Milwaukee, WI: ASQ Quality Press, 2000.

Duffy, Grace L., John W. Moran, and William J. Riley. *Quality Function Deployment and Lean-Six Sigma Applications in Public Health.* Milwaukee, WI: ASQ Quality Press, 2010.

Hayes, Bob E. *Beyond the Ultimate Question: A Systematic Approach to Improve Customer Loyalty.* Milwaukee, WI: ASQ Quality Press, 2010.

Lowenstein, Michael W. *The Customer Advocate and the Customer Saboteur.* Milwaukee, WI: ASQ Quality Press, 2011.

Norausky, Patrick H. *The Customer and Supplier Innovation Team Guidebook.* Milwaukee, WI: ASQ Quality Press, 2000.

Westcott, Russell T., ed. *The Certified Manager of Quality/Organizational Excellence Handbook.* 4th ed. Milwaukee, WI: ASQ Quality Press, 2014, chapters 16–18.

Chapter 11
B. Customer Satisfaction

It's not enough anymore to merely satisfy the customer, customers must be "delighted"—surprised by having their needs not just met, but exceeded.

A. Blanton Godfrey

All of management's efforts for Kaizen boil down to two words: customer satisfaction.

Masaaki Imai

Real profits are generated by loyal customers—not just satisfied customers.

Raphael Aguayo

It's not enough just to give good service; the customer must perceive the fact that he or she is getting good service.

Karl Albrecht and Ron Zemke

> Describe different types of customer feedback mechanisms (formal surveys, informal feedback, official complaints) and describe the importance of using data from these and other sources to drive continuous improvement. (Understand)
>
> **CQIA BoK 2014 IV.B.**

From a customer contact perspective there are three aspects to address: (1) analysis of how the customers feel and react to the products and services an organization delivers, and did those products and services meet their expectations, (2) are customer relationships enhancing customer retention, and (3) what do the customers foresee as their future wants and needs.

Some content for this chapter has been excerpted from *The Certified Manager of Quality/Organizational Excellence Handbook*, 4th ed., ed. Russell T. Westcott (Milwaukee, WI: ASQ Quality Press, 2014), chapter 17.

Customer relationship management (CRM), also referred to as *relationship marketing* or *one-to-one marketing* (serving the unique needs of each customer), is receiving emphasis in the fast-paced, ever-changing environment in which organizations must survive and prosper. CRM relates less to the product or service provided and more to the way business is conducted. In a customer-focused organization, the thrust is usually more toward nurturing the existing customers than a drive to attract new customers. A key principle of good customer relations is determining and ensuring customer satisfaction, and increasing customer loyalty.

Perceptions of customer satisfaction need to be corroborated or rejected through sound means for collecting, analyzing, and acting on customer feedback. Effective systems for utilizing customer feedback involve:

- Formal processes for collecting, measuring, and analyzing customer data and for communicating results to the appropriate business functions for action
- Feedback mechanisms to determine how well an organization is meeting customers' requirements and expectations
- Choice of and combining of several methods to get a more complete understanding of the customers' needs and wants
- Proven techniques are in use to analyze the feedback data and target areas for improvement
- Information that is derived from the analyzed data is stored appropriately and made available to those who need it

CUSTOMER FEEDBACK METHODOLOGIES

Data about customers' satisfaction are found within and outside the organization. Data from within may include:

- Customer complaints
- Past records of claim resolutions
- Product warranty registration cards and guarantee usage
- Customer satisfaction surveys
- Product service records (failure and maintenance)
- Input from internal customer-contact personnel
- Transaction data
- Listening post input
- Lost-customer analysis
- Internal market research

Data from outside the organization may include:

- Focus group data
- Data about competitors' customers

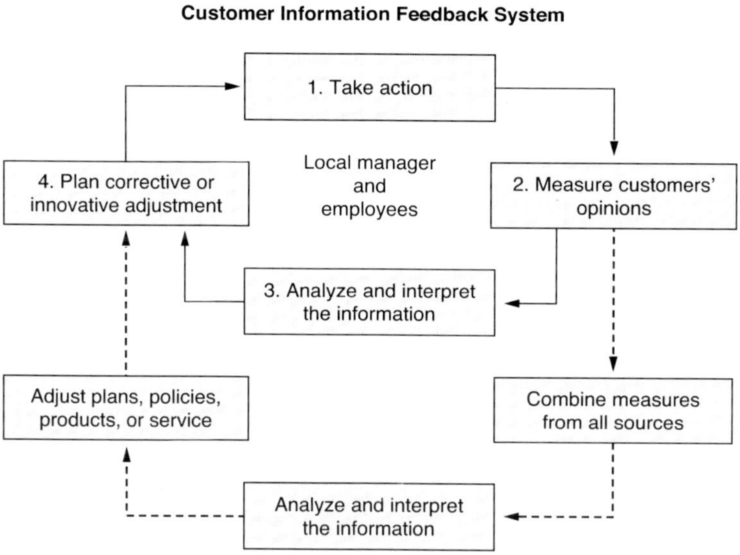

Figure 11.1 System for utilizing customer feedback.

Source: Reproduced by permission from R. T. Westcott, ed., *The Certified Manager of Quality/Organizational Excellence Handbook*, 4th ed. (Milwaukee, WI: ASQ Quality Press, 2014), 461.

- Media research (internet searches, websites, TV and radio, magazines, newspapers, trade journals)
- Public information (customers' and competitors' annual reports, customers' brochures and advertising)
- Industry market research

Figure 11.1 depicts an overview of the primary steps in a system for utilizing customer feedback.

ANALYZING CUSTOMER DATA

Product Warranty Registration (Return Cards and Online Registration)

Product warranty cards are often found in the packages of new products. A consumer who completes the card and sends it in provides some basic customer data that help the seller better understand buyers' needs. Actually, the real value is in analyzing the customer's purchasing decision (by the types of questions asked on the cards), and later, if the consumer files a claim, understanding the cause of the dissatisfaction.

Many warranty registrations are now online. The supplier receives information on the user as well as the user's e-mail address. Some products also provide free information, periodically via the internet, to suppliers on how the device is used and when there are issues.[1]

Complaints

Complaint data, when appropriately captured and analyzed, provide a wealth of information about customers' satisfaction. It's important to recognize that a complaint is not a nuisance; it's a gift. However, it must be realized that the data do not constitute a valid statistical sample: Many customers find it a burden to complain unless there is a very serious problem, and the majority of customers appear to have no complaint to register.

Many organizations openly solicit complaints—think of the restaurant waitperson who inquires about your satisfaction with your food, the organization that serves mail-order customers and includes a self-addressed, stamped reply card, and the hotel that seeks feedback on your satisfaction with your stay at its facility. It has been proved that a buyer's satisfaction is often greatly improved when a complaint is quickly and effectively resolved. Research by the US Office of Consumer Affairs/Technical Assistance Research Programs (TARP) shows that the speed of complaint resolution also affects repurchase intent, which is significantly higher when resolution is achieved quickly.

Customer Surveys

Many organizations solicit customer feedback with formal customer surveys. The aims of a survey are to get as high a response rate as possible so as to obtain the most representative sampling of the customer population surveyed and as much useful data as possible. Designing effective surveys and analyzing the data received are processes involving specialized expertise and knowledge. Administering the survey process can be expensive. Misinterpretation and inappropriate use of the data can be even more expensive.

Surveys may be administered through the following means:

- Mail
- E-mail
- Website
- Telephone
- In person, one-to-one
- In person, group
- In person, panel

Each method has its advantages and disadvantages. The relative effectiveness of one over another also depends on the purpose of the survey, the population to be surveyed, and the benefit-to-cost ratio of conducting the survey. For example, one-to-one interviews can generally reach only a small number of persons and are expensive to conduct, but the personal contact involved often yields great insights. The mailed survey has its costs but can reach unlimited numbers of potential respondents. The response rate can be low and the types of customers responding may not represent a reasonable sample, but this method is far less expensive than one-to-one surveys. Electronic surveys are relatively inexpensive when integrated with other website material, but they can yield very low response rates and may produce responses from only the wildly delighted, the highly dissatisfied customers, and any "loyal" customers willing to help.

Following are points to keep in mind when using surveys:

- Using an annoying methodology, a poor survey design, an overall unappealing presentation, or questions that seem silly, without reason, or not pertinent gives the customer a reason not to respond.
- The organization should not formulate its questions based solely on what it thinks the customer wants to answer. Good survey design calls for the customers to be asked what is most important to them and what they would want to see addressed in a survey. A focus group is sometimes used to initiate ideas for questions to aid the survey design.
- Selecting customers who are neither random nor representative will result in responses that are not statistically valid. This can also happen when a low quantity of responses is analyzed. The analysis ignores the fact that customers at the extremes of satisfaction and dissatisfaction tend to respond to surveys more frequently than those who are neutral.
- Results from inept or misdirected questions can cause the organization to focus on the wrong or least-important improvement effort.
- Designing questions that force an answer where none of the choices are applicable to the customer is unacceptable.
- Failure to write questions at a level that the customer can understand may compromise the validity of the survey.
- Some organizations conduct surveys and then fail to use the results in their strategic planning and continuous improvement efforts.
- Certain types of organizations experiment to determine whether a survey accompanied by an incentive (money, savings coupon, free xyz) increases the volume of responses and whether this strategy literally "buys" the response, perhaps even influencing the level of satisfaction reported. (Some fund-raising entities often include a penny, nickel, dime, or quarter in their literature to lure, or shame, the receiver into making a donation.)

Transaction Data

Organizations frequently collect a wealth of data about their customers through direct one-to-one transactions. Examples include data collected on consumer buying habits through the use of store-issued identification cards (the use of these cards is supported by discount incentives). Analyzing "hits" and "buys" from users of websites is another source of data.

Electronic data interchange (EDI) is the paperless electronic transmission of a customer's order data (requirements) to the supplier's internal order fulfillment system. In some fully automated systems, the EDI data transmitted may trigger the order entry, production of the product, shipping, delivery, and billing—with no or minimum human intervention. EDI is often a contractual requirement from many customers.

Another way to gather transaction data is to engage external "mystery shoppers" to make purchases of the seller's product and provide feedback to the seller-organization about the experience. (The same approach is also used to "shop" the competitors and check out their approaches.)

Data from Established "Listening Posts"

Organizations have many employee categories that periodically or occasionally interact with counterparts in the customers' organizations, for example, engineer to engineer, salesperson to salesperson, CEO to CEO, and delivery person to customer's receiving person, among others. In a majority of these interactions (face-to-face, telephone, e-mail, etc.), the customers' people may express opinions, suggestions, complaints, or compliments about the supplier's organization, the quality of its products/services, delivery, price, and even the personal attention they receive (or don't receive). Excepting severe negative input, these comments, casually and informally made, are seldom captured. By not having a formal process for collecting and analyzing these data (e.g., trending), an organization is unable to spot the early stages of an eventual customer problem. It also misses compliments that should get back to the responsible people as positive feedback.[2]

> *Jan Carlzon, president of Scandinavian Airlines, in his book* Moments of Truth, *discusses the often-unrecognized opportunities all employees have for gathering customer data. A "moment of truth" is any contact a customer has with another organization.*

Understanding Customer Satisfaction Categories

One model used to analyze customer satisfaction data is the Kano model (Figure 11.2). Noriaki Kano developed this model to show the relationship between three types of product/service characteristics, or qualities. These include qualities that must be present, those that are one-dimensional, and those that are delighters.

The presence or absence of must-be characteristics is shown by a curved line in the lower-right quadrant. When a must-be characteristic is not present or is not present in sufficient quantity, dissatisfaction exists. As the characteristic becomes more available or of a higher quality, customer satisfaction increases, but only to a neutral state, represented by the horizontal line. (The characteristic can only serve not to dissatisfy the customer. Its presence will neither satisfy nor delight the customer.)

A one-dimensional characteristic drives satisfaction in direct correlation to its presence, and is represented by a straight line. For example, as the interest rate on a savings account rises, so does customer satisfaction.

The curved line in the upper left to center area represents delighters. If absent, there is no effect on satisfaction. However, when present, these features delight the customer. An example: In the early days of the automobile, there were no cup holders. Gradually, auto manufacturers saw the need, and a series of slide-on, clamp-on, and other less than satisfactory devices evolved. Eventually, built-in cup holders appeared, and for a time became delighters, resulting in great customer satisfaction. Over time, cup holders became a must-have. Having cup holders in the new car just purchased is "no big deal"; not having cup holders or not having a sufficient number of them creates customer dissatisfaction.

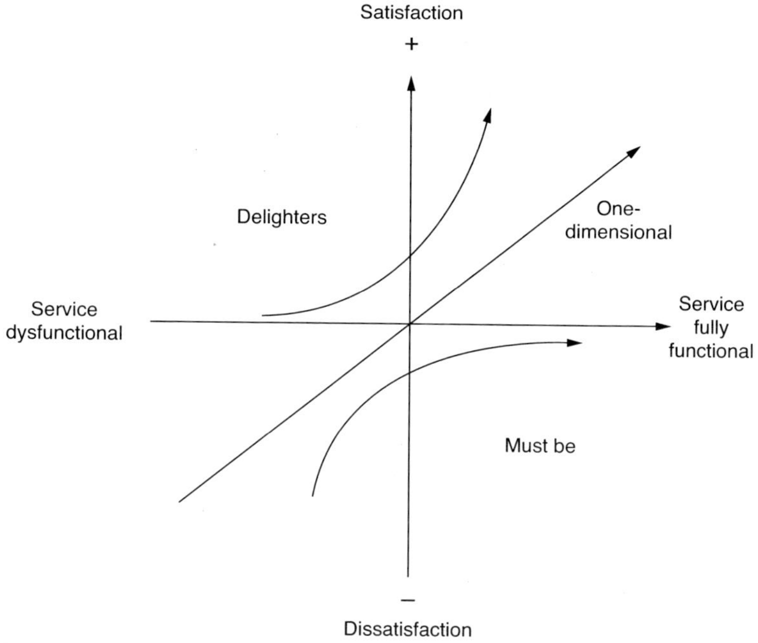

Figure 11.2 The Kano model.

Source: Reproduced by permission from R. Bialek, G. L. Duffy, and J. W. Moran, *The Public Health Quality Improvement Handbook* (Milwaukee, WI: ASQ Quality Press, 2009), 162.

Customer Satisfaction and Loyalty

Customer feedback data, especially complaints, are gifts. Without this feedback, the organization would not know how its customers feel and react to the product and services delivered. And, the organization would not have opportunities to improve its processes to increase its number of loyal customers.

What knowledge may be gained from the information derived from customer data collected? Five basic categories are:

1. May be satisfied?
2. May be dissatisfied?
3. Met their priorities?
4. Just barely met their need?
5. Truly excited or delighted?

Table 11.1 lists some common measures of satisfaction and the impact on customer loyalty.

Thought must be given to whether what is or was delivered or offered only marginally satisfies the customers or has the potential for generating real excitement and delight. The analysis would depend on the types of customers being served as well as the type of product/service and any critical to quality factors. Table 11.2 lists five levels of customer satisfaction, from dissatisfied to committed advocate.

Table 11.1 Commonly used measures of loyalty.

Overall satisfaction with the brand or company	Sensitivity to price
Overall quality of the product/service	Willingness to consider purchasing competitors' products
Advocacy (stated likelihood of telling other people about the product)	Attractiveness of competing products/services
Intent to repurchase/maintain current level of purchases	Willingness to switch to competing products/services
Willingness to continue using/purchasing in the event of problems with service or product	Importance of the product/service category to the respondent
Willingness to expend effort/overcome obstacles in order to purchase	Emotional attachment to the brand

Source: Reproduced by permission from M. Wilburn, *Managing the Customer Experience* (Milwaukee, WI: ASQ Quality Press, 2007), 42.

Table 11.2 Levels of customer satisfaction.

Level	Is Your Customer:	Then Your Customer:
1	dissatisfied?	has probably departed forever.
2	marginally satisfied?	is casual (any supplier will do).
3	basically satisfied?	is borderline, uncommitted.
4	delighted?	is a return customer (retained).
5	a committed advocate?	is loyal, appreciates what you do, and tells others.

Source: Reprinted with permission of R. T. Westcott & Associates.

Utilizing Customer Satisfaction and Loyalty Analysis

A critical factor for the organization is the economic impact of a lost customer. Producing tabulations of customer satisfaction data, trend charts, and so forth is of minimal value unless there is an established objective against which to compare. To make sense of the time and energy involved in collecting the data, there must be a target. To justify the preventive action that may be indicated by the analyzed data, there needs to be a basis for estimating the anticipated gain to be achieved by the action, a means for tracking progress toward achieving the objective, and a basis for evaluating the effectiveness of the action taken.

Knowing what it costs to lose a customer is a good place to start. Improvement in customer retention has the potential for a substantive dollar payoff. The figures have a direct impact on the profit or cost-containment goals of the organization, as well as the qualitative perceptions of the organization within its community.

Tracking, measuring, and reporting on a real-dollar basis is usually more meaningful than doing so on the basis of percentages or quantities alone. Simplified steps for determining what it is worth to retain customers are:

1. Segment the customer base by types of products or services sold to each segment.
2. Select an appropriate time period—for example, for customers buying consumer products, perhaps 2 years; for homeowner insurance buyers, maybe 30 years.
3. Compute the average annual profit each customer segment produces:
   As an example, for the home computer buyer segment, the average initial purchase price (including a three-year service contract) plus the average price of add-ons purchased within the three years, divided by three, times the number of customers in this segment equals the annual value of this segment.
4. Compute the worth to retain the customer:
   To the value of an individual customer in this segment, add the dollar value of upgrading the customer to a new computer at the end of the three-year period. Determine how many customers' upgrades represent a challenging but possible goal. Multiply the individual customer's figure by this number of upgrades. This is what it is worth to retain your customers through their first upgrade.
5. Use your customer satisfaction data to determine what actions are needed in order to retain your present customers, and estimate the cost of these actions.
6. Compute the estimated net gain from customer retention efforts: worth of customers minus cost to retain the customers.[3]
7. Do this for each segment. Note: Not all segments may be worth the added retention effort. You may also discover a segment of customers for which even initial efforts to sell to them may not be economically wise.

> The only large supermarket chain present in a small town estimates that its customers spend an average of $80 a week at the store ($4,160 a year) and that the average customer stays with the store for seven years (total average customer worth equals $29,120). Data analysis shows that customer satisfaction, in addition to the number of retained buyers, is at or above the industry norm for this type of location and store. Great! But the store does lose customers. At an average value of $29,120, it's worth exploring why the lost customers are occurring and what it would be worth to add efforts to retain more of these lost customers. And, as the town grows, the area is attracting other interested store chains. Action now to improve and sustain retention may be wise.

To gain a perspective of the scope and impact of lost customers:

- Create a rating scale for the reasons an organization loses its customers
- Apply the rating to a random sample quantity of customers lost
- Develop a Pareto chart for quantity lost in each rating category
- Create a trend chart showing the losses by category over time
- Initiate preventive action to decrease losses

Customer satisfaction data are analyzed to improve customer satisfaction and retain customers. Retaining customers costs money but is usually much less expensive than seeking new customers.

Organizational Value in Assessing Customer Satisfaction and Loyalty

It should be obvious that the more valid and useful information an organization derives from its customers, the more opportunities are surfaced for process, product, and service improvement. Obvious, yes. Acted on, maybe. A myriad of questions can arise:

- Have enough data been collected, or is there too much?
- Is there enough time and money to make improvements?
- Is management willing to commit to and support change?
- Are there sufficient potential advantages in investing in the changes that customers' feedback indicates are needed?
- Do the organization's vision, mission, strategies, practices, principles, and values support the improvements that the customer information indicates or implies?
- Would all segments of the customer base be affected by indicated changes from customer feedback?
- Does the customer feedback information that would drive organizational improvement suggest that organization culture change would, or should, result from the improvements, and if so, what impact on the organization's stakeholders may result (beneficial or non-beneficial)?

Benefits that the organization should realize from assessing customer satisfaction and loyalty and acting on indicated areas for improvement are the following:

- Reduction or elimination of conflicting encounters between employees and customers
- Increased profitability or cost containment resulting from elimination of waste
- Enhanced reputation for care of customers
- Growth in customer base
- Improved processes leading to improved quality and employee morale

- More word-of-mouth recommendations from present customers to potential new customers
- Widespread approval gained by the organization and recognition for its customers' satisfaction and loyalty
- Possible *unconditional guarantee* policy for the organization's products and services, further enhancing its reputation for quality
- Improvement actions that lead to recognition as the top choice for best-to-work-for organization, a feeling and image that support attracting top talent and employee retention (loyalty)

NOTES

1. Garmin devices use the Garmin Communicator Plugin, a free internet browser plugin that sends and retrieves data from Garmin GPS devices.
2. R. T. Westcott, "Tapping the Customer's Many Voices," in *Stepping Up to ISO 9004* (Chico, CA: Paton Press, 2003), appendix B describes the LCALI (listen, capture, analyze, learn, and improve) process for establishing listening posts and using the information derived.
3. F. Reichheld and C. Fornell present a more sophisticated approach to determining the worth of retaining customers in "What's a Loyal Customer Worth?" *Fortune*, December 1995.

ADDITIONAL RESOURCES

Beecroft, G. Dennis, Grace L. Duffy, and John W. Moran, eds. *The Executive Guide to Improvement and Change.* Milwaukee, WI: ASQ Quality Press, 2003. Chapter 12.

Brown, Stanley A. *Customer Relationship Management.* Toronto: John Wiley & Sons, Canada, 2000.

Carbone, L. P. *Clued In: How to Keep Customers Coming Back Again and Again.* Upper Saddle River, NJ: Financial Times Prentice Hall, 2004.

Chaplin, Ed, and John Terninko. *Customer Driven Healthcare: QFD for Process Improvement and Cost Reduction.* Milwaukee, WI: ASQ Quality Press, 2000.

DeFeo, Joseph A., and Joseph M. Juran, eds. *Juran's Quality Handbook.* 6th ed. New York: McGraw-Hill, 2010. Section 18.

Evans, James R., and William M. Lindsay. *The Management and Control of Quality.* 5th ed. Cincinnati, OH: South-Western, 2002. Chapter 4.

Goldstein, Sheldon D. *Superior Customer Satisfaction and Loyalty: Engaging Customers to Drive Performance.* Milwaukee, WI: ASQ Quality Press, 2010.

Insight Publishing Company. *Real World Customer Service Strategies That Work.* Sevierville, TN: Insight Publishing, 2004.

Newell, Frederick. *Loyalty.com: Customer Relationship Management in the New Era of Internet Marketing.* New York: McGraw-Hill, 2000.

Norausky, Patrick H. *The Customer and Supplier Innovation Team Guidebook.* Milwaukee, WI: ASQ Quality Press, 2000.

Pyzdek, Thomas, and Paul Keller. *The Handbook for Quality Management: A Complete Guide to Operational Excellence.* New York: McGraw-Hill, 2013. Chapter 6.

Schultz, Garry. *The Customer Care & Contact Center Handbook.* Milwaukee, WI: ASQ Quality Press, 2003.

Ulwick, Anthony. *What Customers Want: Using Outcome-Driven Innovation to Create Breakthrough Product and Services.* New York: McGraw-Hill, 2005.

Westcott, Russell T., ed. *The Certified Manager of Quality/Organizational Excellence Handbook.* 4th ed. Milwaukee, WI: ASQ Quality Press, 2014. Chapter 17.

Wilburn, Morris. *Managing the Customer Experience: A Measurement-Based Approach.* Milwaukee, WI: ASQ Quality Press, 2007.

Chapter 12
C. Supplier Management

> Identify supplier performance measures, including quality, price, delivery, and level of service. Describe commonly used metrics, including product defect rates, functional performance, and delivery timeliness; service or process responsiveness, and availability and competence of technical support. (Understand)
>
> **CQIA BoK 2014 IV.C.**

When a customer complains, consider getting down on your knees to offer profuse gratitude because that person has just provided you with priceless advice—free of charge.

Owen Harari, *Management Review*

Supply chain managers work hard to optimize their supply chains. Their main focus is to get products and services to market faster and better. The challenges are growing, however, as customers use new technologies to put even greater demands on suppliers.

Chief supply chain officers are responsible for the "mechanics" of planning, procurement, production, logistics and customer service—and, in many cases, for the receivables and payables of order-to-cash and procure-to-pay processes as well. They have to manage hundreds and thousands of employees and partners in their supply chain ecosystems. They are accountable for controlling costs and increasing efficiencies and productivity, while raising customer satisfaction to an all-time high by delivering the absolute perfect order. And they must do all of this in an environment that is changing rapidly and dramatically.

Given these heavy responsibilities, supply chain managers now urgently need to collaborate with an extensive network of suppliers, logistics providers, manufacturers, and other business partners. They must tap into analytical insights at almost every decision point and, ultimately, create customer-activated supply chains.

A supply chain is complex, made up of many suppliers located around the world, each of which has its own supply chain. The purpose of a supply chain is to place products and services timely and correctly in stores or at customer locations. The supply chain must be designed, directed, and managed as a process, not as a series of order and shipping transactions. Pushing bad logistics processes and practices up or down the supply chain disrupts the smooth flow of products and services. Three root cause areas for improving the overall performance of most supply chains are the following:

- Managing vendor performance is a critical requirement for reducing supply chain cycle time. Suppliers, at the supply chain source, have incredible impact on the supply chain as to time, inventory, and costs—impact that goes far beyond pricing and placing purchase orders. Visibility of purchase orders—at suppliers, in-transit, and at each step in the chain, from the vendor's plant to delivery at the warehouse, store, or customer—is vital.
- Integration up and down the supply chain, both external and internal, is mandatory. Non-integration adds to supply chain time and the lack of responsiveness and dead spots in the cycle time. Demand forecasting or other inventory planning is critical to provide customer requirements to suppliers for their build plans. Everyone should be working from the same data, information, and system or platform. Suppliers and customers must work together to integrate their interests across the entire production process. Sharing data, noncompetitive information, and services adds value to the overall flow of products and services for both customers and suppliers.
- Collaboration with key suppliers and service providers is essential. Work together as partners and be open to mutual exchange. Sending procedures and demanding compliance with requirements is not collaboration. Work to align the process between both parties so that it flows smoothly and within minimal time.

SUPPLIER PERFORMANCE MEASURES

Suppliers need to know how they are performing. This means that for suppliers providing products or services vital to quality, the customer must have a formal process for collecting, analyzing, and reporting supplier performance. Some common assessment and measurement tools for supplier performance are discussed in the following sections.

Questionnaires/Assessments

Suppliers may be asked to complete a survey about how their quality systems are designed and what plans for improvement have been developed. The customer may also conduct on-site assessments. Surveys are usually mailed or e-mailed.

Survey questionnaires may be used to assess prospective or new suppliers or to periodically reassess existing suppliers. Use of questionnaires is one of the ways suppliers are qualified for the customer's qualified supplier list. The same design comments and cautions that apply to customer surveys pertain here as well. The difference between supplier questionnaires and customer questionnaires is that the customer expects a 100% response from suppliers. Many suppliers begrudgingly fill out the questionnaires because not to do so would mean loss of business. Large customers sometimes require lengthy questionnaires of even their smallest suppliers, without considering the burden placed on the suppliers.

Product Data

Suppliers may be requested to provide product quality data from the pertinent production run with each delivery, which is used in place of formal verification by the customer. The customer may then analyze the data for compliance to specification as well as process stability and capability.

Delivery Performance

Supplier performance against delivery requirements (e.g., total number of days early and total late) is typically tracked and compared against order requirements.

Complaints

Tracking and reporting complaints about supplier performance is necessary in order to maintain suppliers' status on the qualified supplier list. An unacceptable number of complaints may result in a supplier's being suspended from the list, placed on probation, or totally removed. Usually a hierarchy of categories (types of reasons) is devised for use in coding complaints. The acceptance tolerance for number of complaints may vary depending on the category.

Corrective Actions

A problem that is reported to a supplier with a formal request for corrective action requires a tracking process for ensuring that the supplier responds. These records should be analyzed to determine whether the supplier has been timely in its responses as well as effective with its corrective actions. Customers typically track defect rates by individual supplier. Service level agreements may be established with critical suppliers to set limits for percentage of defective parts or products. Without good follow-up by the customer, some suppliers will tend to ignore corrective action requests. Making supplier action mandatory through contracts is a way to resolve this situation.

Product Price and Total Cost

Organizations continually try to reduce the cost of raw materials and services, or at least to minimize increases. The ability of suppliers to continually show progress in this arena is encouraged and tracked. Supplier management includes sharing of customer requirements among producers and suppliers for the purpose of achieving the highest value to the customer at the lowest cost across the supply chain.

The price of a service or product is influenced not only by the cost of components used to create the final deliverable but also by intangibles such as administrative costs, quality assurance, and profit margin required to sustain operations for both the producer and the supplier.

REPORTING OF SUPPLIER PERFORMANCE

Reporting of supplier performance is usually done on a regular basis (such as quarterly). Typical indices used in tracking supplier performance are the following:

- Past performance index
- Supplier performance index
- Commodity performance index
- On-time delivery performance index

CERTIFICATION AND SUPPLIER RATING

Some customers have programs for certifying qualified suppliers. Typically, certified suppliers have demonstrated their ability to consistently meet the customer's requirements over a period of time. Suppliers are rated on a predetermined scale that may include most of the measurements already noted, as well as others. As the supplier fulfills the time and rating requirements, it moves up through a two- or three-phase plan to full recognition as a certified supplier. The customer usually provides concessions to the certified supplier, such as no incoming inspection requirement, arrangements to ship directly to stock, a long-term purchasing contract, and "preferred supplier" status.

VALUE IN USING SUPPLIER PERFORMANCE DATA IN DRIVING CONTINUOUS IMPROVEMENT

Material and services from suppliers, when they are direct inputs to the product realization process, can substantially impact the quality of the product, customers' satisfaction, and profitability. Efforts to improve incoming material and services from suppliers (including their correctness, capability, completeness, accuracy, timeliness, and appearance) are often given less attention by the customer than the customer's own internal processes. It should be noted, though, that defective material and inadequate services just received have not yet incurred the added costs of the production process. When a product is rejected at any stage up to and including its use by an end user, *costs have been added at each stage in the cycle.* At any stage, including the failure of a product under warranty, the quality of the incoming material or services could be the real root cause of failure. The tendency of some customers to "work around" supplier deficiencies is no longer acceptable.

Initiatives to continually improve suppliers' performance are critical to build and sustain customers' confidence. As mentioned earlier, the emerging trend of greater collaboration between customers and their suppliers is opening new opportunities for improvement, often developing into partnerships and alliances.

CYCLE FOR IMPROVING CUSTOMER–SUPPLIER RELATIONSHIPS

Plan: Customer focus, a customer satisfaction feedback process design, and customer satisfaction improvement objectives constitute the "plan."

Do: Administration of the plan and collection of the data are the "do."

Check: Analysis of customer satisfaction data and supplier data, measurement against objectives, and identification of areas for improvement constitute the "check."

Act: Development of improvement action plans, implementation of the improvements, and assimilation of the improvements into daily operations are the "act."

The emergence of the focus on supply chain management (SCM) around the globe has created new challenges, but even greater opportunities for the use of existing quality techniques and tools.

THE PROCESS OF SUPPLY CHAINS[1]

While many managers may view SCM and logistics as interchangeable, this is not the case. Following are the current definitions as stated by noted experts:

- Logistics is the process of planning, implementing, and controlling the efficient, cost-effective flow and storage of raw materials, in-process inventory, finished goods, and related information from point-of-origin to point-of-consumption for the purpose of conforming to customer requirements.[2]
- SCM is a set of approaches utilized to efficiently integrate suppliers, manufacturers, warehouses, and stores so that merchandise is produced and distributed at the right quantities, to the right locations, and at the right time in order to minimize system-wide costs while satisfying service level requirements.[3]

Though the concept of SCM can be traced back to the early 1960s, it wasn't until some 35 years later that it became a serious topic of study and discussion outside academic and research circles. The initial supply chains, as they were identified by the National Council on Physical Distribution Management (NCPDM), were a two-factor endeavor: warehousing and transportation.[4]

The meteoric rise of Wal-Mart as the dominant player in the consumer retail marketplace can be tied to a strategy built on superior logistics on an integrated network of information—some of it organic, but most of it shared by an increasingly broad collection of partners. The migration from mainframe computers to networked servers, riding a worldwide web of communications infrastructure (phone lines at first, and then the broader reach of the internet), has resulted in a modern-day approach to SCM that leverages information technologies that operate on several levels. While this more robust approach is referred to as the "integrated SCM stage," others are advocating that the more optimal phrase should be "super-supply chain management."[5]

What is occurring with more frequency is a series of processes, regardless of location or functional responsibility, operating in concert, driven by electronic rather than physical cues. As a result, organizations need to pay more attention to the efficiency and effectiveness of the process steps and the intermediate and final outputs that do not necessarily have the "man in the loop" oversight.

These newer and more complex "process webs" cut across functional areas, making accountability, responsibility, and authority much more difficult to assign, track, and evaluate. As seen in Figure 12.1, there are many stakeholders (customers, suppliers, operators, strategic partners, etc.) in this "contact to cash" supply chain model. Referring back to the SCM definition presented earlier, this figure attempts to show the path to achieving a "perfect order."[6]

As demonstrated in Figure 12.1, what the customer expects from a supply chain and what businesses are attempting to achieve create a natural friction. These competing interests can become a positive or a negative, depending on how they are addressed. Efforts in continuous quality improvement over the past 30 years have effectively run their course within traditional silo functions. Most of the cycle times have been reduced within processes due to the application of qualitative and quantitative techniques such as lean, zero defects, total quality maintenance, and Six Sigma. So, now it is imperative that companies find the next set of challenges to pursue, using quality-based applications. The complex nature of multilevel and multiple player integrated supply chains is a prime target. The differences in sophistication between traditional quality systems and those in the emerging supplier management environment are presented in Figure 12.2.

The SCM-based processes have a series of inherent conflicts built in. This is primarily due to the constant interaction of internal and external customers, many

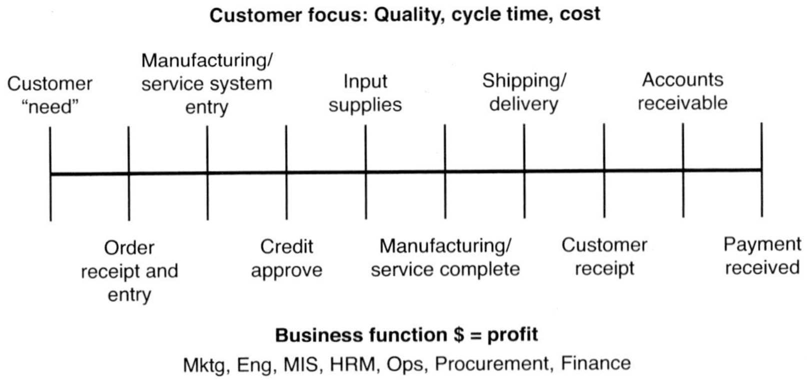

Figure 12.1 Supply chain-contact to cash process management (PM) capable.

Source: Reproduced by permission from G. D. Beecroft, G. L. Duffy, and J. W. Moran, *The Executive Guide to Improvement and Change* (Milwaukee, WI: ASQ Quality Press, 2003), 41.

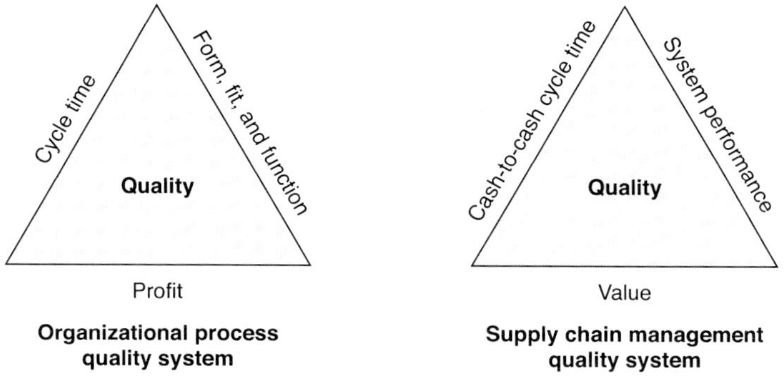

Figure 12.2 Traditional quality versus supply chain quality.

Source: Reproduced by permission from G. D. Beecroft, G. L. Duffy, and J. W. Moran, *The Executive Guide to Improvement and Change* (Milwaukee, WI: ASQ Quality Press, 2003), 41.

with competing interests and performance measures. Following is a representative sample of these conflicts, which can be referred to as supply chain tensions:

- Lot size versus inventory
- Inventory versus transportation
- Product lead time versus transportation
- Product variety versus inventory
- Cost versus service level

These opposites will likely never be fully optimized, but the use of proven and systematic improvement techniques can reduce the amount of negative impact. A pragmatic executive will realize that the goal is not perfection, but reduction in suboptimization of the entire "contact to cash" supply chain system. Effective supply chain system managers spend their time addressing these results. They use the same amount of time wasted on responding to conflict to rein in variability through process-management-based quality techniques.

Figure 12.3 illustrates where people focus their efforts in relation to leading SCM activities. While the quadrants are presented in a symmetric manner for purposes of discussion, this is rarely the case in evaluating supply chains in action.

Lean methodologies do indeed help to optimize these "opposites" by reviewing the total system's impact and then effecting the best balanced solution. Kanbans (see Chapter 8) balance lot size and inventory, just-in-time (JIT) (see Chapter 8) manages inventory and transportation, and so on. The utilization of lean processes is becoming ever more prevalent in both manufacturing and services to manage the optimization of these system conflicts

When managers find the majority of their time, energy, and resources going to quadrants I and II, supply chain system performance suffers and incidences of

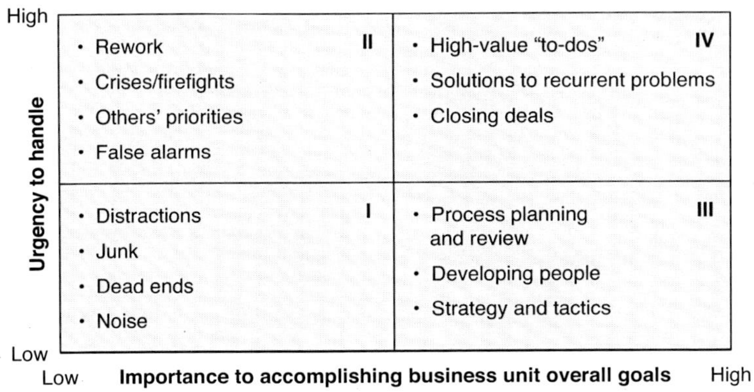

Figure 12.3 What people spend their time on in supply chain processes.
Source: Reproduced by permission from G. D. Beecroft, G. L. Duffy, and J. W. Moran, *The Executive Guide to Improvement and Change* (Milwaukee, WI: ASQ Quality Press, 2003), 43.

suboptimization increase. Symptoms of this reality can be found in the following areas:

- Stock-outs and/or higher inventories
- Increases in cash-to-cash cycle times
- Higher return rates
- Unpredictable operating costs
- Poor service levels—customer dissatisfaction
- Ineffective communication with suppliers at all stages of the supply chain

While these same symptoms are evident in traditional "out of control" business processes, the impacts are even more glaring in integrated supply chains (refer to Figure 12.2). The goal, then, is for managers to focus on activities in quadrants III and IV. As managers, we want to be proactive—designing, operating, and improving high-performing supply chain systems. However, day-to-day malfunctions drain us of the energy to work on the optimization issues presented in the model.

Figure 12.3 looks appealing, but the reality is that models don't magically appear in practical application. The first step in integrating the proactive supply chain is to identify the root causes of system nonperformance. The lack of a true supplier management approach can be categorized in three distinct areas: (1) Information Management, (2) Design and Strategy, and (3) Operational Control.

In evaluating information systems, not just computers, servers, and internet connections, we see some very glaring weaknesses in dysfunctional supply chain processes. For instance, the metrics are scattered at best, and measure the wrong indicators at worst. Typically, cycle time is measured within subprocesses and managed at functional levels. However, the idle time between processes is rarely tracked. Traditionally in organizations, managers are evaluated on the activities that occur within their functional span of control. For example, it takes the average automobile 15 days to travel from the factory to the dealer, but the actual time-in-motion is only one-third of this elapsed duration.[7] In sum, all applicable functional managers are focusing on their areas of responsibility. But who is watching the handoffs? Another deficiency in evaluating the performance metrics is found by inadequate definitions of supply chain service level. Since the breadth of the typical chain is so extensive, what qualifies as the standard in one stage rarely applies throughout. Again, this lack of standard operational definitions can be traced back to an overall lack of singular accountability from the beginning to the end of the process—from the contact of the need through to the point where the cash changes hands.

As to design and strategy, the overwhelming weakness in any supply chain relates to inventories. The advent of JIT, kanban, and the notion of the "lot size of one" have made inventory a chronic waste in many businesses. While there is little debate that increasing inventory turns ultimately reduces carrying costs, capturing true ordering costs has never been easy. While the advent of information technology is assisting development of more accurate supply chain cost structures, it remains a challenge, especially given the large number of variables from the raw materials stage through to final delivery. Idle time of work-in-process inventory is one example of the difficulty in capturing total inventory costs. Another weakness results from a contention by many managers that supply chains are primarily outgrowths of logistics and distribution networks. While transportation, handling, and other movement-related costs are significant, the back end of the process is where the real focus should be. Cash collection to complete the process typically takes 30–45 days, down from the nearly 90 days as recently as the early 1990s. Needless to say, there is ample room for reducing this cash-to-cash cycle even further. Recent advances in transparency and common access to supply chain databases between customers and suppliers is providing some reduction in turnaround time, but there is a long way to go.

Finally, we come to issues of operational control. The biggest hurdle is quantifying the impact of uncertainty and risk across the entire spectrum. From a lean perspective, the Value Stream Map (VSM) (Chapter 8) can be used to lay out the entire process flow from the incoming supply chain components, through on-site production, through product distribution across its various customer types. This analysis identifies where the business losses are being incurred. Given the complexity and numerous variables in play, the ability to perform effective analysis is difficult at best. The many handoffs, numerous internal players, and physical and cultural distances at work make monitoring and controlling an inexact science. Poor coordination between functional areas further exacerbates the problem. The lack of effective control results in bigger gaps between the ideal state and the level of suboptimization in the system.

Difficult problems require strong structures. In order to properly address the three root cause areas presented earlier—cycle time reduction, integration, and collaboration—the concept of process management becomes a driving force.

The ultimate goal of an effective supply chain is customer loyalty. The systematic nature of a process management system works well to address the potential weak links in the chain—strategy and design, information flow, and operational control. As we will see in the following section, there are tools that can assist senior leaders. These combine strategy and tactics, with a focus on organizing efforts around key operational objectives. At the decision-making level, the key to success lies in identifying important process variables and comparing them discretely in sets of two.

For example, Figure 12.4 creates a discussion for evaluating various potential distribution strategies with the factors that impact key supply chain performance criteria. For certain strategy-attribute combinations, there are potential benefits

For example: Distribution processes

Strategy attribute	Direct shipment	Cross docking	Inventory at warehouses
Risk pooling			Take advantage
Transportation costs		Reduced inbound costs	Reduced inbound costs
Holding costs	No warehouse costs	No holding costs	
Demand variability		Delayed allocation	Delayed allocation

Note: a blank box denotes there is insufficient "value" to pursuing a particular strategy–attribute combination.

Figure 12.4 Evaluating cross-functional SCM processes.

Source: Reproduced by permission from G. D. Beecroft, G. L. Duffy, and J. W. Moran, *The Executive Guide to Improvement and Change* (Milwaukee, WI: ASQ Quality Press, 2003), 45.

to be gained if included in the process design. Specifically, in the case of leveraging the distribution component of this particular chain, cross-docking (the movement of in-transit goods between containers at distribution points) can result in the elimination of holding costs. If the inventories in question come with significant holding costs (e.g., cold storage), keeping them in motion through to the final point of delivery may realize considerable savings. This may be desirable in some but not all applications. The results of evaluating process variables tied to performance outcomes better define the scope of the supply chain.

Once performance variables are defined, evaluated, and selected at the macro process level, carrying the "message" down to the execution stages becomes easier. When the manager in charge of supplier qualification works with the supplier to develop the sequence of activities to achieve the particular process objectives, the potential supplier will have to demonstrate ability to cross-dock when it comes to cold storage items. The resulting information flow and control points (process metrics) will be easier to establish and stay tied to the higher-level core process.

At the micro process level, the technicians who carry out their duties and responsibilities should have no doubt as to the outcome if the system of processes is in alignment. Focusing on the inventory management core process, consider the example of a contract with a supplier that provides refrigerated goods. In this case, one of the key measures of performance becomes the use of cross-docking to ensure that *no carrying costs* are incurred during the life cycle of goods from this supplier. The fulfillment of this metric, along with any other pertinent measures, is reported back up through the next higher-level processes. Taken in the aggregate, all micro processes, if planned from the top down and executed from the bottom up, will ultimately perform with more consistency and be in alignment with the overarching goals and objectives of the systems, creating a "value chain." The reason is fairly simple. Design of processes is tied to strategy, and the operational and tactical execution occurs as a natural outcome of the planning. Feedback focuses on the key performance measures at each process level, with operational control in the hands of the appropriate experts. For those organizations that have undertaken process management approaches to supply chain design, measurement, and control, the gains are impressive and will be discussed at the end of this chapter.

In recent years, the number one reason for the increased focus on SCM as a strategic competitive advantage is the enhancement of information technologies (IT) as an underlying enabler. Simply stated, the ability to turn data into information and leverage it as knowledge in complex environments is the engine of the "new economy." If the premise is accepted that SCM is a key to future business success, it is important to understand how IT fits.

One of the largest problems in the IT-SCM merger is misalignment. Enterprise Resource Planning (ERP) software is the standard by which SCM is measured. Business literature is overflowing with case studies of ERP implementations at companies of all sizes. Some tout the value of these centralized databases as the driver of success. On the other side is an equal number of negative incidences where companies were literally brought to their knees, ultimately scrapping IT investments running into the hundreds of millions of dollars. Why the disparity? How can one company achieve breakthrough success with its ERP system, and yet others suffer devastating economic and market loss through implementation of the same software? The answer lies in preparation and a full understanding of the needs of the process flow.

Before an organization invests in ERP-driven IT, its senior leadership must understand the nature of its supply chain. Figure 12.5 provides a way of analyzing supply chain complexity with IT capability.

In his article "Demystifying Supply Chain Management," Peter Metz identifies five key success factors that enable continuing SCM accomplishments:[8]

1. an overriding customer focus;
2. use of cross-functional teams;
3. attention to human factors and organizational dynamics;
4. quantitatively based performance management; and
5. advanced use of IT.

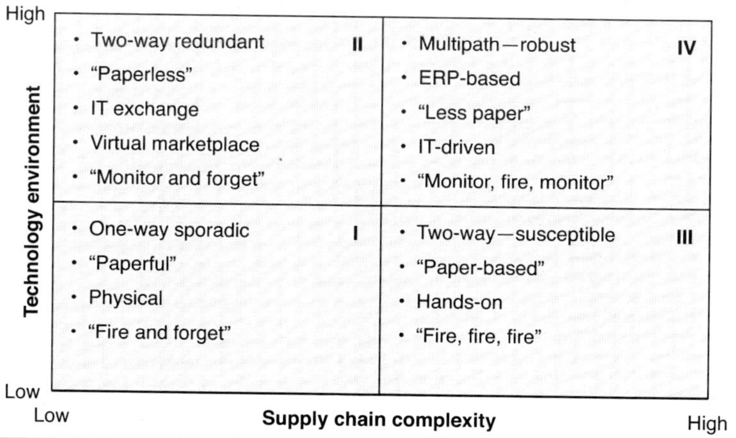

Figure 12.5 Supply chain communication from management.

Source: Reproduced by permission from G. D. Beecroft, G. L. Duffy, and J. W. Moran, *The Executive Guide to Improvement and Change* (Milwaukee, WI: ASQ Quality Press, 2003), 47.

The ability to master the fifth factor drives the first four factors. Take, for instance, the cross-functional nature of supply chain operations, with both physical and virtual teams working together on the design, operation, and control of supply chain activities. During the 1960s, 1970s, 1980s, and well into the 1990s, individual members of supplier management teams were limited by the many legacy (multiple functional database) IT systems. In many cases, similar data were in conflict or difficult to reconcile, making them unusable. With the advent of ERP and internet technologies, team members can focus on using their functional expertise to share and evaluate common information from various perspectives. As a result, the design, operation, and control activities become better defined and managed.

Similarly, customer relationship management (CRM) and organizational dynamics can gain by the use of IT systems. The breaking down, itemizing, and correlating of data is invaluable in deriving root cause. Computer power allows marketing and HR analysts the freedom to envision multiple what-if scenarios, making assumptions, rearranging variables, comparing results, assigning risk, and, ultimately, customizing supply chain activities to better maximize returns to both internal and external customers.

Finally, IT can assist in the "management by fact" focus of SCM. Previously, metrics were managed and reported at the functional level. Manufacturing, distribution, and transportation managers drove operational data, with a focus on evaluating the operations function. Likewise, marketing and sales leaders maintained their vigilance over market share and customer satisfaction indices. At the other end of the spectrum, accounting and finance professionals kept busy determining the flows of the accounts receivable and payable. All of these are critical performance measures, but they are truly enhanced when the discrete measures are integrated into a systematic decision-making process.

KEY SUPPLY CHAIN METRICS

Figure 12.6 establishes the key metrics for integrated SCM. The supply chain operations reference (SCOR) model offers three key result areas, each with specific system metrics and their corresponding units of measure. With a balance between efficiency and effectiveness, the SCOR model brings together two of Metz's five factors directly, with the other three receiving indirect benefits. Additionally, the SCM definition of "quality" becomes possible with this merger of measurement and technology. Going back to process management, upstream and downstream design, operation, and control is tied to one evaluation platform, via centralized IT and integrated performance measures.

At this point we can look at Figure 12.7, a two-by-two matrix that is ideally suited to determine two aspects of SCM performance. First, senior leaders can evaluate current conditions and get a sense of whether the chain is properly aligned (e.g., are the measures appropriate for the level of supply chain sophistication?). The second and more important benefit is validating what attributes are best suited for supply chain performance management as the chain moves forward. Figure 12.7 provides general guidelines for these two evaluations.

For example, a firm that is low in its use of quality tools and techniques in its SCM but is fortunate to be in a low-complexity environment would be well served

Key result areas	Metrics	Unit of measure
Supply chain reliability	• On-time delivery • Order fulfillment lead time • Fill rate • Perfect order fulfillment	• Percentage • Days • Percentage • Percentage
Flexibility and responsiveness	• Supply chain response time • Production flexibility	• Days • Percentage
Assets/utilization	• Total inventory days of supply • Cash-to-cash cycle time • Net asset turns	• Days • Days • Turns

Figure 12.6 Supply chain operations reference (SCOR) model.

Source: Reproduced by permission from G. D. Beecroft, G. L. Duffy, and J. W. Moran, *The Executive Guide to Improvement and Change* (Milwaukee, WI: ASQ Quality Press, 2003), 49.

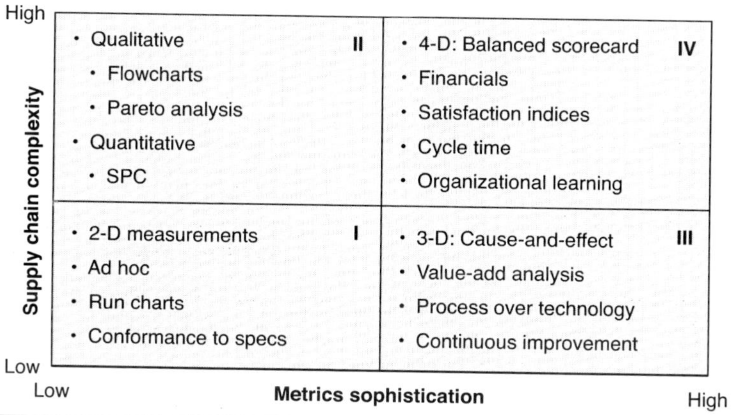

Figure 12.7 Supply chain performance management.

Source: Reproduced by permission from G. D. Beecroft, G. L. Duffy, and J. W. Moran, *The Executive Guide to Improvement and Change* (Milwaukee, WI: ASQ Quality Press, 2003), 50.

to focus on moving from quadrant I to quadrant II instead of trying to stretch into quadrant III or quadrant IV. Eventually, the chain may increase in breadth and depth, necessitating the addition of more robust quality methodologies. In contrast, those organizations with increasing supply chain complexity but that are relatively unsophisticated in their ability to measure, control, and improve will face increasing risk of suboptimization and ultimately supply chain failure.

A properly aligned supply chain has incredible value to those firms engaged in its operations. The model presented in Figure 12.8 is the essence of Deming's exhortation to senior leaders (constancy of purpose, profound knowledge, and continuous improvement). Metz admits that it's not a matter of "rocket science," but rather science and art of due diligence.[9]

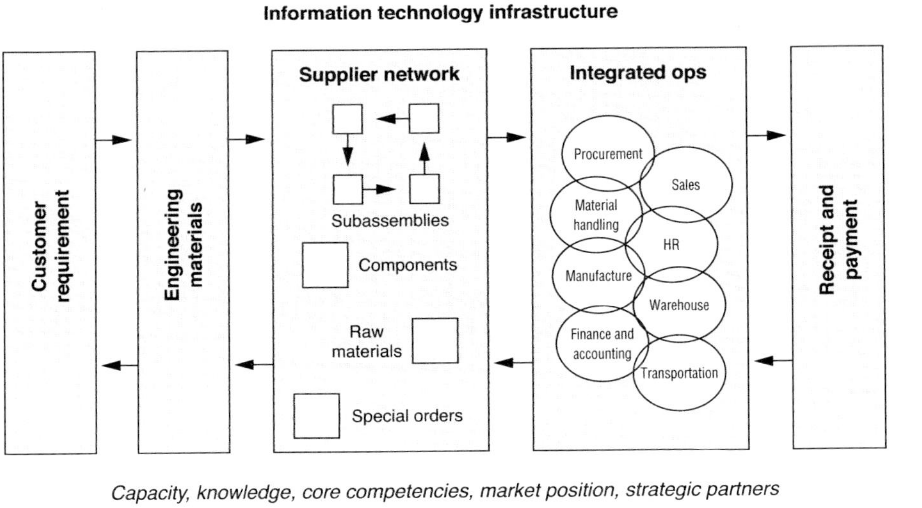

Figure 12.8 Integrated supply chain model.

Source: Reproduced by permission from G. D. Beecroft, G. L. Duffy, and J. W. Moran, *The Executive Guide to Improvement and Change* (Milwaukee, WI: ASQ Quality Press, 2003), 51.

SUMMARY

The key to successful supplier management is to establish an effective system of planning, communication, and measurement. The tools are only as useful as the understanding of the issues. A global supply chain in the automotive industry is no more valuable or better than a local chain that gets the wheat to the local grinding mill and the flour to the local baker and the piping hot bagels to the morning's customers. As long as the tools and rules fit the situation, the SCM is appropriate.

SCM rises or falls on three components—design, operations, and control—all ideally suited for the application of proven "soft" and "hard" quality tools.

NOTES

1. Significant amounts of material in this section are derived from Mike Ensby, "Supply Chain Management," in *The Executive Guide to Improvement and Change*, edited by G. Dennis Beecroft, Grace L. Duffy, and John W. Moran (Milwaukee, WI: ASQ Quality Press, 2003).
2. Council of Supply Chain Management Professionals, http://cscmp.org/search/node/Logistics.
3. David Simchi-Levi, Philip Kaminsky, and Edith Simchi-Levi, *Designing and Managing the Supply Chain: Concepts, Strategies, and Case Studies* (Boston: Irwin McGraw-Hill, 2000), 1.
4. Peter J. Metz, "Demystifying Supply Chain Management," *Supply Chain Management Review* (Winter 1998), 2.
5. Ibid., 3.
6. Donald J. Bowersox, David J. Closs, and M. Bixby Cooper, *Supply Chain Logistics Management* (Boston: Irwin McGraw-Hill, 2002), 3.

7. Simchi-Levi, Kaminsky, Simchi-Levi, *Designing and Managing the Supply Chain*, 5.
8. Metz, "Demystifying Supply Chain Management," 4.
9. Metz, "Demystifying Supply Chain Management."

ADDITIONAL RESOURCES

Bossert, J. L., ed. *The Supplier Management Handbook.* 6th ed. Milwaukee, WI: ASQ Quality Press, 2004.

Bowersox, Donald J., David J. Closs, and M. Bixby Cooper, *Supply Chain Logistics Management.* Boston: Irwin McGraw-Hill, 2002.

Brassard, Michael, and Diane Ritter. *Sailing through Six Sigma: How the Power of People Can Perfect Processes and Drive Down Costs.* Marietta, GA: Brassard & Ritter, 2001.

Lawrence, F. Barry, Ramesh Krishnamurthi, and Norm Clark. *Performance Metric for a Connected Supply Chain.* Review of the Electronic and Industrial Distribution Industries, The NEDA Education Foundation, Vol. 1, No. 1, 2002, pp. 139–161.

Metz, Peter J. "Demystifying Supply Chain Management," *Supply Chain Management Review* (Winter 1998), Russell, J. P., ed. *The ASQ Supply Chain Management Primer.* Milwaukee, WI: ASQ Quality Press, 2013.

Russell, J. P., ed., and ASQ's Customer-Supplier Division. *The ASQ Supply Chain Management Primer.* Milwaukee, WI: ASQ Quality Press, 2013.

Simchi-Levi, David, Philip Kaminsky, and Edith Simchi-Levi, *Designing and Managing the Supply Chain: Concepts, Strategies, and Case Studies.* Boston: Irwin McGraw-Hill, 2000.

Part V

System Integration

Chapter 13
The Organization as a System

INTRODUCTION

An organization's system consists of the parts, functions, and subsystems integrated to accomplish an overall organizational goal. The system has various inputs that are acted on by designated processes to produce outputs, which together achieve the desired goal for the system. For example, consider an organization of many administrative and management functions: product and service departments, support staffs, work groups, and individuals. Changing one part of the system often changes the overall system.

The goal of any organization is to build a high-performance system that continually exchanges operational feedback among its various parts. This constant exchange of information ensures that activities remain closely aligned and focused on achieving the organization's goals. If the performance monitoring process indicates that any of the system's processes or activities have become misaligned, the system must make necessary adjustments to achieve its goals more efficiently.

Duffy, in her book *Modular Kaizen*, emphasizes the interconnectedness of processes into a whole system and identifies the impact that improvement and change will have not only on an individual process but on the fabric of the complete system.[1] The focus is on initial planning to stress the criticality of taking a broad view of the organization and how its individual parts work together to meet the projected outcomes the customer should experience.

A VIEW OF THE ORGANIZATION'S SYSTEM

The persons seeking to improve productivity were aware of the importance of a systems approach for a long time. At the turn of the twentieth century, Frederick Taylor stressed the scientific view of managing the organization by breaking the production process down into individual tasks and standardizing as much as possible to increase productivity. His approach was to keep the worker focused solely at the task level, while management had the responsibility to see that individual tasks were woven together into an efficient flow to meet customer needs.

Later, during and directly after World War II, Dr. Joseph Juran described process improvement as a top-down approach, starting with the overall system to meet the declared need of the user. Juran recognized that processes are made up of many subprocesses and all the individual components are managed through planning, control, and improvement. Each improvement project is managed as one segment of the aggregated organizational processes.

Beginning in the 1980s, Geary Rummler insisted that the place to begin work in an organization is with an organization model and a high-level process architecture. Paul Harmon produced a generic organization model (Figure 13.1) incorporating the concept and issues attributed to Rummler. This model enabled an improvement team to identify the high-level processes and connect them with flow arrows to various external stakeholders. This transparency of process involvement from top management to frontline worker emphasized workforce engagement and clear alignment of daily work to overall organizational performance.

At a minimum, this transparency ensured that everyone in the organization knew exactly what was being discussed when the team focused on a process, such as the "sell widgets" process in Figure 13.1. Note the generic labeling to identify inputs to the organization: people, capital, technology, and materials. The figure shows a hypothetical diagram of operations for an organization making widgets. Although many organizations are now in the service sector, the

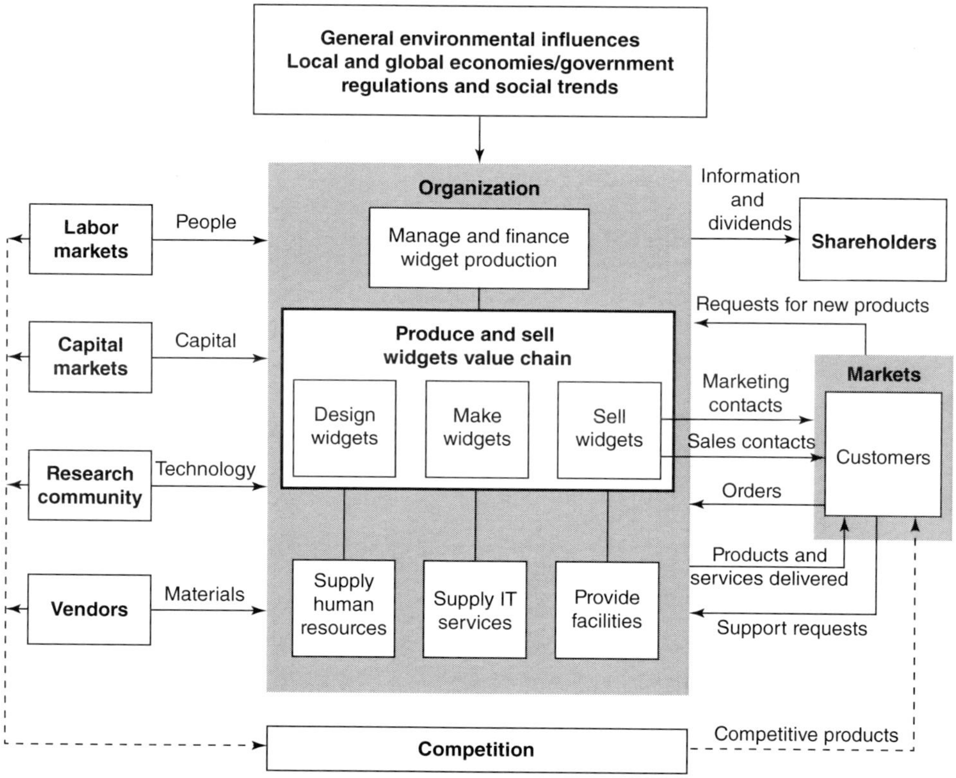

Figure 13.1 A Rummler-type organization model.

Source: Reproduced by permission from G. L. Duffy, *Modular Kaizen* (Milwaukee, WI: ASQ Quality Press, 2014), 44.

concepts are the same. For example, the value chain for a healthcare organization could be:

1. Assess population needs
2. Plan services to meet identified needs
3. Provide services
4. Validate effectiveness through feedback

The organization model was very important to Rummler because he worked primarily with business executives and this was a perfect way to get businesspeople talking about how their organizations worked.[2]

SYSTEM VERSUS PROCESS

When applied to a complex organization such as a corporation or multinational company, systems thinking means focusing on the organization as a whole—and transforming it as a whole—rather than merely paying attention to its individual parts or departments. By focusing on the entire system, solutions can be identified that address as many problems as possible. The positive effect of these solutions leverages improvements throughout the system.

In systems thinking it is vital to identify and examine the interrelationships of the organization's various subsystems and processes. For one subsystem to be improved to the detriment of other subsystems or the overall system is referred to as suboptimization. Balance and alignment across the organization are crucial.

Systems thinking is not about copying other people's best practices. It requires studying the process, testing the process against customer requirements, and reinventing it or readapting it to meet the particular requirements of each new situation. The foundation of systems thinking is continuous improvement and cooperation, not competition among different parts of the organization. The systems outlook is long term rather than short term.

TAKING A SYSTEMS VIEW OF IMPROVEMENT

Certified Quality Improvement Associates should have basic knowledge in each of seven areas identified by these questions:

1. Is the need for alignment of all functions and processes with organizational strategic goals and plans ongoing?
2. How effectively is the organization organized and managed?
3. How are the organization's processes designed, integrated, and operated for optimum performance to meet customers' expectations?
4. How are organizational changes planned and implemented, and the outcomes assessed?
5. How are organizational and individual performance measurements designed and implemented and the results effectively utilized over time?

6. How are process improvements planned, implemented, measured, and assessed for effectiveness?
7. Are the most feasible technologies and quality improvement tools effectively employed to facilitate improvements within the organization's system?

Dr. Juran's concept of Big Q versus little q is illustrated in Table 13.1 as Big "QI" and Little "qi," where "I" and "i" indicate "improvement." This concept appeared in the second edition of Juran's *Planning for Quality.*

Table 13.1 shows how levels of a continuum of quality improvement relate to Big "QI," little "qi," and individual "qi." The *Meso* level (addressed with tools such as QFD and Lean-Six Sigma) acts as an overlay or middle ground between the *Macro* and *Micro* levels as a deployment transition from organizational to unit-specific projects. Table 13.1 also suggests the use of basic and advanced tools of quality within the scope of the organization versus unit activities.

Quality improvement is a never-ending process that pervades the organization when fully implemented. Top organizational leaders address the quality of the system at a macro level (Big Q). In the middle, professional staff members attack problems in programs or service areas by improving particular processes (little q). At the individual level, staff members seek ways of improving their own behaviors and environments (individual q).[3]

When starting a quality journey, organizations tend to embrace little q, which means striving for quality in a limited or specific improvement project or area.

Table 13.1 Quality improvement at three levels.

Topic	Big "QI"—organization-wide	Little "qi"—program/unit	Individual "qi"
System level ⟶ **Quality tools** ⟶	*Macro* *Meso* **Advanced** **QFD/Lean-Six Sigma**	*Micro*	*Individual*
Improvement	System focus	Specific project focus	Daily work level focus
Quality improvement planning	Tied to the strategic plan	Program/unit level	Tied to yearly individual performance
Evaluation of quality processes	Responsiveness to a community need	Performance of a process over time	Performance of daily work
Analysis of processes	Cut across all programs and activities	Delivery of a service	Daily work
Quality improvement goals	Strategic plan	Individual program/unit level plans	Individual performance plans

Source: Reproduced by permission from R. Bialek, G. Duffy, and J. Moran, *Modular Kaizen: Dealing with Disruptions* (Washington, DC: Public Health Foundation, 2011), 49.

Little q can be viewed as a tactical approach to implementing quality and beginning to generate a culture of quality improvement within the organization.

Exploring the CQIA Body of Knowledge (BoK) segment by segment is a typical method for beginning to grasp the individual elements. However, it has one drawback: The BoK in its entirety represents a basic system of knowledge about what constitutes quality and how quality improvement should be addressed. During the time the BoK is initially studied, or shortly thereafter, the reader should begin to formulate hypothetical scenarios or think of work situations where two or more of the BoK segments are interrelated. While the BoK was initially viewed in stand-alone segments, it should now be viewed as one integrated system. Every segment is related in some way with one or more other segments. For example:

> An organization is experiencing customer complaints about the quality of a product or service delivered. The primary concern is "customer satisfaction and retention." In analyzing for the root cause of the problem, specific data must be collected, analyzed (transformed into information), and applied in an improvement action. A four-person team is formed to design and implement an improved process. No team training is done. Because of the conflict developing with team members' time allocation between their primary job and the team, the team is having difficulty coalescing into a focused, viable entity. However, two team members have pushed on to surface some critical information. Multiple suppliers of a key input are utilized, and one supplier has been found to be furnishing a poor-quality item. Incoming inspection has failed to identify the defectives. Using special-cause analysis, certain employees in one of the subsystem processes have been observed "working around" the item when it is found to be substandard.

Without going further, the scenario has taken the reader into every segment of the BoK, and into details of several segments. This brief excursion should demonstrate the value of asking about the applicability of all the BoK segments when approaching an improvement opportunity.

NOTES

1. Grace Duffy, *Modular Kaizen* (Milwaukee, WI: ASQ Quality Press, 2014).
2. Paul Harmon, "Architecture and Process Management," *BPTrends*, April 10, 2012.
3. G. Duffy, J. Moran, and W. Riley, *Quality Function Deployment and Lean-Six Sigma Applications in Public Health* (Milwaukee, WI: ASQ Quality Press, 2010).

Appendix A
The Certified Quality Improvement Associate (CQIA) Body of Knowledge—2014

The topics in this Body of Knowledge include subtext explanations and the cognitive level at which the questions will be written. This information will provide useful guidance for both the Exam Development Committee and the candidate preparing to take the exam. The subtext is not intended to limit the subject matter or be all-inclusive of material that will be covered in the exam. It is meant to clarify the type of content that will be included on the exam. The descriptor in parentheses at the end of each entry refers to the maximum cognitive level at which the topic will be tested. A complete description of cognitive levels is provided at the end of this section.

I. Quality Concepts (30 Questions)

A. Terms, concepts, and principles

1. Quality

Define quality and use this term correctly in various circumstances. (Apply)

2. Quality plan

Define a quality plan, describe its purpose for the organization as a whole, and identify the various functional areas and people that have responsibility for contributing to its development. (Understand)

3. Employee involvement and empowerment

Define and distinguish between employee involvement and employee empowerment, and describe the benefits of both concepts. (Understand)

4. Systems and processes

Define and distinguish between a system and a process and describe the interrelationships between them. Describe the components of a system—supplier, input, process, output, customer (SIPOC)—and how these components impact the system as a whole. (Analyze)

5. Variation

Define and distinguish between common and special cause variation in relation to quality measures. (Understand)

B. Benefits of quality

Describe how using quality techniques to improve processes, products and services can benefit all parts of an organization. Describe what quality means to various stakeholders (e.g., employees, organization, customers, suppliers, community) and how each can benefit from quality. (Understand)

C. Quality philosophies

Describe and distinguish between the following theories and philosophies. (Remember)

1. The Shewhart cycle: plan, do, check, act (PDCA)
2. Deming's 14 points
3. The Juran trilogy
4. The Ishikawa diagram
5. Crosby's zero defects

II. Team Basics (20 Questions)

A. Team organization

1. Team purpose

Describe why teams are an effective way to identify and solve problems, and describe when, where, why, and how teams can be used more effectively than other groups of workers. (Apply)

2. Types of teams

Define and distinguish between various types of teams: process or continuous improvement teams, workgroups or workcells, self-managed teams, temporary or ad hoc project teams, and cross-functional teams. (Apply)

3. Value of teams

Identify how a team's efforts can support an organization's key strategies and effect positive change throughout the organization. (Understand)

B. Roles and responsibilities

Describe the roles and responsibilities of various team stakeholders. (Understand)

1. Sponsor
2. Champion
3. Facilitator
4. Leader
5. Member

C. Team formation and group dynamics

1. Initiating teams

Apply the elements of launching and sustaining a successful team, including establishing a clear purpose and goals, developing ground rules and schedules, gaining support from management and commitment from the team members. (Apply)

2. Selecting team members

Describe how to select team members based on their knowledge and skill sets and team logistics, such as a sufficient number of members in relation to the size or scope of the project, appropriate representation from affected departments or areas, and diversity. (Apply)

3. Team stages

Describe the classic stages of team evolution: forming, storming, norming, and performing. (Understand)

4. Team conflict

Describe the value of team conflict and recognize how to resolve it. Define and describe groupthink and how to overcome it, understand how poor logistics, agendas and lack of training become barriers to team success. (Analyze)

5. Team decision-making

Describe and use different decision-making models such as voting (majority rule, multi-voting) and consensus, and use follow up techniques to clarify the issue to be decided, to confirm agreement on the decision, and to come to closure on the decision made. (Apply)

III. Continuous Improvement Techniques (30 Questions)

A. Continuous improvement

Define and use continuous improvement tools and techniques. (Understand)

1. Brainstorming
2. Plan-do-check-act (PDCA) cycle
3. Affinity diagrams
4. Cost of quality
5. Internal audits to identify improvement opportunities

B. Process improvement

1. Six sigma

Identify key six sigma concepts and tools, including the different roles and responsibilities of green belts and black belts, typical project types that are appropriate for six sigma techniques, and the DMAIC phases: design, measure, analyze, improve, and control. (Understand)

2. Lean

Identify lean tools that are used to reduce waste, including set-up and cycle-time reduction, pull systems (kanban), kaizen, just-in-time (JIT), 5S, and value stream mapping. (Understand)

3. Benchmarking

Define benchmarking and describe how it can be used to develop and support best practices. (Understand)

4. Incremental and breakthrough improvement

Describe and distinguish between these two types of improvements, the steps required for each, and the type of situation in which either type would be expected. (Understand)

C. Quality improvement tools

Select, interpret, and apply the seven basic quality tools. (Apply)

1. Flowcharts
2. Histograms
3. Pareto charts
4. Scatter diagrams
5. Cause and effect diagrams
6. Check sheets
7. Control charts

Describe and interpret basic control chart concepts, including centerlines, control limits, out-of-control conditions.

IV. Customer-Supplier Relations (20 Questions)

A. Internal and external customers and suppliers

Distinguish between internal and external customers and suppliers. Describe their impact on products, services, and processes, and identify strategies for working with them to make improvements. (Understand)

B. Customer satisfaction

Describe different types of customer feedback mechanisms (formal surveys, informal feedback, official complaints) and describe the importance of using data from these and other sources to drive continuous improvement. (Understand)

C. Supplier management

Identify supplier performance measures, including quality, price, delivery, and level of service. Describe commonly used metrics, including product defect rates, functional performance, and delivery timeliness; service or process responsiveness, and availability and competence of technical support. (Understand)

Levels of Cognition

Based on Bloom's Taxonomy—Revised (2001)

In addition to **content** specifics, the subtext for each topic in this BOK also indicates the intended **complexity level** of the test questions for that topic. These levels are based on "Levels of Cognition" (from Bloom's Taxonomy—Revised, 2001) and are presented below in rank order, from least complex to most complex.

Remember. Recall or recognize terms, definitions, facts, ideas, materials, patterns, sequences, methods, principles, etc.

Understand. Read and understand descriptions, communications, reports, tables, diagrams, directions, regulations, etc.

Apply. Know when and how to use ideas, procedures, methods, formulas, principles, theories, etc.

Analyze. Break down information into its constituent parts and recognize their relationship to one another and how they are organized; identify sublevel factors or salient data from a complex scenario.

Evaluate. Make judgments about the value of proposed ideas, solutions, etc., by comparing the proposal to specific criteria or standards.

Create. Put parts or elements together in such a way as to reveal a pattern or structure not clearly there before; identify which data or information from a complex set is appropriate to examine further or from which supported conclusions can be drawn.

Appendix B
The ASQ Code of Ethics

Fundamental Principles

ASQ requires its members and certification holders to conduct themselves ethically by:

1. Being honest and impartial in serving the public, their employers, customers, and clients.
2. Striving to increase the competence and prestige of the quality profession, and
3. Using their knowledge and skill for the enhancement of human welfare.

Members and certification holders are required to observe the tenets set forth below:

Relations with the Public

Article 1—Hold paramount the safety, health, and welfare of the public in the performance of their professional duties.

Relations with Employers, Customers, and Clients

Article 2—Perform services only in their areas of competence.

Article 3—Continue their professional development throughout their careers and provide opportunities for the professional and ethical development of others.

Article 4—Act in a professional manner in dealings with ASQ staff and each employer, customer or client.

Article 5—Act as faithful agents or trustees and avoid conflict of interest and the appearance of conflicts of interest.

Relations with Peers

Article 6—Build their professional reputation on the merit of their services and not compete unfairly with others.

Article 7—Assure that credit for the work of others is given to those to whom it is due.

Appendix C
Quality Glossary

Note: Some items appear in the glossary that are not discussed in the book.

A

A-B-C analysis—A systematic collection and analysis of the observation of an individual's behavior or that of a work group for the purpose of determining the cause of specific behaviors. (A = antecedent [the trigger], B = behavior, and C = consequences)

acceptable quality level (AQL)—The quality level that is the worst tolerable process average when a continuing series of lots is submitted for acceptance sampling.

acceptance sampling—Inspection of a sample from a lot to decide whether to accept or not accept that lot. There are two types: attributes sampling and variables sampling. In attributes sampling, the presence or absence of a characteristic is noted in each of the units inspected. In variables sampling, the numerical magnitude of a characteristic is measured and recorded for each inspected unit; this involves reference to a continuous scale of some kind.

accuracy—A characteristic of measurement that addresses how close an observed value is to the true value. It answers the question, "Is it right?"

ACSI—The American Customer Satisfaction Index is an economic indicator, a cross-industry measure of the satisfaction of US household customers with the quality of the goods and services available to them—both those goods and services produced within the United States and those provided as imports from foreign firms.

action plan—A detailed plan to implement the actions needed to achieve strategic goals and objectives (similar to, but not as comprehensive as, a project plan).

activity network diagram (AND)—*See* arrow diagram.

ad hoc team—*See* temporary/ad hoc team.

affinity diagram—A management and planning tool used to organize ideas into natural groupings in a way that stimulates new, creative ideas.

alignment—The actions taken to ensure that a process or activity allows traceability from an action level upward to support the organization's strategy, goals, and objectives.

alliance—*See* partnership/alliance.

alpha risk—*See* producer's risk.

analogies—A technique used to generate new ideas by translating concepts from one application to another.

analysis of variance (ANOVA)—A basic statistical technique for analyzing experimental data. It subdivides the total variation of a data set into meaningful component parts associated with specific sources of variation in order to test a hypothesis on the parameters of the model or to estimate variance components. There are three models: fixed, random, and mixed.

andon board—A visual device (usually lights) displaying status alerts that can be easily seen by those who should respond.

ANSI—An abbreviation for the American National Standards Institute.

AOQ—*See* average outgoing quality (AOQ).

appraisal costs—The costs associated with measuring, evaluating, or auditing products or services to ensure conformance to quality standards and performance requirements.

AQL—*See* acceptable quality level (AQL).

arrow diagram—A management and planning tool used to develop the best possible schedule and appropriate controls to accomplish the schedule; the critical path method (CPM) and the program evaluation review technique (PERT) expand the use of arrow diagrams.

assessment—An estimate or determination of the significance, importance, or value of an event, organization, process, practice, metric, product, and so on.

assignable cause—*See* special causes.

attribute data—Data that result from counting the number of occurrences or items in a single category of similar items or occurrences. The control charts based on attribute data include fraction defective chart, number of affected units chart, count chart, count-per-unit chart, quality score chart, and demerit chart.

audit—A planned, independent, and documented assessment to determine whether agreed-upon requirements are being met.

audit program—The organized structure, commitment, and documented methods used to plan and perform audits.

audit team—The group of trained individuals conducting an audit under the direction of a lead auditor, relevant to a particular product, process, service, contract, or project.

auditee—The individual or organization being audited.

auditor—An individual or organization carrying out an audit.

autonomation—Features and controls used in production to stop the process if a defect is produced. The Japanese term for this is "jidoka."

average—*See* mean.

average outgoing quality (AOQ)—The expected average quality level of outgoing product or service for a given value of incoming product or service quality.

B

balance sheet—A financial statement showing the assets, liabilities, and owner's equity of a business entity.

balanced scorecard—Translates an organization's mission and strategy into a comprehensive set of performance measures to provide a basis for strategic measurement and management, typically using four balanced views: financial, customers, internal business processes, and learning and growth.

Baldrige Performance Excellence Program (BPEP)—An award established by Congress in 1987, and the criteria published in 1988, to raise awareness of quality management and to recognize US companies that have implemented successful quality management systems. The accompanying *Criteria for Performance Excellence* is updated frequently. Three awards may be given annually in each of five categories: manufacturing businesses, service businesses, small businesses, education institutions, and healthcare organizations. The award is named after the late secretary of commerce Malcolm Baldrige, a proponent of quality management. The US Commerce Department's National Institute of Standards and Technology manages the award, and the American Society for Quality administers it. The major emphasis in determining success is achieving results. The first award was made in 1988.

baseline measurement—The beginning point, based on an evaluation of the output over a period of time, used to determine the process parameters prior to any improvement effort; the basis against which change is measured.

benchmarking—An improvement process in which a company measures its performance against that of best-in-class companies (or others that are good performers), determines how those companies achieved their performance levels, and uses the information to improve its own performance. The areas that can be benchmarked include strategies, operations, processes, and procedures.

benefit-cost analysis—Collection of the dollar value of benefits derived from an initiative and the associated costs incurred and computing the ratio of benefits to cost.

beta risk—Type 2 error; the possibility that a bad product will be accepted by a consumer. *See also* consumer's risk.

bias—An effect that causes a statistical result to be distorted; that is, there is a difference between the true value and the observed value.

Big Q, little q—Terms used to contrast the difference between managing for quality in all business processes and products (Big Q) and managing for quality in a limited capacity (little q).

Black Belt—Full-time leader responsible for implementing Six Sigma process improvement projects using pertinent methodologies such as DMAIC, design of experiments, and others. Usually a Black Belt trains Green Belts and often serves a two-year assignment overseeing 8–10 Six Sigma projects.

Bloom's taxonomy—A hierarchy of terms categorizing levels of cognition. The levels are:

- **Remember** Recall or recognize terms, definitions, facts, ideas, materials, patterns, sequences, methods, principles, etc.
- **Understand** Read and understand descriptions, communications, reports, tables, diagrams, directions, regulations, etc.
- **Apply** Know when and how to use ideas, procedures, methods, formulas, principles, theories, etc.
- **Analyze** Break down information into its constituent parts and recognize their relationship to one another and how they are organized; identify sublevel factors or salient data from a complex scenario.

- **Evaluate** Make judgments about the value of proposed ideas, solutions, etc., by comparing the proposal to specific criteria or standards.
- **Create** Put parts or elements together in such a way as to reveal a pattern or structure not clearly there before; identify which data or information from a complex set is appropriate to examine further or from which supported conclusions can be drawn.

See also Appendix A.

brainstorming—A problem-solving tool used by teams to generate as many ideas as possible that are related to a particular subject. Team members begin by offering all their ideas; the ideas are not discussed or reviewed until after the brainstorming session.

breakthrough improvement—A method of solving chronic problems that results from the effective execution of a strategy designed to reach the next level of quality. Contrasted with incremental improvement, a breakthrough improvement is a one-time major reengineering of change that may cross many interorganizational boundaries. Such change often requires a culture transformation within the organization.

business partnering—The creation of cooperative business alliances between constituencies within an organization or between an organization and its customers or suppliers. Partnering occurs through a pooling of resources in a trusting atmosphere focused on continuous, mutual improvement (*see also* customer–supplier partnership).

business processes—Processes that focus on what the organization does as a business and how it goes about doing it. A business has functional processes (generating output within a single department) and cross-functional processes (generating output across several functions or departments).

C

calibration—The comparison of a measurement instrument or system of unverified accuracy with a measurement instrument or system of a known accuracy to detect any variation from the true value.

capability—The natural tolerance of a machine or process generally defined to include 99.7% of all population values.

capable process—A process is said to be capable if the product or output of the process always conforms to the specifications of the customer—that is, 100% conformance to the customer requirements.

cascading training—Training implemented in an organization from the top down, where each level acts as trainers to those below.

cash flow statement—A critical financial statement showing the flow of cash in and out of an enterprise within a given time period.

cause-and-effect diagram—A tool for analyzing process variables. It is also referred to as the Ishikawa diagram, because Kaoru Ishikawa developed it, and the fishbone diagram, because the complete diagram resembles a fish skeleton. The diagram illustrates the main causes and subcauses leading to an effect (symptom). The cause-and-effect diagram is one of the seven tools of quality and a preliminary approach to identifying root cause.

cell—A layout of workstations and/or various machines for different operations (often in a U shape) in which multitasking operators proceed with a part from machine to machine to perform a series of sequential steps to produce a whole product or major subassembly.

cellular team—The cross-trained individuals who work within a cell.

centerline—A line on a graph that represents the overall average (mean) operating level of the process charted.

central tendency—The propensity of data collected on a process to concentrate around a value situated near the middle between the lowest and highest value.

certification—The receipt of a document from an authorized source stating that a device, process, or operator has been certified to a known standard.

chain reaction—A series of interacting events described by W. Edwards Deming: improve quality → decrease costs → improve productivity → increase market share with better quality and lower price → stay in business, provide jobs and more jobs.

champion—An individual who has accountability and responsibility for many processes or who is involved in making strategic-level decisions for the organization. The champion ensures ongoing dedication of project resources and monitors strategic alignment.

chance cause—A random and uncontrollable cause of variation inherent in the process. Also called *common cause.*

change agent—The person who facilitates change within the organization. May be from either inside or outside the organization, and may or may not be the initiator of the change effort.

characteristic—A property that helps to identify or differentiate between entities and that can be described or measured to determine conformance or nonconformance to requirements.

charter—A documented statement officially initiating the formation of a committee, team, project, or other effort in which a clearly stated purpose and approval is conferred.

check sheet—A simple data-recording device that is custom designed for a particular use, allowing ease in interpreting the results. Formerly referred to as a tally sheet, the check sheet is one of seven basic quality tools. Check sheets should not be confused with checklists.

checklist—A tool for organizing and ensuring that all important steps or actions in an operation have been taken. Checklists contain items that are important or relevant to an issue or situation. Checklists should not be confused with check sheets.

coaching—A continual improvement technique by which people receive one-to-one learning through demonstration and practice and that is characterized by immediate feedback and correction.

code of conduct—The expected behavior that has been mutually developed and agreed upon by an organization or a team.

common causes—Causes of variation that are inherent in any process all the time. A process that has only common causes of variation is said to be stable, predictable, or in control. Also called *chance causes.*

companywide quality control (CWQC)—Term coined by Kaoru Ishikawa, similar to total quality management (TQM).

competence—Refers to a person's ability to learn and perform a particular activity. Competence consists of knowledge, experience, skills, aptitude, and attitude components (KESAA factors).

complaint handling—The process and practices involved in receiving and resolving complaints from customers.

compliance—An affirmative indication or judgment that the supplier of a product or service has met the requirements of the relevant specifications, contract, or regulation; also the state of meeting the requirements.

conflict, team—(1) Team conflict can be positive or negative. (2) Conflict can occur at any stage of the team growth but is most likely in the "forming" and "storming" stages. (3) One way to combat conflict is to use fact-based data to facilitate the appropriate win–win scenario. (4) Facilitators or team leaders should adapt an approach based on the situation to resolve conflict.

conflict resolution—A process for resolving disagreements in a manner acceptable to all parties involved.

conformance—An affirmative indication or judgment that a product or service has met the requirements of a relevant specification, contract, or regulation.

consensus—Finding a proposal acceptable enough that all team members can support the decision and no member will oppose it.

constancy of purpose—Occurs when goals and objectives are properly aligned to the organization's vision and mission (also, the first of Deming's 14 steps)

consumer market customers—End users of a product or service.

consumer's risk—For a sampling plan, refers to the probability of acceptance of a lot, the quality of which has a designated numerical value representing a level that is seldom desirable. Usually the designated value will be the lot tolerance percent defective (LTPD). Also called *beta risk* or *type 2 error.*

continual process improvement—The actions taken throughout an organization to increase the effectiveness and efficiency of activities and processes in order to provide added benefits to the customer and organization. It is considered a subset of total quality management and operates according to the premise that organizations can always make improvements. Continual improvement can also be equated with reducing process variation.

continuous process improvement—Often used interchangeably with *continual process improvement.*

continuous quality improvement (CQI)—Philosophy and attitude for analyzing capabilities and processes and improving them repeatedly to achieve the objective of customer satisfaction.

control chart—A basic tool that consists of a chart with upper and lower control limits on which values of some statistical measure for a series of samples or subgroups are plotted. It frequently shows a central line to help detect a trend of plotted values toward either control limit. It is used to monitor and analyze variation from a process to see whether the process is in statistical control.

control limits—The natural boundaries of a process within specified confidence levels, expressed as the upper control limit (UCL) and the lower control limit (LCL).

control plan—A document, or documents, that provides the characteristics for quality of a product or service, measurements, and methods of control.

core competency—The unique features and characteristics of an organization's overall capability.

corrective action—(1) The implementation of solutions resulting in the reduction or elimination of an identified problem. (2) An action taken to eliminate the root cause(s) and symptom(s) of an existing deviation or nonconformity to prevent recurrence.

correlation—The measure of the relationship between two sets of numbers or variables.

cost of poor quality (COPQ)—The costs associated with the production of nonconforming material.

cost of quality (COQ)—The total costs incurred relating to the quality of a product or service. There are four categories of quality costs: internal failure costs, external failure costs, appraisal costs, and prevention costs (*see also individual entries*).

cost-benefit analysis—*See* benefit-cost analysis.

count chart—A control chart for evaluating the stability of a process in terms of the count of events of a given classification occurring in a sample.

criteria—Stated objectives, guidelines, principles, procedures, and/or standards used for measuring a project, process, product, or performance.

criterion—A standard, rule, or test on which a decision can be based.

critical-to-quality (CTQ)—Characteristics that, from a customer's perception of quality, are critical to the achievement of quality goals, objectives, standards, and/or specifications.

cross-functional team—A group consisting of members from more than one department or work unit that is organized to accomplish a project.

culture—*See* organization culture.

cumulative sum control chart—A control chart on which the plotted value is the cumulative sum of deviations of successive samples from a target value. The ordinate of each plotted point represents the algebraic sum of the previous ordinate and the most recent deviations from the target.

current state map—Flowchart of a process as it is currently performed (*see also* future state map).

customer—Recipient of a product or service provided by a supplier (*see also* external customer; internal customer).

customer council—A group usually composed of representatives from an organization's largest customers who meet to discuss common issues.

customer delight—The result achieved when customer requirements are exceeded in unexpected ways the customer finds valuable.

customer expectations—Customers' perceptions of the value they will receive from the purchase of a product or experience with a service. Customers form expectations by analyzing available information, which may include experience, word of mouth, and advertising and sales promises.

customer loyalty/retention—The result of an organization's plans, processes, practices, and efforts designed to deliver its services or products in ways that create retained and committed customers.

customer relationship management (CRM)—An organization's knowledge of its customers' unique requirements and expectations, and use of that information to develop a closer and more profitable link to business processes and strategies.

customer requirements—Specific characteristics of products and services determined by customers' needs or wants.

customer satisfaction—The result of delivering a product or service that meets customer requirements, needs, and expectations.

customer segmentation—The process of differentiating customers based on one or more dimensions for the purpose of developing a marketing strategy to address specific segments.

customer service—The activities of dealing with customer questions; also sometimes the department that takes customer orders or provides postdelivery services.

customer-oriented organization—An organization whose mission, purpose, and actions are dedicated to serving and satisfying customers.

customer–supplier partnership—A long-term relationship between a buyer and a supplier characterized by teamwork and mutual confidence. The supplier is considered an extension of the buyer's organization. The partnership is based on several commitments. The buyer provides long-term contracts and uses fewer suppliers. The supplier implements quality assurance processes so that incoming inspection can be minimized. The supplier also helps the buyer reduce costs and improve product and process designs.

cycle time—The elapsed time that it takes to complete a process from beginning to end.

cycle-time reduction—The action(s) taken to reduce the overall process time from start to finish.

D

data—Quantitative or qualitative facts presented in descriptive, numeric, or graphic form. There are two kinds of numerical data: measured or variable data (such as "16 ounces," "4 miles," and ".075 inches") and counted or attribute data (such as "162 defects"). Data may also be nonnumeric, expressed as words or symbols.

decision matrix—A matrix used by teams to evaluate problems or possible solutions. The steps are as follows: (1) The team draws a matrix and lists the possible solutions in the far-left vertical column; (2) the team selects criteria to rate the possible solutions, writing them across the top row; (3) the team rates each possible solution on a scale from 1 to 5 for each criterion and the rating is recorded in the corresponding grid; (4) the team adds the ratings of all the criteria for each possible solution to determine its total score. The total score is then used to help decide which solution deserves the most attention.

defect—A product or service's nonfulfillment of an intended requirement or reasonable expectation for use, including safety considerations. They are often classified as the following:

- Class 1, Critical, leads directly to severe injury or catastrophic economic loss
- Class 2, Serious, leads directly to significant injury or significant economic loss
- Class 3, Major, is related to major problems with respect to intended normal or reasonably foreseeable use
- Class 4, Minor, is related to minor problems with respect to intended normal or reasonably foreseeable use (*see also* nonconformity).

defective—A product that contains one or more defects relative to the quality characteristics being measured.

deficiencies—Units of product are considered to have defects. Errors or flaws in a process are described in a hospital setting as "deficiencies." Medical procedures, job tasks, or documented processes, for example, may have deficiencies that reduce their ability to satisfy the patient, physician, or other stakeholder in the organization.

delighter—Feature of a delivered product or service that unexpectedly pleases a customer.

Deming cycle—*See* Plan-Do-Check-Act (PDCA) cycle.

dependability—The degree to which a product or service is operable and capable of performing its required function at any randomly chosen time during its specified operating time, provided that the product or service is available at the start of that period. (Nonoperation-related influences are not included.) Dependability can be expressed by the following ratio: time available divided by (time available + time required).

deployment—(to spread out) Example: Used in strategic planning to describe the process of cascading goals, objectives, and plans throughout an organization.

design of experiments (DOE)—A branch of applied statistics dealing with planning, conducting, analyzing, and interpreting controlled tests to evaluate the factors that control the value of a parameter or group of parameters.

deviation—A nonconformance or departure of a characteristic from specified product, process, or system requirements.

diagnostic journey and remedial journey—A two-phase investigation used by teams to solve chronic quality problems. In the first phase, the diagnostic journey, the team moves from the symptom of a problem to its cause. In the second phase, the remedial journey, the team moves from the cause to a remedy.

DiSC—A profiling instrument that measures characteristic ways in which a person behaves in a particular environment. The four dimensions measured are dominance, influence, steadiness, and conscientiousness.

discrete data—Data where all possible outcomes can be distinctly identified as integers (fractional values are not possible). Examples include family size, good/bad, and SAT scores. Also known as *attributes data.*

discrimination—The ability of a measuring instrument to respond to small changes in the measured characteristic.

dissatisfiers—Those features or functions that the customer or employee has come to expect and that would result in dissatisfaction if they were no longer present.

distribution—Describes the amount of potential variation in outputs of a process; it is usually described in terms of its shape, average, and standard deviation.

DMAIC—Pertains to a methodology used in the Six Sigma approach: Define, Measure, Analyze, Improve, Control.

drivers of quality—Include customers, products/services, employee satisfaction, processes, and total organizational focus on providing quality products/services.

E

effect—That which results after an action has been taken. The expected or predicted impact when an action is to be taken or is proposed.

effectiveness—The state of having produced a decided-upon or desired effect. Increased customer satisfaction, increased employee satisfaction, improved supplier relations, cost reduction, increased efficiency, improved timeliness, greater accuracy, completeness, and profitability are all contributors to effectiveness.

efficiency—The ratio of the output to the total input in a process, with an objective to use minimum amounts of resources, such as time and cost.

efficient—A term describing a process that operates effectively while consuming the minimum amount of resources (such as labor and time).

eighty/twenty (80/20) rule—A term referring to the Pareto principle, which suggests that most defects come from relatively few causes; that is, 80% of the defects come from 20% of the possible causes.

electronic data interchange (EDI)—The electronic exchange of data between customers and suppliers and vice versa; for example, using a dedicated high-speed line, a customer places an order directly with a supplier, and the supplier acknowledges receipt of the order with confirmation of price and shipping date. Some large customers specify that their suppliers must have this capability in order to qualify as approved suppliers.

employee involvement—The practice of involving employees in decisions pertaining to processes, usually within their work units. Such decisions may include suggestions for improving the process, planning, setting objectives, and tracking performance. Natural (work unit) teams, process improvement teams, cross-functional teams, task forces, quality circles, and other vehicles for involvement may be used. Participation in decisions related to legal and/or personnel matters is usually excluded.

empowerment—A condition whereby employees have the authority to make decisions and take action in their work areas, within stated bounds, without prior approval. For example, an operator can stop a production process upon detecting a problem, or a customer service representative can send out a replacement product if a customer calls with a problem.

end users—External customers who purchase products/services for their own use.

Enterprise Resource Planning (ERP)—Business management software that a company uses to collect, store, manage, and interpret data from an integrated suite of applications (e.g., product planning cost and development, manufacturing or service delivery, marketing and sales, inventory management, shipping and payment).

error—The degree of variability between estimates of the same characteristic over repeated samples taken under similar conditions.

error-proofing—Error prevention. Also called *mistake-proofing* and *poka-yoke.*

ethics—An individual's or an organization's adherence to a belief or documented code of conduct that is based on moral principles and that tries to balance what is fair for individuals with what is right for society.

event—An occurrence, incident, or experience, usually of some significance. An outcome or final result, usually of some action. What takes place between the starting and ending point for a task or group of tasks.

excited quality—The additional benefit a customer receives when a product or service goes beyond basic expectations. Excited quality "wows" the customer and distinguishes the provider from the competition. If it is missing, the customer will still be satisfied.

expected quality—The minimum benefit or value a customer expects to receive from a product or service. Also known as *basic quality*.

explicit knowledge—Captured and recorded data, information, or knowledge (*see also* tacit knowledge).

external customer—A person or organization that receives a product, service, or information but is not part of the organization supplying it (*see also* internal customer).

external failure costs—Costs occurring after delivery or shipment of the product, or during or after furnishing of a service, to the customer.

F

facilitator—An individual who is responsible for creating favorable conditions that will enable a team to reach its purpose or achieve its goals by bringing together the necessary tools, information, and resources to get the job done. A facilitator addresses the processes a team uses to achieve its purpose. Specially trained, the facilitator may function as a teacher, coach, and moderator.

failure—The inability of an item, product, or service to perform required functions on demand due to one or more defects.

failure cost—The costs resulting from products or services not conforming to requirements or customer/user needs—the costs resulting from poor quality.

failure mode analysis (FMA)—A procedure to determine which malfunction symptoms appear immediately before or after a failure of a critical parameter in a system. After all the possible causes are listed for each symptom, the product or procedure is designed to eliminate the problems.

failure mode and effects analysis (FMEA)—A procedure in which each potential failure mode in every subitem of an item or process is analyzed to determine its effect on other subitems and on the required function of the item or process.

failure mode, effects and criticality analysis (FMECA)—A procedure that is performed after a failure mode effects analysis to classify each potential failure effect according to its severity and probability of occurrence.

fault tree analysis—A top-down technique for determining the set of components that could cause a failure in a process. Specifically accounts for both single and multiple causes.

feedback—The response to information received in interpersonal communication (written or oral); it may be based on fact or feeling and helps the party who is receiving the information judge how well the other party is understanding him or her. More generally, feedback is information about a process or performance and is used to make decisions that are directed toward improving or adjusting the process or performance as necessary.

fishbone diagram—*See* cause-and-effect diagram.

fitness for use—A term used to indicate that a product or service fits the customer's defined purpose for that product or service.

five Ss—The Americanized version of the Japanese 5S is sort, straighten, scrub, standardize, and sustain. The 5S approach organizes the workplace, keeps it neat and clean, establishes standardized conditions, and maintains discipline to sustain the effort.

five whys—A repetitive questioning technique to probe deeper in order to surface the root cause of a problem. The number of times "why" is asked depends on when the true root cause is reached.

flowchart—A graphical representation of the steps in a process. Flowcharts are drawn to better understand processes. The flowchart is one of the seven basic tools of quality.

focus group—A qualitative discussion group consisting of 8–10 participants, invited from a segment of the customer base to discuss an existing or planned product or service, led by a facilitator working from predetermined questions (focus groups may also be used to gather information in a context other than customers). A focus group may be formed to surface the confusion or displeasure users feel as a step toward developing the questions to be included in a survey of customer satisfaction.

force-field analysis (FFA)—A technique for surfacing, discussing, and analyzing the forces that aid or hinder an organization in reaching an objective. To create an FFA diagram, a large letter "T" is drawn on a piece of paper. The factors that will aid the objective's achievement, called the driving forces, are listed on the left side of the "T." The factors that will hinder its achievement, called the restraining forces, are listed on the right side of the "T."

fourteen points—W. Edward Deming's 14 management practices to help companies increase their quality and productivity: (1) create constancy of purpose for improving products and services; (2) adopt the new philosophy; (3) cease dependence on inspection to achieve quality; (4) end the practice of awarding business on price alone, and instead minimize total cost by working with a single supplier; (5) improve constantly and forever every process for planning, production, and service; (6) institute training on the job; (7) adopt and institute leadership; (8) drive out fear; (9) break down barriers between staff areas; (10) eliminate slogans, exhortations, and targets for the workforce; (11) eliminate numerical quotas for the workforce and numerical goals for management; (12) remove barriers that rob people of pride in workmanship, and eliminate the annual rating or merit system; (13) institute a vigorous program of education and self-improvement for everyone; and (14) put everybody in the company to work to accomplish the transformation.

frequency distribution (statistical)—A table that graphically presents a large volume of data so that the central tendency (such as the average or mean) and distribution are clearly displayed.

frontline personnel—The workforce and their supervisors who produce the product or service provided by the organization, as distinguished from personnel who serve in a staff or support role or represent higher management.

functional organization—An organization organized by discrete functions, for example, marketing/sales, engineering, production, finance, and human resources.

future state map—Flowchart depicting the changed process (*see also* current state map).

G

gage—An instrument or system for testing.

gage repeatability and reproducibility (GR&R)—The evaluation of a gaging instrument's accuracy by determining whether the measurements taken with it are repeatable (i.e., there is close agreement among a number of consecutive measurements of the output for the same value of the input under the same operating conditions) and reproducible (i.e., there is close agreement among repeated measurements of the output for the same value of input made under the same operating conditions over a period of time).

gainsharing—A type of program that rewards individuals financially on the basis of organizational performance.

Gantt chart—A matrix-type, horizontal bar chart used in process/project planning and control to display planned work and finished work in relation to time. It is called a *milestone chart* when interim checkpoints are added.

gap analysis—A technique that compares a company's existing state with its desired state (as expressed by its long-term plans) to help determine what needs to be done to remove or minimize the gap.

gatekeeping—The role of an individual (often a facilitator) in a group meeting in helping to ensure effective interpersonal interactions (e.g., someone's ideas are not ignored due to the team moving on to the next topic too quickly).

goal—A statement of general intent, aim, or desire; it is the point toward which management directs its efforts and resources; goals are usually nonquantitative and are measured by supporting objectives.

ground rules—Norms or agreed-to behaviors concerning how meetings will be run, how team members will interact, and what kind of behavior is acceptable. Each member is expected to respect these rules, which usually prevent misunderstanding and disagreements. Rules may exist regarding attendance, promptness, participation, interruptions, and confidentiality.

group dynamics—The interaction (behavior) of individuals within a team or work group meeting.

groupthink—Occurs when most or all team members coalesce in supporting an idea or decision that hasn't been fully explored, or when some members secretly disagree but go along with the other members in apparent support.

H

Hawthorne effect—The concept that every change results (initially, at least) in increased productivity. (Based on studies by Elton Mayo at the Hawthorne Plant of Western Electric Company, in Chicago in 1924.)

histogram—A graphic summary of variation in a set of data. The pictorial nature of the histogram lets people see patterns that are difficult to see in a simple table of numbers. The histogram is one of the seven tools of quality.

house of quality—A diagram (named for its house-shaped appearance) that clarifies the relationship between customer needs and product features. It helps correlate market or customer requirements (voice of the customer) and analysis of competitive products with higher-level technical and product characteristics and makes it possible to bring several factors into a single figure. Also known as *quality function deployment* (QFD).

I

imagineering—Developing in the mind's eye a process without waste.

improvement—The positive effect of a process change effort. Improvement may result from incremental changes or from a major breakthrough.

in control—A term that describes a situation in which the variations within a process occur only between the computed upper and lower control limits. The process is considered to be stable and therefore predictable. A process in which the statistical measure being evaluated is in a state of statistical control; that is, the variations among the observed sampling results can be attributed to a constant system of chance/common causes (*see also* out-of-control process).

incremental improvement—Frequent improvements that are implemented on a continual basis. These improvements are typically small steps within an overall process contained within a given work unit. (A technique also known as *kaizen*.)

indicators—Predetermined measures used to judge how well an organization is meeting its customers' needs and its operational and financial performance objectives. Such indicators can be either *leading* or *lagging*. Indicators are also devices used to measure physical objects, and mechanical or electronic devices used to measure lengths or flow.

indirect customers—Customers who do not receive process output directly but are affected if the process output is incorrect or late.

information—Data transformed into an ordered format that makes them usable and enables a person to draw conclusions.

information system—Technology-based systems used to support operations, aid day-to-day decision making, and support strategic analysis (other names often used include management information system, decision system, information technology [IT], and data processing).

input—Material, product, service, or information that is obtained from an upstream internal provider or an external supplier and is used to produce an output.

inspection—Measuring, examining, testing, and gaging one or more characteristics of a product or service and comparing the results with specified requirements to determine whether conformity is being achieved for each characteristic.

inspection cost—The cost associated with inspecting the product to ensure that it meets the customer's (internal or external) needs and requirements; an appraisal cost.

intermediate customers—Distributors, dealers, or brokers who make products and services available to the end user by repairing, repackaging, reselling, or creating finished goods from components or subassemblies.

internal audit—An audit conducted within an organization by members of the organization to assess its strengths and weaknesses against its own procedures and/or external standards—a *first-party audit*.

internal customer—The person or department that receives the output of another person or department (product, service, or information) within an organization. Also called *next operation as customer* (NOAC).

internal failure costs—Costs of failures occurring prior to delivery or shipment of the product, or the furnishing of a service, to the customer.

interrelationship digraph—A management and planning tool that displays the relationship between factors in a complex situation. It identifies meaningful categories from a mass of ideas and is useful when relationships are difficult to determine. Typically, it depicts the origin of data, information, material, or product and the single or multiple functions or processes affected.

intervention—An action taken by a leader or a facilitator to support the effective functioning of a team or work group.

Ishikawa diagram—*See* cause-and-effect diagram.

ISO—"equal" (Greek). A prefix for a series of standards published by the International Organization for Standardization. (Note: "ISO" is not the abbreviation of the standards provider.)

ISO 9000 series standards—A set of individual but related international standards and guidelines on quality management and quality assurance developed to help companies effectively document the quality system elements to be implemented to maintain an efficient quality system. The standards have been updated frequently since first published in 1988, and they are not specific to any particular industry, product, or service. The standards were developed by the International Organization for Standardization, a specialized international agency for standardization composed of the national standards bodies of nearly 100 countries.

ISO standards, other—There are ISO standards for industries (automotive, aerospace, telecommunications, etc.), for environmental management, for functions (i.e., laboratories), for products, for materials, and so on.

J

job enlargement and job enrichment—Job enlargement expands the variety or quantity of tasks assigned to a worker. Job enrichment adds responsibility and authority to a worker's assignment.

job specification—A listing of important functional and quality attributes a worker needs to succeed in an assigned job (i.e., knowledge, experience, skills, aptitude, attitude, and other personal characteristics).

Juran's trilogy—*See* quality trilogy.

just-in-time (JIT) manufacturing—An optimal material requirement planning system for a manufacturing process in which there is little or no manufacturing material inventory on hand at the manufacturing site and little or no incoming inspection.

just-in-time training—Providing job training coincidental with, or immediately prior to, an employee's assignment to a new or expanded job. This action is intended to reduce *fade-out*, the loss of knowledge and skill that occurs with the lengthening of time between the training and application on the job.

K

kaizen—Incremental improvement; a Japanese term that means gradual unending improvement by doing little things better and setting and achieving increasingly higher standards. Masaaki Imai made the term famous in his book *Kaizen: The Key to Japan's Competitive Success.*

kaizen blitz/event—An intense, short-time-frame (typically 3–5 consecutive days) team approach to apply the concepts and techniques of continual improvement (e.g., to reduce cycle time, increase throughput, and reduce waste).

kanban—A method for providing material/product to a succeeding operation by signaling the preceding operation when more material/product is needed. Originally, this "pull" type of process control employed a kanban (a card or signboard) attached to a lot of material/product in a production line, signifying the delivery of a given quantity. When all of the material/product has been processed, the card/sign is returned to its source, where it becomes an order to replenish. Presently, some type of electronic notification might replace the card. The key advantages of this method are that unnecessary buildup of work-in-process inventory is eliminated, space is saved, and the risk of loss due to defective material/product is decreased (less work-in-process inventory is produced before a defect is detected).

Kano model—Three classes of customer requirements as described by Dr. Noriaki Kano: satisfiers—what customers say they want; dissatisfiers—what customers expect and what results in dissatisfaction when not present; delighters/exciters—new or unexpected features that customers do not expect. It is observed that what a customer originally perceived as a delighter will become a dissatisfier if it is no longer available. A delighter ultimately becomes a must-have.

KESAA factors—*See* competence.

key process—A major system-level process that supports the mission and satisfies major customer requirements. The identification of key processes aids the organization to focus its resources on what is important to the customer.

key result area (KRA)—A major category of customer requirements that is critical for the organization's success.

key success factors (KSFs)—Those factors that point toward answers to key questions, such as "How will we know if we're successful?" "How will we know when we're heading for trouble?" and "If we are moving away from our organizational strategy and targets, what corrections should we make?" KSFs are selected to measure what is truly important to an organization: customer satisfaction, employee satisfaction, financial stability, and important operational factors.

KJ method—The affinity chart was created by Jiro Kawakita in the 1960s (*see also* affinity diagram).

knowledge management (KM)—Involves transforming data into information, the acquisition or creation of knowledge, and the processes and technology employed in identifying, categorizing, storing, retrieving, disseminating, and using information and knowledge for the purposes of improving decisions and plans. Broadly, KM addresses the transformation hierarchy: data → information → knowledge → wisdom.

L

lateral thinking—A process that includes recognizing patterns, becoming unencumbered with old ideas, and creating new ones.

LCALI—A process for operating a listening-post system for capturing and using formerly unavailable customer feedback ("listen," "capture," "analyze," "learn," "improve").[1]

leader—An individual recognized by others as the person to lead an effort. One cannot be a leader without one or more followers. The term is often used interchangeably with "manager" (*see also* manager). A leader may or may not hold an officially designated management-type position.

leadership—An essential part of a quality improvement effort. Organization leaders must establish a vision, communicate that vision to those in the organization, and provide the tools, knowledge, and motivation necessary to accomplish the vision.

lean—Producing the maximum sellable products or services at the lowest operational cost while optimizing inventory levels. Lean focuses on reducing cycle time and waste. "Lean" and "agile" are terms often used interchangeably

life cycle—A product life cycle is the total time frame from product concept to the end of its intended use; a project life cycle is typically divided into five stages: concept, planning, design, implementation, and evaluation and closeout.

listening post—An individual who, by virtue of her or his potential for having contact with customers, is designated to collect, document, and transmit pertinent feedback to a central collection authority within the organization. Such feedback is analyzed for emerging trends or recurring problems, which are reported to management. Preventive actions are taken when the information indicates the need. Positive feedback is passed on to the organizational function or person responsible for a customer's expression of satisfaction.

listening-post data—Customer data and information gathered from designated listening posts.

little q, Big Q—The difference between managing for quality in a limited capacity (q) of daily operations and managing for quality across all business processes and products (Q), Attributed to J. M. Juran.

logistics—Management of the flow of goods between the point of origin and the point of consumption in order to meet stated requirements, for example, of customers or corporations. The resources managed in logistics can include physical items, such as food, materials, animals, equipment, and liquids, as well as abstract items, such as time, information, particles, and energy.

loss function—*See* Taguchi loss function.

lost customer analysis—An analysis to determine why a customer or segment of customers was lost or defected to a competitor.

lot—A defined quantity of product accumulated under conditions that are considered uniform for sampling purposes.

lower control limit (LCL)—Control limit for points below the central line in a control chart.

M

maintainability—The probability that a given maintenance action for an item under given usage conditions can be performed within a stated time interval when the maintenance is performed under stated conditions using stated procedures and resources. Maintainability has two categories: (1) serviceability, the ease of conducting scheduled inspections and servicing, and (2) repairability, the ease of restoring service after a failure.

management by fact—A business philosophy that decisions should be based on data.

management by walking around (MBWA)—A manager's planned, but usually unannounced, walk-through of the organization to gather information from employees and make observations; may be viewed in a positive light by virtue of giving employees the opportunity to interact with top management, but also has the potential of being viewed negatively if punitive action is taken as a result of information gathered.

management levels—A typical hierarchy of management levels is top management (executive level, upper management, top team, C-suite), middle management (directors, general managers, plant managers, department managers), and first-level supervision (persons directly supervising workers).

management review—An internal, scheduled review and evaluation by management of the status and adequacy of the quality/environmental management system(s) in relation to the organization's strategic objectives, policy, and any certification requirements.

management styles—Managing styles used include authoritarian, autocratic, combative, conciliatory, consensual, consultative, democratic, disruptive, ethical, facilitating, intimidating, judicial, laissez-faire, participative, promotional, secretive, shared, and shareholder management.

manager—An individual who manages and is responsible for resources (people, material, money, time). A person officially designated with a management-type position title. A manager is granted authority from above, whereas a leader's role is derived by virtue of having followers. However, the terms "manager" and "leader" are often used interchangeably.

matrix chart/diagram—A management and planning tool that shows the relationships among various groups of data; it yields information about the relationships and the importance of task/method elements of the subjects.

mean—A measure of central tendency; the arithmetic average of all measurements in a data set.

mean time between failures (MTBF)—The average time interval between failures for repairable product or service for a defined unit of measure, for example, operating hours, cycles, miles.

measles chart—Type of "check sheet" in which a diagram, map, or picture is used in the background and data points are placed on the image relative to the place of data origin. Example: data points from a group of people, representing infections from each individual in the group, are placed on a diagram of a human body where the infections originated to show areas of concentration and aid in prioritizing for decision making.

measure—The criteria, metric, or means to which a comparison is made with output.

measurement—The reference standard or sample used for the comparison of properties.

median—The middle number or center value of a set of data when all the data are arranged in an increasing sequence.

metric—A standard of measurement or evaluation.

metrology—The science and practice of measurements.

micromanaging—Managing every little detail (e.g., an executive approving the purchase of paper clips).

milestone chart—A Gantt chart on which the starting time, interim check points, and end time are indicated for each event or task displayed.

mind map—Visual representation (words, symbols, pictures, etc.) of issues, concerns, ideas, or suggestions that results from a group formed to explore the thinking and understanding of a situation, event, or problem and the relationships of the data presented. Usually the mind map is created by a facilitator as individuals in the group express their thoughts. The completed mind map tends to look similar to an octopus, from a distance.

mission statement—An explanation of purpose or reasons for existing as an organization; it provides the focus for the organization and defines its scope of business.

mistake-proofing—*See* poka-yoke.

mode—The value that occurs most frequently in a data set.

moment-of-truth (MOT)—Jan Carlzon, former CEO of Scandinavian Air Services, described a MOT as "any episode where a customer comes into contact with any aspect of your company, no matter how distant, and by this contact, has an opportunity to form an opinion about your company."[2]

motivation—Two types of motivation are *extrinsic* (influence from outside the person) and *intrinsic* (feelings from inside the person). One person cannot directly "motivate" another person, but instead must create an environment in which the affected person feels motivated.

muda—Japanese term for waste.

multivoting—A decision-making tool that enables a group to work through a long list of ideas to identify priorities.

Myers-Briggs Type Indicator (MBTI)—A method and instrument for identifying a person's "personality type" based on Carl Jung's theory of personality preferences.

N

n—Sample size (the number of units in a sample).

natural team—A team of individuals drawn from a single work group; similar to a process improvement team except that it is not cross-functional in composition and it is not usually temporary.

next operation as customer (NOAC)—The concept that the organization is made up of service/product providers and service/product receivers or "internal customers."

NIST—An abbreviation for the National Institute of Standards and Technology (US).

nominal data—Data used for classifying information without an implied order or use of numbers for identification purposes.

nominal group technique (NGT)—A technique similar to brainstorming that is used by teams to generate ideas on a particular subject. Team members are asked to silently come up with as many ideas as possible and write them down. Each member is then asked to share one idea, which is recorded. After all the ideas are recorded, they are discussed and prioritized by the group.

nonconformity—The result of nonfulfillment of a specified requirement.

nondestructive testing and evaluation (NDT)—Testing and evaluation methods that do not damage or destroy the product being tested.

non-value-added—Refers to tasks or activities that can be eliminated with no deterioration in product or service functionality, performance, or quality in the eyes of the customer.

norm—A behavioral term relating to how a person or group will behave in a given situation based on established protocols, rules of conduct, or accepted social practices.

normal distribution—A bell-shaped distribution for continuous data where most of the data are concentrated around the average, and it is equally likely that an observation will occur above or below the average.

O

objective—A statement of future expectations and an indication of when the expectations should be achieved; it flows from and supports goals and clarifies what people must accomplish. An objective includes measurable end results to be accomplished by specific teams or individuals within time limits. It is the "how, when, and who" for achieving a goal (*see also* S.M.A.R.T. W.A.Y.).

objective evidence—Verifiable qualitative or quantitative observations, data, information, records, or statements of fact pertaining to the quality of an item or service or to the existence and implementation of a quality system element. (Auditing is seeking and assessing objective evidence.)

on-the-job-training (OJT)—Training that is usually conducted at the workstation, typically done one-on-one.

operational planning—Planning for the operation of day-to-day processes.

ordinal number—Any number in a series of numbers used to indicate position, but the size of the number is not important.

organization culture—The collective beliefs, values, attitudes, manners, customs, behaviors, and artifacts unique to an organization.

outcome—The measurable result of a project, a quality initiative, an improvement, and so on. Usually, some time passes between the completion of the action and the realization of the outcome.

outlier—An observation extremely different in some respect from the other observations in a set of data. More loosely, any extremely different or unusual event.

out-of-control process—A process in which the statistical measure being evaluated is not in a state of statistical control (i.e., the variations among the observed sampling results cannot all be attributed to a constant system of chance causes; special or assignable causes exist) (*see also* in control).

output—The deliverables resulting from a project, a quality initiative, an improvement, and so on. Outputs include data, information, documents, decisions, and tangible products. Outputs are generated from both the planning and management of the activity (e.g., project) and the delivered product, service, program, and so on. Output is the item, document, or material delivered by an internal provider/supplier to an internal receiver/customer.

overall equipment effectiveness (OEE)—A measure of the efficiency and effectiveness of a process. OEE combines the measurement of availability, performance, and quality.

P

Pareto chart—A basic tool used to graphically rank causes from most significant to least significant. It uses a vertical bar graph in which the bar height reflects the frequency or impact of causes.

partnership/alliance—A strategy leading to a relationship with suppliers or customers aimed at reducing costs of ownership, maintenance of minimum stocks, just-in-time deliveries, joint participation in design, exchange of information on materials and technologies, new production methods, quality improvement strategies, and the exploitation of market synergy.

payback period—The number of years it will take for the results of a project or capital investment to recover the investment monies.

Plan-Do-Check-Act (PDCA) cycle—A four-step process for quality improvement. In the first step (plan), a plan to effect improvement is developed. In the second step (do), the plan is carried out, preferably on a small scale. In the third step (check), the effects of the plan are observed. In the last step (act), the results are studied to determine what was learned and what can be predicted. The PDCA cycle is sometimes referred to as the Shewhart cycle (Walter A. Shewhart discussed the concept in his book *Statistical Method from the Viewpoint of Quality Control*) and as the Deming cycle (W. Edwards Deming introduced the concept in Japan). The Japanese subsequently called it the Deming cycle. Sometimes referred to as Plan-Do-Study-Act (PDSA).

poka-yoke—A Japanese term that means to mistake-proof a process by building safeguards into the system that avoid or immediately find errors. It comes from *poka*, which means "inadvertent error," and *yokeru*, which means "to avoid."

policy—An overarching plan (direction) for achieving an organization's goals.

population—A collection or set of individuals, objects, or measurements whose properties or characteristics are to be analyzed.

ppm—An abbreviation for parts per million. The number of times an occurrence happens in one million chances.

precision—A characteristic of measurement that addresses the consistency or repeatability of a measurement system when the identical item is measured a number of times.

prevention costs—Costs incurred to keep internal and external failure costs and appraisal costs to a minimum.

prevention vs. detection—A term used to contrast two types of quality activities. Prevention refers to those activities designed to prevent nonconformances in products and services. Detection refers to those activities designed to detect nonconformances already in products and services. Another phrase used to look at this distinction is "designing in quality vs. inspecting in quality."

preventive action—Action taken to eliminate the potential causes of a nonconformity, defect, or other undesirable situation in order to prevent further occurrences.

probability—Refers to the likelihood of occurrence.

problem solving—A rational process for identifying, describing, analyzing, and resolving situations in which something has gone wrong without explanation.

procedure—The steps to be taken in a process. A document that answers the following questions: What has to be done? Where is it to be done? When is it to be done? Who is to do it? Why do it? (contrasted with a work instruction, which answers: How is it to be done? With what materials and tools is it to be done?); in the absence of a work instruction, the instructions may be embedded in the procedure.

process—An activity or group of activities that takes an input, adds value to it, and provides an output to an internal or external customer; a planned and repetitive sequence of steps by which a defined product or service is delivered.

process capability—A statistical measure of the inherent process variability for a given characteristic.

process control—The methodology for keeping a process within boundaries; minimizing the variation of a process.

process decision program chart (PDPC)—A management and planning tool that identifies events that can go wrong and the appropriate countermeasures for those events. It graphically represents all sequences that lead to a desirable effect.

process improvement—Refers to the act of changing a process to reduce variability and cycle time and make the process more effective, efficient, and productive.

process improvement team (PIT)—A natural work group or cross-functional team whose responsibility is to achieve needed improvements in existing processes. The duration of the team is based on the completion of the team purpose and specific goals.

process management—The collection of practices used to implement and improve process effectiveness; it focuses on holding the gains achieved through process improvement and ensuring process integrity.

process mapping—The flowcharting of a work process in detail, including key measurements.

process owner—The person who coordinates the various functions and work activities at all levels of a process, has the authority or ability to make changes in the process as required, and manages the entire process cycle so as to ensure performance effectiveness.

process reengineering—*See* reengineering.

producer's risk—For a sampling plan, refers to the probability of not accepting a lot, the quality of which has a designated numerical value representing a level that is generally desirable. Usually the designated value is the acceptable quality level. Also called *alpha risk* and *type 1 error*.

product or service liability—The obligation of a company to make restitution for loss related to personal injury, property damage, or other harm caused by its product or service.

product warranty—The organization's stated policy that it will replace a product, repair a product, or reimburse a customer for a defective product providing the product defect occurs under certain conditions and within a stated period of time.

profound knowledge, system of—W. Edwards Deming stated that learning cannot be based on experience only; it requires comparisons of results with a prediction, a plan, or an expression of theory. Predicting why something happens is essential to understand results and to continually improve. The four components of the system of profound knowledge are appreciation for a system, knowledge of variation, theory of knowledge, and understanding of psychology.

project life cycle—Refers to the five sequential phases of project management: concept, planning, design, implementation, and evaluation.

project management—Refers to the management of activities and events involved throughout a project's life cycle.

project team—A designated group of people working together to produce a planned project's outputs and outcome.

pull system—*See* kanban.

Q

qualitative variables—Describes the sample collected and measures more abstract things—variables whose values are categories such as man, woman, and child; red, green, and blue; Democrat, Republican, Liberal, Conservative, and independent.

quality—A subjective term for which each person has his or her own definition. In technical usage, quality can have two meanings: (1) the characteristics of a product or service that bear on its ability to satisfy stated or implied needs, and (2) a product or service free of deficiencies. The following definitions are in common use:

- Crosby defined quality as "conformance to requirements."
- Deming believed that quality should be focused on the needs of the consumer, present and future, and that quality begins with intent, adopted by management and translated into plans, specifications, tests, and production.
- Juran defined quality as "fitness for use."
- Garvin expands the definition to include eight dimensions: performance, features, reliability, conformance, durability, serviceability, aesthetics, and perceived quality.
- Customers define quality as "what I expect" and "I'll know it when I see it."

quality assessment—The process of identifying business practices, attitudes, and activities that enhance or inhibit the achievement of quality improvement in an organization.

quality assurance/quality control (QA/QC)—Two terms that have many interpretations because of the multiple definitions of the words "assurance" and "control." For example, assurance can mean the act of giving confidence, the state of being certain, or the act of making certain; control can mean an evaluation to indicate needed corrective responses, the act of guiding, or the state of a process in which variability is attributable to a constant system of chance causes. One definition of quality assurance is: all the planned and systematic activities implemented within the quality system that can be demonstrated to provide confidence that a product or service will fulfill requirements for quality. One definition of quality control is: the operational techniques and activities used to fulfill requirements for quality. Often, however, "quality assurance" and "quality control" are used interchangeably, referring to the actions performed to ensure the quality of a product, service, or process.

quality audit/assessment—A systematic, independent examination and review to determine whether quality activities and related results comply with planned arrangements and whether those arrangements are implemented effectively and are suitable to achieve the objectives.

quality characteristics—The unique characteristics of products and services by which customers evaluate their perception of quality. For example, performance, price, durability, safety, maintainability, and ease of disposal are characteristics of products; responsiveness, competence, accuracy, courtesy, security, timeliness, safety, and completeness are characteristics of services.

quality circles—Quality improvement or self-improvement study groups composed of a small number of employees (10 or fewer) and their supervisor, who meet regularly with an aim to improve a process.

quality costs—*See* cost of quality.

quality function—The entire spectrum of activities through which an organization achieves its quality goals and objectives, no matter where those activities are performed.

quality function deployment (QFD)—A multifaceted matrix in which customer requirements are translated into appropriate technical requirements for each stage of product development and production. The QFD process is often referred to as listening to the voice of the customer. Also called *house of quality.*

quality loss function—Loss created by the product to society from the time the product is shipped. Included may be reworking, scrapping, maintenance, downtime due to equipment failure, and warranty claims. In addition are costs to the customer from poor product performance and reliability that lead to further losses to the manufacturer due to loss of market share. Attributed to Dr. Genichi Taguchi.

quality management—All activities of the overall management function that determines the quality policy, objectives, and responsibilities and implements them by means such as quality planning, quality control, quality assurance, and quality improvement within the quality system.

quality management system (QMS)—The organizational structure, processes, procedures, and resources needed to implement, maintain, and continually improve quality management.

quality manual—Document stating the organization's quality policy and describing the organization's quality management system.

quality philosophy—Fundamental principles that are the basis for the organization's beliefs and actions in support of day-to-day operations and continual improvement.

quality plan—The document, or documents, setting out the specific quality practices, resources, specifications, and sequence of activities relevant to a particular product, project, or contract.

quality planning—The activity of establishing quality objectives and quality requirements.

quality policy—An organization's formally stated beliefs about quality, how it will occur, and the expected result.

quality principles—Rules, guidelines, or concepts that an organization believes in collectively. The principles are formulated by senior management with input from others and are communicated and understood at every level of the organization.

quality tool—An instrument or technique that is used to support, sustain, and/or improve the activities of process quality management and improvement.

quality trilogy—A three-stage approach to managing for quality. The three stages are quality planning (developing the products and processes required to meet customer needs), quality control (meeting product and process goals), and quality improvement (achieving unprecedented levels of performance). Attributed to Joseph M. Juran.

quality-level agreement—*See* service-level agreement.

quantitative variables—Variables whose values are numbers.

quincunx—A teaching tool that creates frequency distributions. Beads tumble over numerous horizontal rows of pins, which force the beads to the right or left. After a random journey, the beads are dropped into vertical slots. After many beads are dropped, a frequency distribution results. In the classroom, quincunxes are often used to simulate a manufacturing process. English scientist Francis Galton invented the quincunx in the 1890s.

R

random cause—A cause of variation due to chance and not assignable to any factor (*see also* chance cause; common causes of variation).

random sampling—A commonly used sampling technique in which sample units are selected in such a manner that all combinations of *n* units under consideration have an equal chance of being selected as the sample.

range—The measure of dispersion in a data set; highest value minus lowest value.

red bead experiment—An experiment developed by W. Edwards Deming to illustrate that it is impossible to put employees in rank order of performance for the coming year based on their performance during the past year, because performance differences must be attributed to the system, not to employees. Four thousand beads, of which 20% are red and the rest are white, in a jar and six people are needed for the experiment. The participants' goal is to produce white beads because the customer will not accept red beads. One person begins by stirring the beads and then, blindfolded, selects a sample of 50 beads. That person hands the jar to the next person, who repeats the process, and so on. When everyone has his or her sample, the number of red beads for each is counted. The limits of variation between employees that can be attributed to the system are calculated. Everyone will fall within the calculated limits of variation that could arise from the system. The calculations will show that there is no evidence one person will be a better performer than another in the future. The experiment shows that it would be a waste of management's time to try to find out why, say, John produced 4 red beads and Jane produced 15; instead, management should improve the system, making it possible for everyone to produce more white beads.

reengineering—Completely redesigning or restructuring a whole organization, an organizational component, or a complete process. It's a "start over from the beginning" approach, sometimes called a "breakthrough." In terms of improvement approaches, reengineering is contrasted with incremental improvement (kaizen).

reference material—Material or substance, one or more of whose property values are sufficiently homogeneous and well established to be used for the calibration of an apparatus, for the assessment of a measurement method, or for assigning values to materials.

registration—The act of including an organization, product, service, or process in a compilation of those having the same or similar attributes. Sometimes incorrectly used interchangeably with the term "certification." A quality management system for an organization may be "certified" and the organization "registered" in a listing of organizations having achieved ISO 9001 certification. The respective terms for the documents involved are "certificate" and "register."

regression analysis—A statistical technique for determining the best mathematical expression describing the functional relationship between one response and one or more independent variables.

reinforcement of behavior—The practice of providing positive consequences when an individual is applying the correct knowledge and skills in performing the assigned job. Often described as *catching people doing something right and recognizing their behavior.* (Caution: less than desirable behavior can be unintentionally reinforced.)

reliability—In measurement system analysis, reliability refers to the ability of an instrument to produce the same results over repeated administration—to measure consistently. In reliability engineering, it is the probability of a product performing its intended function under stated conditions for a given period of time (*see also* mean time between failures [MTBF]).

repeatability—Precision under repeatability conditions, that is, conditions where independent test results are obtained with the same method on identical test items by the same operator using the same equipment within short intervals of time.

representative sample—A sample that contains the characteristics of the corresponding population.

reproducibility—Precision under reproducibility conditions, that is, conditions where test results are obtained with the same method on identical test items with different technicians using the same equipment or procedure.

resource requirements matrix—A tool to relate the resources required to the project tasks requiring them (used to indicate types of individuals needed, material needed, subcontractors, funds, etc.).

return-on-investment (ROI)—ROI is an umbrella term for a variety of ratios used to measure an organization's business performance. It is calculated by dividing some measure of return by a measure of the investment to produce the return, and multiplying by 100 to give a percentage. In its most basic form, ROI indicates what remains from all money taken in after all expenses are paid.

rework—Action taken on a nonconforming product or service to return it to meet specified requirements.

right the first time—A term used to convey the concept that it is beneficial and more cost-effective to take the necessary steps up front to ensure that a product or service meets its requirements than to provide a product or service that will need rework or not meet customers' needs. In other words, an organization should focus more on defect prevention than defect detection.

risk assessment/management—The process of determining what present or future potential risks are possible in a situation (a project plan, for example) and what actions might be taken to eliminate or mitigate the risks.

robustness—The condition of a product or process design that remains relatively stable with a minimum of variation even though factors that influence operations or usage, such as the environment and wear, are constantly changing.

root cause analysis—Use of a variety of quality tools to find the source of defects or problems. It is a structured approach that focuses on the decisive or original cause of a problem or condition. The technique probes well below the obvious "symptom" level to uncover the true cause or causes.

run chart—A line graph showing data collected during a run or an uninterrupted sequence of events. A trend is indicated when the series of collected data points head up or down.

S

sample—A finite number of items of a similar type taken from a population for the purpose of examination to determine whether all members of the population would conform to quality requirements or specifications.

sample size—The number of units in a sample chosen from the population.

sampling—The process of drawing conclusions about the population based on a part of the population.

satisfier—The term used to describe the quality level received by a customer when a product or service meets expectations.

scatter diagram—A graphical technique to analyze the relationship between two variables. Two sets of data are plotted on a graph, with the y-axis being used for the variable to be predicted and the x-axis being used for the variable to make the prediction. The graph will show possible relationships (although two variables might appear to be related, they might not be; those who know the most about the variables must make that evaluation). The scatter diagram is one of the seven tools of quality.

schedule—A plan showing when each activity in a project should begin and end.

scientific management—Aimed at finding the one best way to perform a task so as to increase productivity and efficiency.

scope—The total number of products, services, processes, people, and operations that will be affected by an initiative, project, or other action. Scope creep is when the initial scope is enlarged without due consideration of the effect of the increase.

SCOR (supply chain operations reference) model—A process that enables users to address, improve, and communicate supply chain management practices within and between all interested parties in the supply chain.

secondary customer—Individuals or groups from outside the process boundaries who receive process output but who are not the reason for the process.

selective listening—When a person hears only what he or she is predisposed to hear.

self-control—Workers' self-control comprises three elements: knowing what they are supposed to do, knowing what they are actually doing and how well, and being able to control the process.

self-inspection—Employees inspect their own work according to specified rules.

self-managed team—A team that requires little supervision and manages itself and the day-to-day work it does; self-directed teams are responsible for whole work processes, with each individual performing multiple tasks.

service—Work performed for others. Services may be internal (e.g., support services including payroll, engineering, maintenance, hiring, and training) or external (such as legal services, repair services, and training).

service-level agreement (SLA) —Agreement between an internal service provider and a service receiver that clarifies the expectations of the receiver and the capability of the provider to meet those expectations. The documented SLA also provides the criteria for measuring the provider's performance in delivering the service or product expected. Also referred to as a *quality-level agreement*.

setup time—The time taken to change over a process to run a different product or service.

seven basic tools of quality—Tools that help organizations understand their processes in order to improve them. The tools are the cause-and-effect diagram, check sheet, control chart, flowchart, histogram, Pareto chart, and scatter diagram (*see also individual entries*).

seven management tools of quality—The tools used primarily for planning and managing are the activity network diagram (AND) or arrow diagram, affinity diagram (KJ method), interrelationship digraph, matrix diagram, priorities matrix, process decision program chart (PDPC), and tree diagram.

Shewhart cycle—*See* Plan-Do-Check-Act (PDCA) cycle.

shift—An abrupt change in an important variable in a process. Examples of causes of shifts are broken tools, dropped gages, parts that have slipped, stopped oil flow, and ingredients omitted in a mix.

ship-to-stock—An approved or certified supplier ships material for a process directly to the buying organization without incoming inspection.

sigma—Greek letter (σ) that stands for the standard deviation of a process.

silo—An organization consisting of mostly single-purpose functions working autonomously on their own objectives with little or even no regard for the interface with other internal organizations and little concern for the impact of their actions on the overall organizational system.

single minute exchange of die (SMED)—A goal for reducing the setup time required to change over to a new process; the methodologies used in devising and implementing ways to reduce setup time.

SIPOC—A macro-level analysis of the suppliers, inputs, processes, outputs, and customers.

situational leadership—A leadership theory and style that maintains that leadership decisions should be based on the situational conditions present and supported by varying degrees of leader behavior. "It depends" becomes a common expression.

Six Sigma approach—A quality philosophy; a collection of techniques and tools for use in reducing variation; a process of improvement.

Six Sigma quality—A term used generally to indicate that a process is well controlled, that is, process limits $\pm 3\sigma$ from the centerline in a control chart and requirements/tolerance limits $\pm 6\sigma$ from the centerline. The term was initiated by Motorola.

S.M.A.R.T. W.A.Y.—A guide for setting objectives in which each objective is specific, measured, achievable, realistic, time-based, worth doing, assigned, and yields results.[3]

span of control—The number of subordinates a manager can effectively and efficiently manage.

special causes—Causes of variation that arise because of special circumstances. They are not an inherent part of a process. Special causes are also referred to as *assignable causes* (*see also* common causes).

specification—The engineering requirement used for judging the acceptability of a particular product/service based on product characteristics, such as appearance, performance, and size. In statistical analysis, specifications refer to the document that prescribes the requirements to which the product or service has to perform.

sponsor—The person who supports a team's plans, activities, and outcomes; the team's "backer." The sponsor provides resources and helps define the mission and scope to set limits. The sponsor may be the same individual as the "champion."

stages of team growth—Teams typically move through four stages as they develop maturity over time: forming, storming, norming, and performing.

stakeholder—The aggregate of people, departments, organizations, and communities that have an investment or interest in the success or actions taken by the organization.

standard—A statement, action, specification, or quantity of material against which measured outputs from a process may be judged as acceptable or unacceptable.

standard deviation—A calculated measure of variability that shows how much the data are spread around the mean.

standardized work—Documented and agreed-upon procedures and practices to be used by all persons doing the same type of work.

statistical process control (SPC)—The application of statistical techniques to control a process.

statistical quality control (SQC)—The application of statistical techniques to control quality. Often the term "statistical process control" is used interchangeably with "statistical quality control," although statistical quality control includes acceptance sampling as well as statistical process control.

statistical thinking—A philosophy of learning and action based on fundamental principles:

- All work occurs in a system of interconnected processes
- Variation exists in all processes
- Understanding and reducing variation are vital to improvement

statistics—Descriptive: A field that involves the tabulating, depicting, and describing of data sets. Inferential: A formalized body of techniques characteristically involving attempts to infer the properties of a large collection of data from inspection of a sample of the collection.

steering committee—A special group established to guide and track initiatives or projects.

storyboarding—A technique that visually displays thoughts and ideas and groups them into categories, making all aspects of a process visible at once. Often used to communicate to others the activities performed by a team as they improved a process.

strategic planning—A process to set an organization's long-range goals and identify the objectives and actions needed to reach the goals.

stratified sampling—A type of random sampling. The technique can be used when the population is not homogeneous. The approach is to divide the population into strata or subgroups, each of which is more or less homogeneous, and then take a representative sample from each group.

structural variation—Variation caused by regular, systematic changes in output, such as seasonal patterns and long-term trends. Occurrences of structural variation will, on a control chart, often look like special causes, but are not, inasmuch as structural variation is inherent in the process.

supplier—Any provider whose information, materials, products, or services may be used at any stage in the production, design, delivery, or use of another company's products or services. Suppliers include businesses (such as distributors, dealers, warranty repair services, transportation contractors, and franchises) and service suppliers (such as healthcare, training, and education). Internal suppliers provide materials or services to internal customers.

supplier audit—Audits conducted by a buying organization, or a buyer's subcontractor, of a supplier's organization to verify contractual compliance or conformance to a standard or requirement.

supplier quality assurance—Confidence that a supplier's product or service will fulfill its customers' needs. This confidence is achieved by creating a relationship between the customer and the supplier that ensures the product or service will be fit for use with minimal corrective action and inspection. According to J. M. Juran, nine primary activities are needed: (1) define product and program quality requirements, (2) evaluate alternative suppliers, (3) select suppliers, (4) conduct joint quality planning, (5) cooperate with the supplier during the execution of the contract, (6) obtain proof of conformance to requirements, (7) certify qualified suppliers, (8) conduct quality improvement programs as required, and (9) create and use supplier quality ratings.

supply chain—The series of processes and/or organizations that are involved in producing and delivering a product to the end user. For example, in the automotive industry the supply chain may extend from the extraction of iron ore to the delivery of the completed automobile to the dealer (intermediate customer), and on to the end user.

supply chain management (SCM)—The process of effectively integrating and managing components of the supply chain.

support systems—Starting with top-management commitment and visible involvement, support systems are a cascading series of interrelated practices or actions aimed at building and sustaining support for continuous quality improvement. Such practices/actions may include the mission statement, transformation of company culture, policies, employment practices, compensation, recognition and rewards, employee involvement, rules and procedures, quality-level agreements, training, empowerment, methods and tools for improving quality, tracking-measuring-evaluating-reporting systems, and so on.

surveillance—Continual monitoring of a process.

survey—An examination for some specific purpose; to inspect or consider carefully; to review in detail (*survey* implies the inclusion of matters not covered by agreed-upon criteria). Also, a structured series of questions designed to elicit a predetermined range of responses covering a preselected area of interest. May be administered orally by a survey-taker, by paper and pencil, or by computer. Responses are tabulated and analyzed to surface significant areas for improvement.

SWOT analysis—An assessment of an organization's key strengths, weaknesses, opportunities, and threats. It considers factors such as the organization's industry, the competitive position, functional areas, and management.

symptom—An indication of a problem or opportunity.

system—A network of connecting processes and people that together strive to achieve a common mission.

system of profound knowledge (SoPK)—*See* profound knowledge, system of.

systems approach to management—A management theory that views the organization as a unified, purposeful combination of interrelated parts; managers must look at the organization as a whole and understand that activity in one part of the organization affects all parts of the organization. Also known as *systems thinking*.

T

tacit knowledge—Unarticulated, undocumented knowledge "stored" within individuals. The knowledge and wisdom that have developed within a person over time and are not captured for use by others; the knowledge that is no longer available when a person leaves an organization.

tactical plans—Short-term plans, usually of one to two years' duration, that describe actions the organization will take to meet its strategic business plan.

Taguchi loss function—Quality loss is defined as loss imparted by the product to society from the time the product is shipped. Included are not only loss to the company from costs of rework, scrap, maintenance, downtime from equipment failure, and warranty claims, but also the costs to the customer from poor product performance and reliability, leading to further losses in market share. Any points beyond the center (target) of the process, in either direction, even though within specifications, Taguchi considers a loss.

Taguchi method—A prototyping method that enables the engineer or designer to identify the optimal settings to produce a robust product that can survive manufacturing time after time, piece after piece, in order to provide the functionality required by the customer.

takt time—The available production time divided by the rate of customer demand. Operating to takt time sets the production pace to customer demand.

tampering—Action taken to compensate for variation within the control limits of a stable system. Tampering increases rather than decreases variation.

task—A specific, definable activity to perform an assigned function, usually within a specified time frame.

team—A group of two or more people who are equally accountable for the accomplishment of a purpose and specific performance goals; it is also defined as a small number of people with complementary skills who are committed to a common purpose.

team building/development—The process of and techniques for transforming a group of people into a team and developing the team to achieve its purpose.

team dynamics—The interactions that occur among team members under different conditions.

team facilitation—Addresses both the role of the facilitator on the team and the techniques and tools for facilitating the team.

team leader—A person designated to be responsible for the ongoing success of the team; keeps the team focused on the task assigned.

team maturity and stages of growth—Team growth progresses through four development stages: forming, storming, norming, and performing. Adjourning is added to cover closing down a team's work.

team member—A participant in the project planning and control processes. A team member may also be a manager of one or more activities, or a source of technical information. A key attribute for team members is that they value teamwork in the problem-solving process. Effective team members are expected to help, encourage and support other team members.

team performance evaluation—Special metrics are needed to evaluate the work of a team (to avoid focus on any individual on the team) and as a basis for recognition and rewards for team achievements.

temporary/ad hoc team—A team, usually small, formed to address a short-term mission or emergency situation.

theory X and theory Y—A theory developed by Douglas McGregor that maintains there are two contrasting assumptions about people, each based on the manager's view of human nature. Theory X, the negative view, assumes most employees don't like work and try to avoid it. Theory Y, the positive assumption, is that employees want to work, will seek and accept responsibility, and can offer creative solutions to organizational problems.

third-party audit—External audits conducted by personnel who are neither employees of the organization nor a supplier, but are usually employees of certification bodies or of registrars.

TJC—An abbreviation for The Joint Commission, formerly the Joint Commission on Accreditation of Healthcare Organizations (JCAHO).

top management commitment—Participation of the highest-level officials in the organization's quality improvement efforts. Their participation includes establishing and serving on a quality committee, establishing quality policies and goals, deploying those goals to lower levels of the organization, providing the resources and training that the lower levels need to achieve the goals, participating in quality improvement teams, reviewing progress organization-wide, recognizing those who have performed well, and revising the current reward system to reflect the importance of achieving the quality goals. Commitment is top management's visible, personal involvement as supportive and as seen by others in the organization.

total productive maintenance (TPM)—Methodologies for reducing and eliminating equipment failure; preventive maintenance.

total quality control (TQC)—A systematic or total approach to quality requiring the involvement of all functions of the organization in the quality process. Attributed to Dr. Armand V. Feigenbaum, considered to be the originator of TQC.

total quality management (TQM)—A term initially coined by the Naval Air Systems Command to describe its management approach to quality improvement. TQM has taken on many meanings. Simply put, TQM is a management approach to long-term success through customer satisfaction. TQM is based on the participation of all members of an organization in improving processes, products, services, and the culture they work in. TQM benefits all organization members and society. The methods for implementing this approach are found in the teachings of such quality leaders as Philip B. Crosby, W. Edwards Deming, Armand V. Feigenbaum, Kaoru Ishikawa, J. M. Juran, and others.

traceability—The ability to track the history, application, or location of an item or activity, and like items or activities, by means of recorded identification.

training—Identifying the needed skills that employees require to perform to established standards, specifications, and work practices pertaining to their present assigned tasks, and the process of providing those skills.

training evaluation—Techniques and tools for evaluating the effectiveness of training.

tree diagram—A management and planning tool that shows the complete range of subtasks required to achieve an objective. A problem-solving approach can be aided from this analysis.

trend—Consecutive data points plotted in relation to a time period that shows a pattern of performance and helps identify any unexpected occurrences (*see also* run chart).

trend analysis—Refers to the charting of data over time to identify a tendency or direction.

trilogy—*See* quality trilogy.

type 1 error—A supplier organization's incorrect decision to reject something (such as a statistical hypothesis or a lot of products) when it is acceptable. Also known as *producer's risk* and *alpha risk.*

type 2 error—A customer's incorrect decision to accept something when it is unacceptable. Also known as *consumer's risk* and *beta risk.*

U

unconditional guarantee—An organizational policy of providing customers an unquestioned remedy for any product or service deficiency.

upper control limit (UCL)—Control limit for points above the central line in a control chart.

V

validation—Confirmation by examination of objective evidence that a specific intended use and/or specific requirements are met.

validity—The ability of a feedback instrument to measure what it is intended to measure.

value stream—The primary actions required to take a product from concept to placing the product in the hands of the end user.

value stream mapping (VSM)—Detailed mapping of a process in two stages. The first stage is a very detailed visual "as is" representation of every process in the material and information flows. The second stage is a future map of the "to be" process. VSM is a detailed graphical flowcharting technique that shows material and informational flow.

value-added—Refers to tasks or activities that convert resources into products or services consistent with customer requirements. The customer can be internal or external to the organization. Parts of the process that add worth from the external customers' perspective.

values—Statements that clarify the behaviors that the organization expects in order to move toward its vision and mission. Values reflect an organization's personality and culture.

variable data—Data resulting from the measurement of a parameter or a variable. Contrast with *attribute data.*

variance—The difference between a planned amount (usually money or time) and the actual amount.

variation—A change in data, a characteristic, or a function that is caused by one of four factors: special causes, common causes, tampering, or structural variation (*see also individual entries*).

verification—The act of reviewing, inspecting, testing, checking, auditing, or otherwise establishing and documenting whether items, processes, services, or documents conform to specified requirements.

virtual team—A boundaryless team functioning without a commonly shared physical structure or physical contact, using technology to link the team members.

vision—A statement that explains what the company wants to become and what it hopes to achieve.

visual control—The technique of positioning all tools, parts, production activities, and performance indicators so that the status of a process can be understood at a glance by everyone. Also, provides visual cues to aid the performer in correctly processing a step or series of steps in order to reduce cycle time, cut costs, smooth the flow of work, and improve quality.

vital few, useful many—A term used by J. M. Juran to describe his use of the Pareto principle, which he first defined in 1950. (The principle was used much earlier in economics and inventory control methodologies.) The principle suggests that most defects come from relatively few causes; that is, 80% of the defects come from 20% of the possible causes. The 20% of the possible causes are referred to as the "vital few"; the remaining causes are referred to as the "useful many."

voice of the customer—An organization's efforts to understand the customers' needs and expectations ("voice") and to provide products and services that truly meet such needs and expectations.

W

walk the talk—Means not only talking about what one believes in but also being observed acting out those beliefs. Employees' buy-in of the total quality management (TQM) concept is more likely when management is seen involved in the process, every day.

warranty—A manufacturer's published statement that defective or deficient product or service experienced by the customer, within a specified period of time, and perhaps additional constraints, will be remedied by the manufacturer.

waste—Activities that consume resources but add no value; visible waste includes scrap, rework, and downtime, and invisible waste includes inefficient setups, wait times of people and machines, and inventory.

what-is/what-is-not chart—A tool for analyzing the presence or absence of a step, activity, item, event, behavior, and so on.

win–win—Outcome of a negotiation that results in both parties being better off.

wisdom—The culmination of the continuum from data to information to knowledge to wisdom.

work analysis—The analysis, classification, and study of the way work is done. Work may be categorized as value-added (essential) or non-value-added (waste). Collected data may be summarized on a Pareto chart showing how people within the studied population work. The need for and value of all the work is then questioned, and opportunities for improvement identified.

work breakdown structure (WBS)—A project management planning tool by which a project is decomposed into tasks, subtasks, and units of work to be performed and displayed as a tree-type chart.

work group—A group composed of people from one functional area who work together on a daily basis and whose goal is to improve the processes of their function.

work instruction—A document that answers the question "How is the work to be done?" (*see also* procedure).

world-class quality—A term to indicate a standard of excellence; the best of the best.

X, Y, Z

yield—Ratio between salable goods produced and the quantity of raw materials and/or components input at the beginning of the process.

zero defects—A performance standard popularized by Philip B. Crosby to address a dual attitude in the workplace: People are willing to accept imperfection in some areas, whereas in other areas, they expect the number of defects to be zero. This dual attitude developed because people are human and humans make mistakes. However, the zero-defects methodology states that if people commit themselves to watching details and avoiding errors, they can move closer to the goal of zero defects.

NOTES

1. Defined by Russell T. Westcott in *The Certified Manager of Quality/Organizational Excellence Handbook,* 4th ed. (Milwaukee, WI: ASQ Quality Press, 2014).
2. Defined by Jan Carlzon, *Moments of Truth* (New York: HarperBusiness, 1987).
3. Westcott, *The Certified Manager of Quality/Organizational Excellence Handbook.*

Appendix D
Additional Reading

The following pages list additional resources for readers wishing to acquire more knowledge about many of the topics covered in this handbook. The books have been selected from the hundreds of books available. In no way is it implied that any of the books on this list are required reading.

Note: Many of the cited texts are available through ASQ. Call 1-800-248-1946 to request a current catalog, or visit the online store at http://asq.org/quality-press.

POCKET GUIDES

Publisher—GOAL/QPC, Salem, New Hampshire

Advanced Project Management Memory Jogger, 2006.

Black Belt Memory Jogger, 2002.

Coaching in the Workplace: Strategies and Tools for Powerful Change, 2008.

Creativity Tools Memory Jogger: for Creative Thinking, 1998.

Facilitation at a Glance, 2nd ed., 2008.

Hoshin Kanri Memory Jogger, 2013.

Lean Enterprise Memory Jogger, 2002.

Memory Jogger 2: Tools for Continuous Improvement and Effective Planning, 2nd ed., 2010.

Problem Solving Memory Jogger: Seven Steps to Improved Processes, 2000.

Process Management Memory Jogger: Building Cross-Functional Excellence, 2008.

Project Management Memory Jogger, 1997.

Six Sigma Memory Jogger II: Tools for Six Sigma Teams, 2002.

Team Memory Jogger, 1995.

Time Management Memory Jogger: Create Time for the Life You Want, 2008.

Value Methodology: Reduce Cost and Improve Value through Function Analysis, 2008.

Publisher—ASQ Quality Press, Milwaukee, Wisconsin

The ASQ Pocket Guide for the Certified Six Sigma Black Belt, 2013.

The ASQ Pocket Guide to Failure Mode and Effect Analysis (FMEA), 2015.

The ASQ Pocket Guide to Root Cause Analysis, 2013.

The ASQ Pocket Guide to Statistics for Six Sigma Black Belts, 2015.

The ASQ Quality Improvement Pocket Guide, 2013.

Continual Improvement Assessment Guide: Promoting & Sustaining Business Results, 2004.

Effective Writing for the Quality Professional: Creating Letters, Reports & Procedures, 2005.

The Internal Auditing Pocket Guide: Preparing, Performing, Reporting and Follow-up, 2nd ed., 2007.

The Process Auditing and Techniques Guide, 2nd ed., 2010.

Six Sigma Project Management, 2002.

Virtual Teams Guidebook for Managers, 2003.

BASIC QUALITY PRINCIPLES AND PRACTICES

ASQ. *Certified Quality Improvement Associate*. ASQ CQIA Brochure #B1158. Milwaukee, WI: ASQ Quality Press.

Beecroft, G. Dennis, Grace L. Duffy, and John W. Moran, eds. *The Executive Guide to Improvement and* Change. Milwaukee, WI: ASQ Quality Press, 2003.

Deming, W. Edwards. *Out of the Crisis*. Cambridge, MA: MIT Center for Advanced Engineering Study, 1986.

Duffy, Grace L., ed. *The ASQ Quality Improvement Pocket Guide*. Milwaukee, WI: ASQ Quality Press, 2013.

Evans, James R., and William M. Lindsay. *Managing for Quality and Performance Excellence*. 9th ed. Cincinnati, OH: South-Western College Publishing, 2014.

Juran, Joseph M., and A. Blanton Godfrey, eds. *Juran's Quality Handbook*. 5th ed. New York: McGraw-Hill, 1999.

Pyzdek, Thomas, and Paul Keller. *The Handbook for Quality Management: A Complete Guide to Operational Excellence*. 2nd ed. New York: McGraw-Hill, 2013.

Westcott, Russell T., ed. *The Certified Manager of Quality/Organizational Excellence*. 4th ed. Milwaukee, WI: ASQ Quality Press, 2014.

ASSESSMENTS AND AUDITS

Arter, Dennis R. *Quality Audits for Improved Performance*. 3rd ed. Milwaukee, WI: ASQ Quality Press, 2003.

Fisher, Donald C. *Homeland Security Assessment Manual: A Comprehensive Organizational Assessment Based on Baldrige Criteria*. Milwaukee, WI: ASQ Quality Press, 2005.

Russell, J. P., ed. *The ASQ Auditing Handbook*. 4th ed. Milwaukee, WI: ASQ Quality Press, 2013.

———. *Continual Improvement Assessment Guide: Promoting and Sustaining Business Results*. Milwaukee, WI: ASQ Quality Press, 2004.

Stimson, William A. *Internal Quality Auditing: Meeting the Challenge of ISO 9001*. 2nd ed. Chico, CA: Paton Professional, 2010.

BALDRIGE AWARD

Blazey, Mark L. *Insights to Performance Excellence 2013–2014: Understanding the Integrated Management System and the Baldrige Criteria*. Milwaukee, WI: ASQ Quality Press, 2006.

Leonard, Denis, and Mac McGuire. *The Executive Guide to Understanding and Implementing the Baldrige Criteria*. Milwaukee, WI: ASQ Quality Press, 2007.

NIST. *Baldrige Performance Excellence Program: Criteria for Performance Excellence*. (Criteria for: Business, Health Care, or Education). Baldrige National Quality Program, National Institute of Standards and Technology, Technology Administration, United States Department of Commerce, Administration Building, Room A600, 100 Bureau Drive, Stop 1020, Gaithersburg, MD 20899-1020. Telephone: 301-975-2036, Fax: 301-948-3716, e-mail: nqp@nist.gov, website: http://www.baldrige.nist.gov. One copy of the criteria appropriate to your organization is available free.

CERTIFICATION PREPARATION—ASQ

Benbow, Donald W., and Hugh W. Broome. *The Certified Reliability Engineer Handbook.* 2nd ed. Milwaukee, WI: ASQ Quality Press, 2013.

Borror, Connie M., ed. *The Certified Quality Engineer Handbook.* 3rd ed. Milwaukee, WI: ASQ Quality Press, 2009.

Bucher, Jay L., ed. *The Metrology Handbook.* Milwaukee, WI: ASQ Quality Press, 2012.

Christensen, Chris, Kathleen M. Betz, and Marilyn S. Stein. *The Certified Quality Process Analyst Handbook.* 2nd ed. Milwaukee, WI: ASQ Quality Press, 2014.

Daugherty, Taz, ed. *Fundamental Concepts for the Software Quality Engineer.* Milwaukee, WI: ASQ Quality Press, 2002.

Kubiak, T. M. *The Certified Six Sigma Master Black Belt Handbook.* Milwaukee, WI: ASQ Quality Press, 2012.

Kubiak, T. M., and Donald W. Benbow. *The Certified Six Sigma Black Belt Handbook.* 2nd ed. Milwaukee, WI: ASQ Quality Press, 2009.

Munro, Roderick A., Matthew J. Maio, Mohamed B. Nawaz, Govindarajan Ramu, and Daniel J. Zrymiak. *The Certified Six Sigma Green Belt Handbook.* Milwaukee, WI: ASQ Quality Press, 2008.

Russell, J. P., ed. *The ASQ Auditing Handbook.* 4th ed. Milwaukee, WI: ASQ Quality Press, 2013.

Walker, H. Fred, Donald W. Benbow, and Ahmad K. Elshennawy. *The Certified Quality Technician Handbook.* 2nd ed. Milwaukee, WI: ASQ Quality Press, 2013.

Walker, H. Fred, Ahmad K. Elshennawy, Bhisham C. Gupta, and Mary McShabe-Vaughn. *The Certified Quality Inspector Handbook.* 2nd ed. Milwaukee, WI: ASQ Quality Press, 2013.

Westcott, Russell T., ed. *The Certified Manager of Quality/Organizational Excellence Handbook.* 4th ed. Milwaukee, WI: ASQ Quality Press, 2014.

Westfall, Linda. *The Certified Software Quality Engineer Handbook.* Milwaukee, WI: ASQ Quality Press, 2010.

CONTINUOUS AND BREAKTHROUGH IMPROVEMENT

Andersen, Bjørn. *Business Process Improvement Toolbox.* 2nd ed. Milwaukee, WI: ASQ Quality Press, 2008.

Andersen, Bjørn, and Tom Fagerhaug. *Root Cause Analysis: Simplified Tools and Techniques.* 2nd ed. Milwaukee, WI: ASQ Quality Press, 2006.

Andersen, B., T. Fagerhaug, B. Henriksen, and L. F. Unseen. *Mapping Work Processes.* Milwaukee, WI: ASQ Quality Press, 2008.

ASQ Statistics Division. *Improving Performance through Statistical Thinking.* Milwaukee, WI: ASQ Quality Press, 2000.

Duffy, Grace L. *Modular Kaizen: Continuous and Breakthrough Improvement.* Milwaukee, WI: ASQ Quality Press, 2014.

Escoe, Adrienne. *The Practical Guide to People-Friendly Documentation.* Milwaukee, WI: ASQ Quality Press, 2001.

Hutton, David W. *From Baldrige to the Bottom Line: A Road Map for Organizational Change and Improvement.* Milwaukee, WI: ASQ Quality Press, 2000.

Jones, Russ. *Proving Continuous Improvement with Profit Ability.* Milwaukee, WI: ASQ Quality Press, 2008.

Okes, Duke. *Root Cause Analysis: The Core of Problem Solving and Corrective Action.* Milwaukee, WI: ASQ Quality Press, 2009.

Plenert, G. *Strategic Continuous Process Improvement: Which Quality Tools to Use, and When to Use Them.* New York: McGraw-Hill, 2012.

ReVelle, Jack B., ed. *Manufacturing Handbook of Best Practices: An Innovation, Productivity, and Quality Focus.* Boca Raton, FL: St. Lucie Press, 2002.

———. *Quality Essentials: A Reference Guide from A to Z.* Milwaukee, WI: ASQ Quality Press, 2004.

Siebels, Don. *The Quality Improvement Glossary.* Milwaukee, WI: ASQ Quality Press, 2004.

Tague, Nancy R. *The Quality Toolbox.* 2nd ed. Milwaukee, WI: ASQ Quality Press, 2005.

CUSTOMERS

Brown, Stanley A. *Customer Relationship Management: A Strategic Imperative in the World of e-Business.* New York: John Wiley & Sons, 2000.

Fornell, Claes. *The Satisfied Customer: Winners and Losers in the Battle for Buyer Preference.* New York: Palgrave MacMillan, 2007.

Goldstein, Sheldon D. *Superior Customer Satisfaction and Loyalty: Engaging Customers to Drive Performance.* Milwaukee, WI: ASQ Quality Press, 2010.

Hayes, Bob E. *Beyond the Ultimate Question: A Systematic Approach to Improve Customer Loyalty.* Milwaukee, WI: ASQ Quality Press, 2010.

Hayes, B. E. *Measuring Customer Satisfaction and Loyalty: Survey Design, Use, and Statistical Analysis Methods.* 3rd ed. Milwaukee, WI: ASQ Quality Press, 2008.

Naumann, Earl, and Steven H. Hoisington. *Customer-Centered Six Sigma: Linking Customers, Process Improvement, and Financial Results.* Milwaukee, WI: ASQ Quality Press, 2001.

Schultz, Garry. *The Customer Care & Contact Center Handbook.* Milwaukee, WI: ASQ Quality Press, 2003.

Wilburn, Morris. *Managing the Customer Experience: A Measurement-Based Approach.* Milwaukee, WI: ASQ Quality Press, 2007.

EDUCATION

ASQ. *Successful Applications of Quality Systems in K–12 Schools.* Milwaukee, WI: ASQ Quality Education Forum/Division, 2003.

Jenkins, Lee. *Improving Student Learning: Applying Deming's Quality Principles in the Classroom.* 2nd ed. Milwaukee, WI: ASQ Quality Press, 2003.

HEALTHCARE—MEDICAL

American College of Medical Quality. *Core Curriculum for Medical Quality Management.* Sudbury, MA: Jones and Bartlett Publishers, 2005.

Duffy, Grace L., John W. Moran, and William J. Riley. *Quality Function Deployment and Lean-Six Sigma Applications in Public Health.* Milwaukee, WI: ASQ Quality Press, 2010.

Harnack, Gordon. *Mastering and Managing the FDA Maze: Medical Device Overview.* Milwaukee, WI: ASQ Quality Press, 1999.

Pauley, Judith Ann, and Joseph F. Pauley. *Establishing a Culture of Patient Safety.* Milwaukee, WI: ASQ Quality Press, 2011.

Ransom, Scott B., Maulik Joshi, and David Nash. *The Healthcare Quality Book: Vision, Strategy, and Tools.* Chicago: Health Administration Press, 2005.

Sperl, Todd, Rob Ptacek, and Jayant Trewn. *Practical Lean Six Sigma for Healthcare.* Milwaukee, WI: ASQ Quality Press, 2013.

ISO 9000

Myhrberg, Erik Valdemar. *A Practical Field Guide for ISO 9001:2008.* Milwaukee, WI: ASQ Quality Press, 2009.

West, John E., and Charles A. Cianfrani. *Unlocking the Power of Your QMS: Keys to Business Process Improvement.* Milwaukee, WI: ASQ Quality Press, 2004.

LEADERSHIP AND MANAGEMENT—GENERAL

Andersen, Bjørn. *Bringing Business Ethics to Life: Achieving Corporate Social Responsibility.* Milwaukee, WI: ASQ Quality Press, 2004.

Barker, Tom. *Leadership for Results: Removing Barriers to Success for People, Projects, and Processes.* Milwaukee, WI: ASQ Quality Press, 2006.

Bellman, Geoffrey. *Getting Things Done When You Are Not in Charge.* San Francisco: Berrett-Koehler Publisher, 2001.

Ducoff, Neil. *No-Compromise Leadership: A Higher Standard of Leadership Thinking and Behavior.* Sanford, FL: DC Press, 2009.

Evans, G. Edward, Patricia Layzell Ward, and Bendik Rugas. *Management Basics for Information Professionals.* New York: Neal-Schuman Publishers, 2000.

Hofstede, G., G. J. Hofstede, and M. Mikov. *Cultures and Organizations.* 4th ed. New York: McGraw-Hill, 2010.

Kouzes, James M., and Barry Z. Posner. *The Leadership Challenge.* 4th ed. San Francisco, CA: Jossey-Bass (Wiley), 2008.

PROJECT MANAGEMENT

Kerzner, Harold. *Project Management: A Systems Approach to Planning, Scheduling and Controlling.* 8th ed. New York: John Wiley & Sons, 2003.

McGhee, Pamela, and Peter McAliney. *Painless Project Management: A Step-by-Step Guide for Planning, Executing, and Managing Projects.* New York: John Wiley & Sons, 2007.

Phillips, Jack J., Timothy W. Bothell, and G. Lynne Snead, *The Project Management Scorecard; Measuring the Success of Project Management Solutions.* New York: Butterworth-Heinemann, 2002.

Westcott, Russell T. *Simplified Project Management for the Quality Professional.* Milwaukee, WI: ASQ Quality Press, 2005.

QUALITY COSTS AND METRICS

Okes, Duke. *Performance Metrics: The Levers for Process Management.* Milwaukee, WI: ASQ Quality Press, 2013.

Wood, Douglas C. *The Executive Guide to Understanding and Implementing Quality Cost Programs: Reduce Operating Expenses and Increase Revenue.* ASQ Quality Management Division Economics of Quality Series. Milwaukee, WI: ASQ Quality Press, 2007.

———, ed. *Principles of Quality Costs: Financial Measures for Strategic Implementation of Quality Management.* Milwaukee, WI: ASQ Quality Press, 2013.

RISK MANAGEMENT

Frame, J. D. *Managing Risk in Organizations: A Guide for Managers.* New York: John Wiley & Sons, 2003.

Stamatis, D. H. *Failure Mode Effect Analysis: FMEA from Theory to Execution.* 2nd ed. Milwaukee, WI: ASQ Quality Press, 2003.

Westcott, Russell T. *Stepping Up to ISO 9004.* Chico, CA: Paton Press, 2005. Chapter 4.

SOFTWARE QUALITY

Daugherty, Taz, ed. *Fundamental Concepts for the Software Engineer.* Milwaukee, WI: ASQ Quality Press, 2002.

Faris, Thomas H. *Safe and Sound Software: Creating an Efficient and Effective Quality System for Software Medical Device Organizations.* Milwaukee, WI: ASQ Quality Press, 2006.

Westfall, Linda. *The Certified Software Quality Engineer Handbook.* Milwaukee, WI: ASQ Quality Press, 2010.

STATISTICS

ASQ Statistics Division. *Improving Performance through Statistical Thinking.* Milwaukee, WI: ASQ Quality Press, 2000.

Crossley, Mark L. *The Desk Reference of Statistical Quality Methods.* Milwaukee, WI: ASQ Quality Press, 2000.

Durivage, Mark Allen. *Practical Engineering, Process, and Reliability Statistics.* Milwaukee, WI: ASQ Quality Press, 2015.

SUPPLIER QUALITY

Ayers, James B. *Supply Chain Project Management.* 2nd ed. Boca Raton, FL: CRC Press, 2010.

Bolstorff, Peter, and Robert Rosenbaum. *Supply Chain Excellence: A Handbook for Dramatic Improvement Using the SCOR Model.* 2nd ed. New York: AMACOM, 2007.

Bossert, James L., ed. *The Supplier Management Handbook.* 6th ed. Milwaukee, WI: ASQ Quality Press, 2004.

Dittmann, P. J. *Supply Chain Transformation: Building and Executing an Integrated Supply Chain.* Milwaukee, WI: ASQ Quality Press, 2013.

Hoover, Bill, Eero Eloranta, Kati Huttunen, and Jan Holmstrom. *Managing the Demand Chain: Value Innovations for Supplier Excellence.* New York: John Wiley & Sons, 2001.

Russell, J. P., ed. *The ASQ Supply Chain Management Primer.* Milwaukee, WI: ASQ Quality Press, 2013.

TEAMS

Scholtes, Peter R., B. L. Joiner, and B. J. Streibel. *The Team Handbook.* 3rd ed. Madison, WI: Joiner Associates, 2003.

TOTAL QUALITY MANAGEMENT

Beecroft, G. Dennis, Grace L. Duffy, and John W. Moran, eds. *The Executive Guide to Improvement and Change.* Milwaukee, WI: ASQ Quality Press, 2003.

Berk, Joseph, and Susan Berk. *Quality Management for the Technology Sector.* New York: Butterworth-Heinemann, 2000.

Gryna, Frank, Richard C. H. Chua, and Joseph A. DeFeo. *Quality Planning and Analysis for Enterprise Quality.* 5th ed. New York: McGraw-Hill, 2007.

Shearer, Clive. *Everyday Excellence: Creating a Better Workplace through Attitude, Action, and Appreciation.* Milwaukee, WI: ASQ Quality Press, 2006.

Index

Note: Page numbers followed by *f* or *t* refer to figures or tables, respectively.

D

T

U

V

W

Y

Z

About the Editors

RUSSELL T. WESTCOTT

Russ Westcott is:

- A Fellow of the American Society for Quality (ASQ)
- ASQ Certified: Manager of Quality/Organizational Excellence (CMQ/OE) and Quality Auditor (CQA)
- Editor: *The Certified Quality Manager of Quality/Organizational Excellence Handbook*, 4th ed. (ASQ Quality Press, 2014)
- Instructor: ASQ's Certified Manager of Quality/Organizational Excellence Exam Preparation Course
- Coeditor: *The Quality Improvement Handbook*, 3rd ed. (ASQ Quality Press, 2015).
- Advisor to Council and chair of the Professional Development Committee, ASQ Quality Management Division (QMD)
- Career coach: Provides work-life planning and career coaching for individuals
- Writer: *ASQ Quality Progress;* ASQ *Quality Management Division Forum, the Auditor*, publication of Paton Professional; *ASQ Journal of Quality and Participation*; and other publications
- Author: *Stepping Up to ISO 9004:2000* (Paton Press, 2003); *Simplified Project Management for the Quality Professional* (ASQ Quality Press, 2005)
- Member of ASQ Thames Valley Section (308) Executive Board
- Frequent speaker on quality management and training topics

Russ's industry experience includes management and consulting within the following industries:

- Public utility, aerospace systems, business financing, consumer financing, manufacturing, defense systems, and insurance
- Small business manufacturing, state and federal government, banking, educational institutions

Russ Westcott, president of R.T. Westcott & Associates, Old Saybrook, Connecticut, guides clients in:

- Organizational performance improvement projects
- Implementing quality management systems (ISO 9001)
- Project planning and management
- Strategic planning
- Implementing Baldrige-criteria-driven management systems
- Coaching in work-life planning and the career-change process

He is a graduate of Boston University and of GE's three-year financial training program.

Russ is celebrating his 36th year as an independent consultant, business writer, and career coach.

GRACE L. DUFFY

Grace L. Duffy provides services in organizational and process improvement, leadership, quality, customer service, and teamwork. She designs and implements effective systems for business and management success. She is coeditor of *The Quality Improvement Handbook; The Executive Guide to Improvement and Change, The Public Health Quality Improvement Handbook*; coauthor of *Executive Focus: Your Life and Career, QFD and Lean Six Sigma for Public Health; Modular Kaizen: Dealing with Disruption; Tools and Applications for Starting and Sustaining Healthy Teams, The Encyclopedia of Quality Tools*; editor of *The Quality Improvement Pocket Guide*; and author of *Modular Kaizen: Continuous and Breakthrough Improvement*.

Ms. Duffy has over 40 years' experience in successful business and process management in corporate, government, education, healthcare, not for profit, and small business. She is a recognized specialist in leadership and executive performance. Grace uses her experience as president, CEO, and senior manager to assist organizations and individuals in performance excellence. She is a frequently requested keynote and conference speaker on organizational and professional performance. She is an active coach and mentor to senior leaders in large corporations as well as entrepreneurs, focusing on strategic alignment of individual skills to organizational outcomes.

Grace holds a master's in business administration from Georgia State University and a bachelor's in archaeology and anthropology from Brigham Young University. She is an ASQ Certified Manager of Quality/Organizational Excellence, Certified Quality Improvement Associate, and Certified Quality Auditor. Grace is a Certified Lean-Six Sigma Master Black Belt and Manager of Process Improvement.

Grace is a member of ATD, ISPI, and ASQ. She is an ASQ Fellow and past vice president within the ASQ Office of the President, 2014 recipient of the ASQ Distinguished Service Medal, and Quality Magazine's 2014 Quality Person of the Year. She served as chair of ASQ's Quality Management Division (QMD) and remains active as an advisor to the QMD Council.